WADHURST IN THE SECOND WORLD WAR
LIFE IN A WEALDEN MARKET TOWN 1939 - 1945

A PUBLICATION OF
THE WADHURST HISTORY SOCIETY

Wadhurst History Society

Set in 11pt Times New Roman and published
for the Wadhurst History Society
by
Greenman Enterprise
Greenman Farm, Wadhurst, East Sussex TN5 6LE

Printed on Evoke 75% recycled paper
by
The Ink Pot
Southbank House, Victoria Road, Southborough, Kent TN4 0LT

ISBN 978-0-9545802-8-5

We have sought permission to include material from other sources and have
attributed it, wherever possible. We apologise for any we have missed.

WADHURST IN THE SECOND WORLD WAR
LIFE IN A WEALDEN MARKET TOWN 1939 - 1945

CONTENTS

ABBREVIATIONS AND EXPLANATIONS

For many of our readers, little explanation is needed for any of the contents of this book. However, for some, it may be helpful if the abbreviations used are defined from the beginning:

ARP	Air Raid Precautions
ATC	Air Training Corps
BSI	British Standards Institute
CO	Commanding Officer
DSC	Distinguished Service Cross
HG	Home Guard
JP	Justice of the Peace
LDV	Local Defence Volunteers
LEA	Local Education Authority
MAF	Ministry of Agriculture
MC	Military Cross
NAAFI	Navy, Army and Air Force Institute
POW	Prisoner of War
RDC	Rural District Council
RE	Royal Engineers
SSAFA	Soldiers, Sailors, Airmen and Families Association
TD	Territorial Defence medal
UD	Urban District
VAD	Voluntary Aid Detachment
WI	Women's Institute
WLA	Women's Land Army
WRNS	Women's Royal Naval Service 'Wrens'
WVS	Women's Voluntary Service

Finally a note for younger readers: rather than translate pre-decimal coinage every time it is mentioned in the text, the following note may help:

The pound used to be divided into twenty shillings, each equivalent to 5 new pence; the shilling was divided into 12 old pennies, each equivalent to 5/12 of a new penny – to put it another way one new penny is worth 2.4 old pennies. The old style currency was written £1/ 2 /6, £1 2s 6d or £1-2-6; in speech "*one pound two shillings and sixpence*" or "*one pound two and six*", equivalent to £1.125 today. A 'tanner' was a sixpence and a 'bob' was a shilling; half a crown was 2/6. The cost of living has increased over 50-fold since 1936; a carter earning 12/6 a week [p. 142] in the 1930s would be paid £230 for a 40-hour week on today's minimum wage.

i

PREFACE

WADHURST in the SECOND WORLD WAR - **Life in a Wealden Market Town 1939 - 1945** has its origins in Wadhurst's celebrations in 2005 to mark the 60th anniversary of the end of the War. The community responded to that week-end's activities with thanksgiving and with nostalgia. Members of the Wadhurst History Society subsequently recorded and retrieved the memories of many people who had experienced village life during the years of War.

Like all communities in Britain, Wadhurst [which includes Tidebrook] reflected the challenges of that time. Its location underlined those dangers. Had Hitler launched Operation Sea Lion and invaded the country, the coast was not far away. Occupied France was just across the Channel and villagers heard the reverberations during the raid on Dieppe in 1942. Several regiments were billeted in the area in preparation for D-Day, and beforehand. Luftwaffe squadrons passed overhead on their way to London during the Battle of Britain, and often jettisoned bombs; and during the closing months of the War the village lay firmly in 'Doodlebug Alley'. At the same time, especially during the isolation of 'Fortress Britain' in the early years of the War, the farming community was called on to increase production radically, and people learnt to fend for themselves.

Whilst the book highlights the years 1939-45, it also provides the background context and refers to the aftermath. It makes no claims to be a definitive history of Wadhurst during the War, but is a series of studies by members of the focus groups which constitute the core of the research of the History Society.

There are, of course, variations in approach and style among the different contributors. While the chapters that follow have been attributed to named authors, there have been many others involved in the work and much of the research has been collective and benefited from group discussion. A group, consisting of Arthur Dewar, David James and Heather Woodward, perhaps presumptuously but probably appropriately called 'Overlords' in view of the Normandy operation, has tried to provide a co-ordinated approach across the articles. We are grateful to all who have given their permission to use their illustrations and photographs, especially to Wadhurst Parish Council, Stan Cosham and the Trustees of the Bocking Collection. The final preparations for publication have been the work of Michael Harte.

The editorial team has very much appreciated the suggestions, contributions and support from many members of the History Society and of the wider community. Like many residents who have been interviewed, we have continued to refer to Wadhurst as a 'village', ignoring the 1253 Charter granting Wadhurst the status of market town.

We hope that this publication provides a perspective of life in Wadhurst at such a critical time in its history. We hope also that readers will be able to fill in the gaps in our knowledge - and maybe identify the un-named people in local photographs. We apologise for any errors and omissions and hope that the articles will become the platform for further research, debate and correction, and that readers will be stimulated to offer responses for the History Society to publish in its future Newsletters.

November 2008

TO AN ENGLISH ROSE - from a Canadian soldier

I sailed across the ocean blue
In the year of '42
And I landed on a friendly shore
To fight in this, the last great war.

We settled at last in Sussex green
Where I met a young lady from Sparrows Green.
A shy little lady with nice blonde hair
With always a laugh and a smile to spare.

In both her cheeks was a dimple rare
Whenever she smiled you see them there.
Abundant in health with eyes so blue
And twinkled, as if filled with morning dew.

I left Sussex that was green
And I forget the names of the places I've seen
And now that I'm back with my folks once more
My thoughts return to that friendly shore.

Maybe you've met her of whom I speak
With the laughing eyes and rosy cheeks.
Well, if you meet her, and I hope you do
Tell her I'll be back over that ocean blue.

Barry Barrowman 21 Aug 1946

This poem was written about the young June Usherwood

PERSONAL SOURCES

In putting together this book, all the authors have drawn heavily - and freely - on the recollections of many individuals who were in Wadhurst during and after the War: some people were formally interviewed and their words recorded on disc or tape for future reference; some interviews were fully recorded in type; some people wrote down their reminiscences for us to use and many were simply gained through face to face or telephone conversation.

Without them, this book would be the poorer and we therefore list here all those, who have given us their memories and agreed that we may use them in this book, and those who have sourced information for us:

Joyce Anscombe	Jennifer Hawkins	Roma Ogilvy Watson
Josephine Bailey	Jennet Hemsley	Jim Overy
Peggy Bartholomew	Don Henderson	Rosemary Pope
Frank Bishop	Colin Hodder	Rosemary Potter
Gillian Briggs	Walter Hodder	Heather Russell
Molly Codd	Betty Hunter	Ruth Skilton
Jan Comerford	Ken Jones	Nellie Thompsett
Hans Degenkolb	Hans Kaupert	Val Tunbridge
Doreen Drury	John Lamplugh	John Turley
Norman Gingell	Nora Manktelow	Nora Tweedley
Jim Gray	Des Mansfield	William Whitehorn
David Hawken	Sheila Mansfield	Peter Wicker
	Kathy Mitchell	

Sadly, not all of these are still alive to read the results of their co-operation. We also heard, just before going to print, that Oliver Mason, historian of Wadhurst, had died.   He was an honorary member of the History Society. We valued his active involvement in, and support of, the Society; his book *Wadhurst - Town of the High Weald* has been an inspiration to us all.

The Overlords

TIME LINE OF EVENTS

World Events		Events in Wadhurst	
		1939	
		May	German refugees arrive in Wadhurst
1 Sep	German invasion of Poland		
3 Sep	Great Britain and France declare war on Germany	Sep	War Agriculture Committee set up
Sep	Sinking of 26 British merchant ships by German U-boats	2 Sep	Evacuated staff and students of Brockley County Grammar School arrive. Billeting arranged at Commemoration Hall
		1940	
		Jan	Rationing of butter, bacon and sugar introduced. Further goods added throughout the War
		Jan	First market held under government control
9 Apr	German invasion of Denmark and Norway		
10 May	German invasion of the Low Countries	May - Jun	South Wales Borderers stationed in the area in anticipation of German invasion
3 Jun	Evacuation of British troops from Dunkirk		
11 Jun	Italy declares war on Great Britain		
22 Jun	France capitulates to the Germans	Jun	Church bells silenced
29 Jun	German occupation of the Channel Islands		
		Jul	Home Guard units established
		Jul-Oct	5th Loyal North Lancashire Regiment stationed in the area
8 Aug - 31 Oct	German Luftwaffe offensive against Great Britain (the Battle of Britain)	4 Sep	German aircraft crashes at Little Butts. Four more crash between Sep and Oct
27 Sep	Tripartite pact by Germany , Italy and Japan	19 Sep	Bombs destroy Buttons Farm resulting in two fatalities
			Over 2,000 high explosive and incendiary bombs land in the parish, most during the first half of the war
		1941	
11 Mar	USA Senate pass Lend-Lease Bill	9 Mar	Four bombs hit Sparrows Green destroying Newington's Stores and adjoining cottages and damaging partially-built new primary school
		14-21 Mar	Wadhurst Warship Week
6 Apr - 31 May	German invasion of mainland Greece; Battle of Crete	19-26 Apr	Wadhurst War Weapons Week
22 May	German invasion of Russia (Operation Barbarossa)	17 May	Rose Ede presented with the George Medal by King George VI for her bravery in saving children from the ruins of Buttons Farm
24-24 May	Sinking of HMS Hood by the German battleship Bismarck; sinking of the Bismarck		

Wadhurst in the Second World War

World Events		Events in Wadhurst	
		1941 [cont]	
		Jun	Comprehensive survey of 78 Wadhurst farms conducted by MAF
		Jul	Monks Park opened as a hostel for old people bombed in London
12 Aug	Signing of Atlantic Charter by Churchill and President Roosevelt		
18 Nov	Launch of British offensive in Western Desert		
7 Dec	Japanese attack on Pearl Harbour		
8 Dec	USA and Great Britain declare war on Japan	Dec	First Canadian troops arrive
9 Dec	Siege of Tobruk ends		
11 Dec	Germany and Italy declare war on USA		
		1942	
15 Feb	Singapore falls to the Japanese	1942/43	Canadian troops engage in training manoeuvres over parish land, often involving local Home Guard units
30 May	First RAF '1000 bomber' raid on Cologne	12 Apr	Church services to celebrate work of Home Guard
19 Aug	Dieppe Raid (Op.Jubilee) by 2nd Canadian Div and British Commandos	19 Aug	Some Canadian troops stationed in Wadhurst participate in Dieppe Raid
		2 Nov	Introduction of school meals
4 Nov	Allies defeat German/Italian army at El Alamein	15 Nov	Church bells rung to celebrate victory in North Africa
		1943	
31 Jan	Surrender of German 6th Army at Stalingrad		
May	End of Battle of the Atlantic with final victory over German U-boats		Wadhurst 'Wings' week
13 May	Surrender of Axis forces in Tunisia		
10 Jul	Allied invasion of Sicily	July?	Italian POWs start arriving at Wadhurst Park
1 Sep	Allied invasion of Italy		
8 Sep	Italy surrenders		
18 Nov	RAF raid on Berlin		
		1944	
22 Jan	Allies land at Anzio	Jan-Jun	Canadian troops leave Wadhurst in advance of D-Day. Many other troop movements through the village
18 Mar	RAF drops 3,000 tons of bombs on Hamburg		
		6-13 May	Wadhurst 'Salute the Soldier' week
4 Jun	Allies capture Rome		
6 Jun	D-Day invasion of Normandy	13 Jun	First V1 observed crossing Wadhurst
13 Jun	Flying bomb (V1) attacks on Britain commence	Jun-Oct	A total of 18 V1s land in the parish
June	Defeat of Japanese in India		Royal Artillery Light Air Defence Units stationed in the area to combat V1s

Wadhurst in the Second World War

World Events		Events in Wadhurst	
		1944 [cont]	
		29 Jul	V1 destroys eight cottages in Green Square, resulting in two fatalities
		3 Aug	V1 destroys Tidebrook school
25 Aug	Liberation of Paris	6 Aug	V1 explodes on the railway near the Faircrouch Lane road bridge
8 Sep	Rocket bomb (V2) attacks on Britain commence		
17 Sep	The Battle of Arnhem begins		
10 Oct	Americans re-land on the Philippines		
16 Dec	Battle of the Bulge in Ardennes	Dec	Home Guard units disbanded
		1945	
17 Jan	Russians capture Warsaw		
9 Feb	British and Canadian troops reach the Rhine		
13/14 Feb	Allied bombing of Dresden		
30 Apr	Hitler commits suicide		
2 May	Russians capture Berlin	2 May	Air Raid Wardens' "stand down"
5 May	Unconditional surrender of all German forces	3 May	Last time of lighting of lamp at first aid post at Cousley Wood
8 May	Churchill and President Truman proclaim VE Day	8 May	Informal VE Day celebrations including closure of school for two days, bonfires and small parties
26 Jul	Labour Government elected		
8 Aug	First atomic bomb dropped on Hiroshima		
9 Aug	Atomic bomb dropped on Nagasaki		
14 Aug	Japan agrees to unconditional surrender		
15 Aug	VJ Day	15 Aug	Schools closed for two days for further celebrations
5 Sep	British forces re-enter Singapore		
		1946	
		Jan	Revd. E Mannering announces his retirement
		June	German POWs arrive at Wadhurst Park
21 Jul	Bread rationing introduced - 9 oz a day		
		1947	
		Jan	'Welcome Home Gathering'
		March	'ITMA' comes to Wadhurst

WADHURST PARISH NEWS

THE CHURCH OF | S? PETER & S? PAUL

JAN., 1936 | ENTER INTO HIS GATES WITH THANKSGIVING | PRICE 2D.

CHAPTER 1: THE RÔLE OF THE CHURCH
MICHAEL HARTE

A fairly complete set of Parish magazines has been made available to us by the East Sussex Record Office [PAR 498/7/4]; over the eleven-year period from January 1936, 92 issues [or 70%] of the Parish magazines were available for analysis. Study of the issues from January 1936 to November 1946 has provided a good insight into the effects the War had on the Church and the influence the Church had on daily life and on the support given by the community to each other and to those on active service. Throughout the period - until June 1946 when the Revd. David Rice arrived - the vicar was the Revd. Ernest Mannering, Rural Dean of Etchingham, and the Parish magazine had a monthly commentary from him, often on events in the outside world. Coverage in the magazine not only included matters relating strictly to the Church and Church worship but also details of activity in the community, some aimed at supporting the War effort but much more giving an insight into more mundane matters. Throughout, but particularly in the vicar's own letter starting 'MY DEAR FRIENDS', the theme is one of comfort and support; in this chapter, the extracts concentrate on purely Church matters and the outside world. Throughout, his writing flows with smooth and elegant cadences.

Worship

Before the outbreak of war, the routine of Church worship at St Peter & St Paul was:

Sundays	11:00 15:00 18:30
Holy Communion	every Sunday 08:00
1st Sunday	07:00 [during summer]
1st Sunday	12:00
3rd Sunday	10:00
5th Sunday	- after Evensong

Great Festivals	06:00 07:00 08:00 12:00
Thursday	08:00 [when no Saint's Day]
Last Thursdays	12:00 [specially for invalids]
Holy Baptism	1st Sunday 15:00
Weekdays	09:45
Saint's Days	08:00
Churchings	after any service or by arrangement.

In addition, at the Mission Church in Faircrouch Lane there were services of Holy Communion every fourth Sunday at 08:00, and Evensong every Sunday at 18:30, and another celebration of Evensong at Cousley Wood School every Sunday at 15:30.

By March 1941 there had been minor changes to the times of some services: there were no longer four services of Holy Communion to mark the Great Festivals, and the Litany was being said on Wednesday and Friday every week at 12:00. Holy Communion was being celebrated at Cousley Wood School [from August 1938] at 10:00, and a Children's service every Sunday [from January to November 1940] at 14:45. A Sunday School was running in the Institute at 10:00 and at Cousley Wood School at 14:30 by August 1942, continuing until after the end of the war. These – and other alterations and special services - were announced in the Parish magazine:

September 1940: Naturally the completion of the first year of the war prompts us to reflection. On September 8th we are again summoned by our King to a Day of National Prayer. .... May I call your attention specially to the announcement that there will be a United Service in the Parish Church at 3 pm.

October 1940: Times of Services. On and after Sunday, October 20th, the Evening Service will be at 3 pm. There will be no separate Children's Service, but we hope to make the Afternoon Service a "Family Service", to which parents and children can come together. At the Mission Church, which can be "blacked out", Evensong will still be at 6.30 pm. During the winter months there will not be a celebration of Holy Communion at 7 am. on the first Sunday of the month.

November 1940: Time of services: Owing to the extension of "Summertime" to the whole winter, on and after November 24th, early Celebrations of Holy Communion will be at 9 am. instead of 8 am.

and Under existing circumstances the services which have been held for twenty years on "Remembrance" Sunday must be considered to have come to an end. But it is felt that a United Service, at which members of the Home Guard, ARP Services and other bodies would parade, would better meet the needs of today. The Commandant of the Home Guard has asked for this service, and the Chief Warden has promised to support it. I hope that the Salvation Army Band may lead the singing, and that a considerable cross-section of the present population of Wadhurst may be present, so that together we may strengthen our hearts in God for the immediate task.

September 1941: In connection with the second anniversary of the outbreak of war, Sunday, September 7th, will be observed as a National Day of Prayer and in addition to the usual services there will be a United Service in the afternoon at 3 pm., to which I should like to invite all people of goodwill to be present. The collection at this service will be for the "Comforts Fund".

and The second anniversary of the outbreak of war may also be regarded as the first anniversary of the mass assault upon this country

3

from the air, which we now call "The Battle of Britain," and Sunday, September 21st, is to be observed as a Day of Thanksgiving for the deliverance from the peril from the air a year ago. The suggestion has been made that the collections throughout the country on this day should be given to the Royal Air Force Benevolent Fund, and we hope to fall in with that suggestion here.

April 1942: Sunday, April 12th, is being kept throughout Sussex as "Home Guard" Sunday, and we shall be glad to welcome the Wadhurst Home Guard to a special service at 3 pm. We all realise the greatness of the task which the Home Guard would have to shoulder in the event of an invasion, and the importance of maintaining it both in its efficiency and in numbers. It will be good for them, and for us, to go to church together on April 12th, and we bid them welcome.

September 1942: On September 3rd, we are summoned to keep yet again a National Day of Prayer. There are special reasons why we should do so. The war seems to be moving towards its climax and is increasing in sternness and severity. The Day of Prayer is to be held on a weekday, the third anniversary of the declaration of war, and therefore on the part of many a special effort will be needed if they are to attend a service. .... I hope, too, that it may be possible, if hop-picking has started by then, to have some quite short Services in the hop-gardens. There will also be a Service at Cousley Wood School at 6.30 pm. The shops and business houses will close for an hour from 10 am. to enable their people to come to church at 11, as this will take place at the exact time of the declaration of war on September 3rd, 1939. I am sure that we shall all appreciate their readiness to help in this way.

and TIMES OF SERVICE. On Sunday, September 27th, the time of Evensong must be put back to 5.30 pm. There will not be a celebration of the Holy Communion at the Mission Church on that day.

August 1943: Once again we are asked to keep September 3rd, the fourth anniversary of the outbreak of war, as a day of National Prayer and Dedication. But this year the word Thanksgiving is inserted before 'Prayer and Dedication' in the title, and we can all understand the reason for it. Since last September the strategic and political outlooks have entirely changed, and enormously to the advantage of the United Nations. Many of those, whose faith in the ultimate victory of good has never faltered, and who therefore believed that systems based on force and fraud must some day come crashing down, were hard put to see exactly how victory could be achieved. But now we can at least descry the outline of the prospect, which opens up before us, even though the way to complete victory may yet be hard and long.

December 1943: Among the 'minor inconveniences' may be reckoned the disturbance of the hours of church worship and the absence of the facilities upon which many have relied in order to get to church. For some the laying up of cars and the absence of buses during Sunday forenoon have led to a break in the life-long habit of worship. But would it not be possible for some, who have been accustomed to come to church on Sunday morning, to come in the afternoon when buses do run? .... Those who have come to the 8 am. war-time Christmas celebrations in the dark at the Parish Church when the Christmas hymns are sung from memory, and the only light comes from a few candles, have found it deeply impressive and inspiring.

June 1944: EMPIRE YOUTH SUNDAY. There was a fine gathering of Young People for the Empire Youth Service on May 21st. The ATC, Cadets, Guides, Rangers, Junior Red Cross Detachment, Methodist Guild, Hill House Girls' Club, and Wadhurst College were present in force, and we were only sorry that the Youth Group was elsewhere. Flt. Sergt. Denis Page [ATC] acted as Churchwarden, and read the Bidding. Lessons were read by Sergt. Ken Midmer [ATC], Audrey Farley [Rangers], Arthur Bryan [Methodist Guild] and Eliza White [Wadhurst College]. Prayers were led by Ian Sharpe [Methodist Guild]. Others distributed service sheets and took the collection, which was for the Princess Tsahai Memorial Hospital, Addis Ababa, and amounted to £2 10s 0d.

July 1944: War Intercessions are held daily in the Parish Church, as follows: Monday, Wednesday, Friday 12 noon; Tuesday, Thursday, Saturday 8 pm.

October 1944: Turning to matters domestic it appears that it will be possible to continue evensong at 6.30 pm. with certain modifications in the lighting arrangements. This will mean that the evening congregation will have to sit in the centre of the church, if they want any light, but there should be no difficulty about that.

November 1944: There will be a United Service in the Parish Church at 3 pm. on Sunday, November 5th. This is the British Legion's service, primarily, but members of the Home Guard and Civil Defence services, also the ATC and Cadets, are invited to parade in uniform, if they so desire.

May 1945: On the day when hostilities with Germany are declared to be at an end, short United Services of Thanksgiving will be held in the Parish Church at 3.30 pm. and 7.30 pm. On the following day there will be a celebration of Holy Communion at 8 am. Later on - on the appointed day - there will be a United Service of Thanksgiving and Dedication. The time will be announced later. Whatever may have been the case in 1918, this time the end of the war in Europe will find us in no mood for undue exaltation

September 1945: RAF SUNDAY: We are asked to keep Sunday September 16th as a day of remembrance of the 'Battle of Britain'. The collection on that day will be for the RAF Benevolent Fund.

and THE MISSION CHURCH: We are sorry to say that it has been found necessary to close the Mission Church, except for the monthly service of Holy Communion at 8 am. on the fourth Sunday. It is hoped that those who attend evensong at the Mission Church will be able to

come to the Parish Church.

November 1945: Some of us were wondering what would happen this year with regard to the keeping of Armistice Day. The King's Order has made it clear that it is to be retained, and the 'Two Minutes' Silence' will again be observed. We shall remember not only those who gave their lives in the 1914-1918 war, but those who gave their lives in the 1939-1945 war, linking the two wars by the sacrifice of life, which both involved. Here in Wadhurst, in order that the Silence may be kept as it should be, the congregation are asked to be in their places by 10.55 am. In the afternoon, at 3 pm., there will be a United Service, which the British Legion is sponsoring, and it is hoped that there may be a really good gathering of ex-Service men and women at this, the first post-war Remembrance Day Service. The Revd. J Walton Acres will be the preacher. We shall be able, by means of the collections on this day, to help Earl Haig's Fund, which does so much in so many ways for ex-Service men.

March 1946: For the present the Mission Church must be closed. Should it be possible to arrange a service, notice will be given.

Church Personnel

Personnel changes within the church hierarchy were remarkably few. In July 1936, the Revd. D E Rice, living at Fernlea, Old Station Road, was an additional clergy until he left in July 1938; the vicar wrote:

Soon after the "Parish News" appears we shall be losing Mr Rice. Though we cannot regret the reason, we do regret the fact. During his time at Wadhurst he has shown himself a good worker, and he will be much missed, not only by the lads whom he has made his special care, but by the many friends whom he has made. On August 9th at 2.30 pm. he is to be married to Miss Elisabeth New at the Parish Church.

Mr Rice was replaced in December 1938 by the Revd. C H Cartwright BA, who lived at Great Durgates, until September 1941; from then on the Revd. E Mannering was on his own until replaced by the Revd. David Rice in June 1946.

Church Wardens	Start date	End date
Lt Col A R Cheale, TD Buckland House	Jan 1936	Jul 1938
Mr T B Miller JP, Stone Cross	Jan 1936	Jun 1944
Mr M G Woods, Moseham	Aug 1938	Feb 1941
Mr M Watts, Byeways	Mar 1941	Nov 1946
Mr E Burns-Pye, Buckhurst Manor	Jul 1944	Nov 1946
Clerk and Sexton		
Mr H J Halford, Balburnie	Jan 1936	Nov 1946
Organist		
Miss Moren, Durgates	Jan 1936	Jan 1946

Her retirement was noted in the Parish magazine for May 1946:

> On the occasion of Miss Moren's retirement from the post of Organist
> at the Parish Church, the Parochial Church Council wished to show
> their appreciation of her loyal and faithful service for so many years
> and so a resolution was passed at a meeting of the Council that a cheque
> for 100 guineas should be presented to Miss Moren. In addition to this,
> a sum of £18 was subscribed by various parishioners who also wished
> to show their appreciation of Miss Moren's services, so a cheque for
> £123 was sent to her, representing both these amounts.

Mr Noel Gallup, Best Beech	Mar 1946	Nov 1946
Church Schools		
Mr C Mould and Miss M E Larcombe	Jan 1936	Nov 1946
Members of the Parochial Church Council on active service		
Mr J T Casterton	Mar 1941	
Mr P R G Charters	Mar 1941	Dec 1945
[Major from April 1943]		
Mr A McQueen	Mar 1941	Dec 1945
Mr H G Meech	Mar 1941	Dec 1945
Mr F H Bond	Apr 1941	Dec 1945

The magazines also list the District visitors – a remarkably stable list of between 27 and 31 married and spinster ladies of the parish; between May and August 1943, Mr Woods joined the throng. In June 1941, when the list was longest, 18 unmarried and 13 married women, headed by Miss Dorothea Courthope, made up the team; the full list was the Misses Dorothea Courthope, Brian, Marshall, McKechnie, Milne, Oliver, Parsons, Previte, Rowntree, Scott, Smith, Stephenson, Crossley Taylor, Denton Thompson,

Walker, O Walker, E Watson, and Whitty, and the Mrs Austen, C Bell, Bryant, Burns-Pye, Bye, Hartnell, Heath, Hopkins, Keyser, McCormick, Roberts, Sykes, and Whitten.

Baptisms, Marriages and Burials

There was no obvious change of pattern or other interference with the regular routines of baptisms, marriages and burials throughout the War years.

Over the period of these issues of the Parish magazine, 365 deaths were recorded. The ages of all but nine of these were printed: 19 were under two years old - the youngest *'only lived three hours'* and six others only lived for a week or less. At the other end of the scale, the oldest was 95 and five others were nonagenarians. One six-year old boy's death was recorded: *'the only son of his mother, and she a widow, died as a result of an injury accidentally inflicted'*.

under 2	19	51 - 60	50
3-20	10	61 - 70	78
21-40	17	71 - 80	92
41-50	13	Over 80	77

Analysis of recorded burials

In January 1939 the magazine printed this:

> "HAND - On December 10th, 1938, at Fir Bank, Wadhurst, Samuel Hand, "John", for 67 years the faithful servant and beloved friend of the family of the late A G Watson, formerly of Harrow School, and Uplands, Wadhurst, aged 84."

> The above, which appeared in the columns of the Times for 15th December, epitomizes the life story of Mr Samuel Hand, who had been living in quiet retirement for some years. Recently he had failed considerably, and for some months had kept to his room. It was always a privilege to visit him and to minister to him, and one could not help feeling that the rock foundation of his fine character was his simple Christian faith, and that he loved his Lord, the family which he served so long, and his friends.

139 marriages were recorded in St Peter & St Paul over the same period.

257 baptisms, 113 girls and 144 boys, were recorded over the period, 4 at the Cousley Wood school, 2 in Tidebrook, 3 privately; the remainder, including one adult, were in the Parish church.

In 12 instances, the names of the parents are not printed; six children were adopted.

Musical Activity

The Parish magazines also record some events relating to the church bells and to the choir – other aspects of the life of the church:

> **August 1938**: It has been brought to our notice that there is something a little amiss with one of the bells, and it was decided to obtain expert opinion as to what should be done. The help of Messrs. Mears and Stainbank, the famous bell founders, was called in, and their report says that it is the fifth bell which needs attention. .... Messrs. Mears and Stainbank [*at the Whitechapel Bell Foundry*] add to their report some details about the bells which may be of interest:
>
> "All your bells, except the third, were cast at this foundry, the treble and fifth in 1764, the second and tenor in 1752 and the fourth in 1753. We re-cast the tenor in 1872 and the second in 1925. In 1891 we quarter-turned the five smaller bells, and re-hung the six with new headstocks, bearings, pulleys etc and strengthened the bell-frame with tie bolts. The bearings on the smaller bells have therefore done 47 years' service. The third bell was cast in 1670 by John Hodson, a London founder.
>
> "The following are the inscriptions on the bells:-
>
> *Tenor*: Thos Vigor & John Elliott, Ch Wardens. 1752. Thos Lester & T Pack fecit 13-2-11
> *Fifth*: Lawrence Kemp & Wm Collens Ch Wardens. Lester & Pack, of London, fecit 1764
> *Fourth*: C Russel, J Elliott C Wardens. T Diamond. 1753. 9-0-6
> *Third*: John Hodson made me. 1670. Nathaniel Johnson. John Barham Church-wardens. CH
> *Second*: This bell was raised by voluntary subscriptions, 1752. Thos Vigor & John Elliott Ch Wardens. Thos Lester & T Pack fecit 5-3-1. Recast June 1925, Harry C Corke Ernest Leete Churchwardens
> *Treble*: Lester & Pack, of London, fecit, 1764."

August 1940: Shortly before the ban of silence was imposed upon all church bells, the belfry was examined by an expert from Messrs. Mears & Stainbank, after complaints had been made by the ringers about the increasing difficulty of ringing. .... It would not be safe to ring the bells in their present state, so in view of the report, and as an act of faith in ultimate victory, the Parochial Church Council has decided to put these repairs in hand, in order that when the bells can be rung again there may be no question of danger arising from the state of the bell-frame.

December 1942: We have all been heartened and encouraged by the good news from the various war fronts during the past month and, without any risk of being accused of wishful thinking, we may feel expectant and even confident that it will be followed by favourable developments. Our mood found expression in the ringing of the bells on November 15th, and the relaxation of the ban, which was very welcome. When we heard once again the familiar summons of the bells to thanksgiving and prayer, we realised how much we have missed them, and it is to be hoped that the ban may be further relaxed in the future, and not only for victories!

March 1944: Now that the sound of bells is again heard pealing forth on Sundays, we should like to say how much we appreciate the work of the ringers. Undismayed by the fact that nearly all our keen young ringers have joined the Forces, the older ringers have gathered round them some new recruits, including some ladies, and right well they are learning their craft.

November 1944: THE CHOIR: During the war the Choir has had to contend with difficulties. Full practices in the evening have not been possible, owing to the black-out and other reasons. Now that it is possible to use the church in the evening, it is hoped to resume full practices at 7.30 pm. To sing with feeling and intelligence is something that needs constant practice. Especially is this true of the singing of the psalms and canticles. During the black-out years we have dropped back a good deal in our Choir singing. Now is the time for the present members of the Choir, who have carried on so steadily, to begin to build up again the tradition of good choir singing, which was for so long a feature at Wadhurst Parish Church.

March 1946: The time has come for regular practice to be resumed. The first full practice will be at 8 pm. on Friday, March 8th. Tenors and basses and altos will be welcome, and it is hoped to make a start with a few boys shortly. What is wanted is not only voices, but keenness and a readiness to use the gift of song for the glory of God.

June 1946: The Choir are making valiant efforts to make our services bright and colourful, but they need the presence of a great many more voices, both lusty and gentle, in the body of the Church, if their efforts are to be crowned with success. Even then the picture would still be incomplete without the sombre background of those few young men who, like their Vicar, find it almost impossible to make anything that could be described as a pleasant noise.

Another important regular event, linked to the Parish church, was the Sunday Schools' outing. Before the war it involved a train trip to Hastings, with accommodation reserved in advance:

July 1936: COMBINED SUNDAY SCHOOLS OUTING - to Hastings, Wednesday, July 22nd. Will all please be at Wadhurst Station at 7.30 am. Will all adults please purchase their tickets from Mrs H T Manktelow, Primmers Green, on or before July 20th, so that sufficient accommodation may be assured. It is hoped that all who possibly can will travel by the Special Train, which has to be registered, so that all may go in comfort. Fares: Adults 2/6; Children 1/3.

Once war began, this became impossible to arrange and alternatives were needed:

February 1943: SUNDAY SCHOOL PARTY. There must have been nearly 200 children in the Commemoration Hall for the Annual Sunday School Party. .... We all enjoyed ourselves and had a thoroughly good time. Once more we owe a debt of gratitude to Mrs Manktelow and her helpers, and to all who worked hard to make a happy and successful treat.

But peace brought the chance to return to happier times and the special train again was used to take children and their parents for a day by the sea:

August 1945: SUNDAY SCHOOL OUTING: For the first time since 1939 the United Sunday School Outing was held again this year, and on July 18th about 450 children and parents went by special train to Hastings, and thoroughly enjoyed a long summer day by the sea. .... The organisation of such an outing is no small matter, and we are most grateful to Mrs Manktelow for all her work. Everyone voted the outing a great success. Our thanks are also due to those who responded, so kindly and readily, to the appeal for help towards the expenses; and last but not least, to those who supplied lorries and cars to convey the children to their homes at the end of a happy day.

Comments on Current Affairs

Throughout the period, the vicar used his monthly letter to share his thoughts with his parishioners. Often these included carefully worded phrases about the progress of political and military affairs, written to avoid giving any comfort to our enemies – and therefore not always easy today to link back to specific events of the time.

> **January 1936**: The year opens in circumstances of unusual difficulty and great uncertainty, as far as the international outlook is concerned. Italy is still engaged in what she professes to regard as her "civilizing mission" in Abyssinia, though fifty nations have adjudged her action to be an "act of aggression". During the past month we have had the astonishing spectacle of a British Cabinet Minister agreeing to and defending a series of terms - suggested as a basis for negotiation - which seemed to make the way of aggressors easy, and were rightly rejected by public opinion, which made itself speedily and effectively felt. The net result has been that the Government has extricated itself from an awkward situation - not without some loss of prestige; a trusted Minister [*the British Foreign Secretary - Samuel Hoare*], of whom much was hoped, has had to resign, and the whole process of dealing with the situation has been slowed down. But if it has revealed that the greater part of the nation is determined that aggression shall not pay, if means can be found to prevent it, and has aroused other nations to the implications of collective action the crisis will not have been in vain.

> **February 1936**: It is difficult to realise that the King [*King George V*], who for more than twenty-five eventful years had borne the cares and burdens of the throne, whose voice many of us heard speaking to us on Christmas Day, is no longer with us. .... To the Queen [*Mary*] our hearts

go out in deepest sympathy, and to our new King [*King Edward VIII*], now called to take his father's place, we pledge our loyalty and prayers.

May 1936: During the past few weeks the turn which world affairs have taken has given cause for great anxiety. At the present moment it does look as if the wanton aggression of Italy may possibly achieve the end in view, the collapse and dismemberment of Abyssinia. It also seems clear that pledges given by dictators on behalf of a totalitarian state are not worth the paper on which they are written, and that, in spite of the horror expressed almost throughout the world at the methods of warfare adopted by Italy, those methods are what we must expect whenever war breaks out in future. .... It is little to be wondered at that Germany chose this moment for her own bit of treaty-breaking [*the Treaty of Locarno*], thereby making a difficult position more difficult still, and diverting attention from the Abyssinian tragedy, even though she may think she has saved her own soul.

April 1937: Then in some six weeks' time we shall be in the midst of the Coronation rejoicings [*King George VI*]. These will be tempered by the circumstances which preceded this particular Coronation [*the Abdication of King Edward VIII in December 1936*]. It is all the more important therefore that the religious element should be duly emphasised. .... I hope to make arrangements for the broadcast of the Coronation to be heard in Church.

June 1937: As we think of the Coronation in retrospect, the most wonderful thing about it would seem to be that millions of the King's subjects were able, by means of the broadcast, to share in the service at Westminster Abbey, and to understand, as never before, something of the meaning of that splendid rite. .... We are very grateful to Mr C Baldwin, who not only took great pains to ensure that the reception in Church should be as good as possible by installing no less than three receiving sets, but made no charge to the Church for doing so, a piece of voluntary service which we deeply appreciate. As regards the rest of the day, the rain came down when the procession, which was most imposing, started, and continued until well into the afternoon. In spite of it there was a good gathering for the sports at the field, and about 1500 teas were served by Mrs Manktelow and her small army of helpers.

August 1938: That there has been a distinct easing in the international situation during the past few weeks is a matter for thankfulness, though there is nothing in the immediate outlook, which gives ground for any but a limited optimism. Indeed, as long as the ethics of the jungle prevail in world relations - and there is only too much evidence of that - we must expect to live under a perpetual liability to shocks, excursions and alarms.

October 1938: During the past month, affairs in Europe have drifted rapidly to a stage of crisis, and it seems probable that we shall know more clearly by the time that the PARISH NEWS appears which way the crisis will be resolved. In circumstances such as these, events have a way of making anything that is written beforehand look foolish, and all we can do is to hope that a peaceful solution to the problems which beset us may be found, and that it may be a real solution, and not merely a postponement until another crisis arises. The minds of many in these days have gone back to 1914, but there is this difference between 1914 and 1938. The peoples of Europe and - it is to be hoped - their leaders too are more alive today to the dangers which would threaten humanity if a European war did break out, and the prospect is one from which they rightly shrink. In that factor lies the main hope of a peaceful solution - the peoples do not want war. At the same time it must be admitted that the mentality which lies behind dictatorship makes for war, and not inconceivably might make it inevitable. There lies the danger. .... We should pray for Herr Hitler and Signor Mussolini as well as for Mr Chamberlain, M. Daladier [*of France*] and President Benes [*of Czechoslovakia*].

November 1938: It is now nearly a month since "The Crisis" came to an end, but there is as yet no sign that the spate of speeches and letters about it is ceasing. This shows that people were profoundly moved and shaken by the events of the last fortnight of September. With hardly an exception, people felt that Mr Chamberlain's action [*meeting Hitler in Munich*] was right, that it averted war, and that it gave effect to the inmost desires of a vast majority of the people of Europe. .... After our experience last month, we dare not leave to haphazard and last-minute arrangements such matters as ARP and other emergency measures. In these things I believe we are prepared to be led, and that we look to those in authority to give us a lead. We may not be willing to forego our right to criticise - no Englishman could dream of doing that! But we are willing to be told what is wanted of us. It will mean sacrifice - of time, convenience, money and much else - but the time for letting things slide has gone by, and we have to justify our right to exist as a free and intelligent democracy by showing that we are prepared to submit to discipline, and to show a spirit of service as strong as any that can be found elsewhere.

December 1938: During the past month the whole world, outside "Greater Germany", has been shocked by the appalling measures taken by the German Government against their Jewish and "non-Aryan" minorities, and both in the press and in private conversation there has been abundant evidence that the feelings of humanity have been deeply stirred by these excesses. But it may be doubted how far knowledge of these things has been allowed to penetrate to where it is most desirable that they should be known, i.e. in Germany itself. It may be doubted also whether any appeals, on humanitarian grounds, would have any effect on the present rulers of Germany. .... But I venture to think that this Christmas we shall all have the "refugees" on our minds and hearts, and shall want to do something extra and something special for them. In order that, as a congregation, we may give corporate effect to this desire, there will be retiring collections on Sunday, December 11th, for Refugees in Czechoslovakia and elsewhere.

March 1940: A big question haunts the minds of most people at the present moment. Will spring be heralded by an intensification of warfare on land and in the air? We shall soon know the answer to that question now. But it is at least possible that the anticipated "flare-up" may not come at all, and probably that, if it does come, it will not come in the way expected. Let us then not get into the way of thinking that the present phase can only be resolved by some titanic clash. It may even be, though the outlook is unpromising, that a way to peace might open up unexpectedly. We just cannot tell. But it is clear that we must be ready for every eventuality.

April 1940: A thoughtful young man, who loathing war and all that it means, felt it to be his duty to join up at the beginning, and deliberately chose the infantry as the branch of the service which incurred most risk and took the hardest knocks, recently said that he felt he could not pray about this war. It was all too big, and he could not see how prayer about it could do any good or make any difference. I expect that many are inclined to feel like that about it in these days. War breeds a spirit of fatalism. This is not altogether a bad thing, as otherwise things might become intolerable. .... These reflections are suggested by the fact that the extra war-time services during the past six months have met with little or no support, and therefore after Easter we shall be going back to our pre-war ways. If the prayerfulness of Wadhurst in war-time is to be judged in this way, the position is grievous.

May 1940: A partial answer has already been given to the question asked in this letter two months ago. If we were shocked by the swiftness of the German blows in Denmark and in Norway, we have been greatly heartened by the Allied riposte, delivered in the first instance by the Navy and the Air Force, and now being driven home by the Army. It must surely be clear to all now that we are fighting against an evil thing. We have a cause of which none need to be ashamed. It is our part to see that we live worthy of the principles, which we are seeking to maintain. It is true that Nazism threatens our very existence, but it does so by trampling underfoot the right of smaller nations to live their own lives in peace and quietness.

June 1940: We have learnt in recent days [*the evacuation from Dunkirk*], and by more than one example, how quickly the features of the situation may change, and so far the changes have been for the worse. The war is at our very doorstep, and only the existence of "the moat" [*the English Channel*] has prevented us so far from suffering as Holland, Belgium and France have suffered. We have now to be prepared for the possibility of the extension of the conflict by one means or another to the soil of our own land. In this grave situation, grave but not hopeless, it may be of help to remember certain things:
[1] the cause for which we fight is as good and splendid to-day as it was at the beginning of September last, and to have the better cause is no small asset;
[2] from the realist point of view it has yet to be proved that they are wrong who say that sea-power counts more than any other form of power in war, and will still be the deciding factor;
[3] that faith and courage will carry us through.

17

July 23 1940: I am sure that many have been helped and encouraged by Lord Halifax's [*Foreign Secretary*] re-statement of Britain's position, yesterday. We recognised there the authentic Christian note, which has not been too conspicuous in the utterances of statesmen so far during this war.

November 1940: The shape of things to come seems to be emerging a little more clearly. The doubtful blessings of the new world order are to be extended to the Near East, unless the British Empire can prevent it, and Hitler, foiled of his plans for the invasion and subjugation of Britain, is attempting with the aid of his faithful partners in the Axis [*Nazi Germany and Fascist Italy*], and of as many other peoples as he can cajole or threaten, to accomplish the same end by other means. Meanwhile, the process of destruction from the air will go on, though we may hope that as winter draws on and counter measures develop, it will become less and less.

Rommel with the 15th Panzer Division in Libya 1941 [www.ww2db.com]

May 1941: One of the many things that makes this war so different from the last is the startling rapidity with which events happen, when they do happen. Almost overnight, certainly in a week, as we have known to our cost recently, the whole situation in an important area may be transformed. Thus after a short period of great success on land

and sea, we have met with a series of set-backs, and a number of ugly possibilities are beginning to show themselves. [*Rommel's attack on Agheila began on March 31; 7-14 April the Allied retreat to Tobruk.*]

August 1941: Who amongst us could have foreseen, three months ago, that we were going to have as quiet a summer as we have enjoyed so far? Who would have guessed that once more Hitler would break a solemn pact and invade Russia [*Op. Barbarossa*]? Who would have thought that the Russian Army would have put up as stout a fight as it is doing? Let us try and assess this event against the background of world events. Not so very long ago there was a possible danger of Britain and America being faced by an Axis Quadrilateral - Germany, Russia, Japan and Italy. That danger is now passed. Japan seems to be left to her own devices, and it takes no great effort of the imagination to believe that Italy wishes that she were well out of it. Of course what has happened is the kind of thing that was bound to happen, so long as the code of honour among nations is on a level with or below that which is said to prevail among thieves. At the worst our position is not a little improved through Germany's pre-occupation with her traditional foe in the East. At the best we may be on the threshold of great events, though it would probably be "wishful thinking" to anticipate any very speedy "issue out of all our afflictions."

January 22, 1942: Once more we find ourselves "in the trough of the wave," and those who follow the late Lord Salisbury's advice and "study large maps" are the first to realise how serious a threat to the Empire the entry of Japan into the war constitutes [*the Japanese attack on Pearl Harbour - December 1941- which brought the USA into the war*], and how large a measure of success has already attended their adventurous and carefully planned strategy. It is nothing less than a tragedy that the Japanese should have absorbed from Europe the doctrines which have their home in modern Germany, rather than the more ancient Christian tradition, which is the real source of all that is best in European culture and civilisation.

June 1942: On the titanic struggle which appears to be developing in Russia the fate of Europe may well depend, and with its issue our own destiny is profoundly involved. Russia at present stands between us and our deadliest foe. This fact should make us keenly appreciative of the magnificent effort that she is making against the invaders of her soil, and should stimulate us to help her in every way that we can.

May 1943: At this season, in the previous years of this war, our thoughts have turned to the possibility of spring offensives, and so far it has been mainly offensives by our enemies that we have had in mind. But this year a change has come over the scene and we think rather of his spring 'defensive.'

June 1943: Victory, complete and final, has come in North Africa, and for that we give thanks, as many did on May 16th. Whatever happens this summer or during the later course of the war, we shall continue to enjoy certain strategic advantages, hitherto denied to us, the prospect of which was opened up by the Allied landing in last November *['Operation Torch' - U.S. and British landing in French Morocco and Algeria]*, and of which we are now in a position to make use. With the words of the Prime Minister [*Winston Churchill*] to Congress fresh in our minds, there is no need to enlarge upon the greatness of the tasks that remain, but at least it may be claimed that a considerable instalment of his promise, *'Give us the tools, and we will finish the job',* has been made good. .... It was never more important than it is this year that the harvest should be abundant, and for that reason, though not for that reason alone, we propose to mark the Rogation Days by a procession to some fields and allotments, making three or four halts, when prayers will be offered and a verse or two of a hymn sung.

August 1943: Now that it seems possible, at long last, to say that the road to victory is in sight, and at a time when great possibilities are unfolding themselves before our eyes, it is more than ever important to maintain a sense of direction and destination. 'After Victory - what?' is the question that is arising in many minds, and it is important that some kind of answer should be given.

November 1943: The future may have much in store for us, which will test our powers of endurance to the utmost. The day of the 'Grand Assault' is not yet, and when it comes it will make great demands upon us. We have had reminders lately that Germany's power to strike and destroy is still great, and that her power is not yet broken. In this great contest, when force meets force, and endurance is matched by endurance, the side that can hold out longest will win. We believe that we know which side that will be, but we do not all apparently realise that if we are to be in a position to say 'God is our hope and strength' certain demands of a moral and spiritual nature are made upon us.

January 1944: All the signs point to 1944 as likely to be "the year of decision" as far as this great struggle in Europe is concerned, and we salute its dawn with mingled feelings; with fear, because it seems inevitable that the sum total of sorrow and misery caused by this war must be greatly increased, and it is natural to men to fear when they "enter into the cloud"; with hope, because in the last twelve months a long stride has been taken towards the victory of the cause which we took up in September 1939, and we are now in a measure prepared for the final ordeal that lies ahead.

May 21 1944: At the time of writing we are still waiting for the great and critical moment towards which things have been moving. I only want to say just one thing about it now. When "D Day" comes, please remember that the church is always open for private prayer during the hours of daylight.

Royal Marine Commandos landing at Juno 'Nan Red' Beach from 6 June 1944
[www.ww2db.com]

Jul 1944: Since the last issue of Parish News the first great step towards the liberation of Western Europe has been taken, and the forces of the United Nations are firmly established in Normandy. We all knew that it must come, and that the most careful preparations had been made for it, and that nothing less than a complete and decisive victory was the aim of the allied commanders.

September 1944: We approach the fifth anniversary of the commencement of the war with feelings far removed from those which marked the four previous anniversaries, for the pattern of victory can be discerned on every front. Things have moved so swiftly during the past few months that it now looks as if it may not be very long before the Nazi dragon is finally cornered and overcome. Four years ago that seemed a remote contingency, a matter of faith rather than hope, but now it is coming to pass before our eyes. We have had much for which we can only be thankful: steadfast and far-sighted leadership, a real unity, both in purpose and in action, amongst the Allies, such as has never been achieved before; unstinted bravery, devotion and sacrifice on the part of the Forces, who have sustained in three elements the full rigour of the struggle; a patient and persistent courage on the part of the peoples behind the fronts, who have borne sufferings undaunted and losses without complaint, because they knew that the cause was worthy.

October 1944: Seldom can so much that is encouraging have happened in so short a time as during the past few weeks. October finds the Allied armies in some cases across the German frontier, in some knocking at the gates. All are wondering how and when hostilities in the West will cease, and hoping that the time will not be long. Some of us remember the last hundred days of the first world war, and how rapidly things moved then to the final capitulation. But on psychological grounds, and in view of the Nazi frame of mind, it seems possible that the end of hostilities may be much more untidy than it was last time, and that the Nazi leaders, for whom the future holds no hope, and the most fanatical of their followers may fight it out to the last moment. So whilst we must be aware of thinking that it is all over bar the shouting - and even then there is Japan - we approach the time of transition from war to peace, for which we have all longed.

December 1944: If we had been told, at Christmas 1939, that five years later, at Christmas 1944, our nation would still find itself deeply engaged in a horrible war, we should have been appalled. But human nature is very adaptable, and we have become so inured to horrors, that even the disappointment of our hopes of a speedy and clear-cut decision in the West has not in any great degree diminished either our will or our capacity to endure 'jusqu' au bout', as the French used to say in the last war, and if we must say 'The end is not yet' at least the tokens of victory are clear and unmistakable.

April 1945: The Easter note is the note of Victory - and victory is in the air today. There is the victory of life over death, to which the recurrent miracle of the spring bears witness; there is the victory on the western and eastern fronts - may it be speedy and complete; there is victory over this or that form of evil, as envisaged in the five freedoms and in all planning for social reform and reconstruction. There is also "the victory that overcometh the world, even our faith."

June 1945: May 8th, the day which saw the end of hostilities in Europe, was one which will remain a landmark in the lives of all. Long expected, and not unheralded, when it came it was difficult to realise that the struggle which had lasted more than five years and eight months was over. There was, of course, the fact that the Far Eastern war was yet to be won, and the feeling that the difficulties of "winning the peace" really begin when the shooting stops, to curb exuberance. .... To those deep feelings the services held on VE-Day and on the Sunday following sought to give expression. We had a cause, which no man need be ashamed to have sustained, even by the dread arbitrament of war. We have been blessed with great leadership in the State, and in operations by sea and land and in the air.

September 1945: The world is at peace again. For that fact we can only feel profound thankfulness and relief. In one way the end of the Far-Eastern War came as an anti-climax, for most people could not help feeling more directly affected by the end of the war in Europe. But we do rejoice that now the second World War has definitely come to an end. Our ship of state has weathered the storm, and though not without loss and damage, is still taut and well-founded. The old pilot [*Winston Churchill*] who had steered it through the worst of the storm was dropped in the last month of the voyage - a consequence which no doubt many of those who brought it about rather regretted - and a new pilot, with a crew largely new, [*Clement Attlee and the Labour Government*] has taken over. .... We have just held our Day of Thanksgiving for Victory and Peace, and large congregations were present to take part in them. The motive of Dedication was present as well as that of Thanksgiving. There was also the sense that the shattering and shocking revelation of the power of the atomic bomb had rendered all our previous notions of political and military thought obsolete over-night, and that we were on the threshold of a new era. This new and terrible power must either be controlled, or it will destroy humanity. And what power, short of a world organisation, can control it, it is difficult to see. Henceforward national frontiers are going to mean little, national armies and navies and air forces are of little or no use, except for police duties.

The mushroom cloud resulting from an atomic bomb, Nagasaki, 9 Aug 1945
[www.ww2db.com]

The Impact of the War on the Local Community

July 1940: Our hearts go out in sympathy to Mr and Mrs Miller, Col and Mrs Cheale, and Mrs Playfoot in the loss of their sons in action, and to those who are still in anxiety and suspense concerning their loved ones. It is the tragedy of war that it is the young who have to bear the brunt of it, and to us with our limited vision, it seems as if they of all people can least be spared. On the other hand, a number of our men have come safely back from Dunkirk, and we have been glad to hear of the good progress of some who were wounded.

October 1940: Now that London is going through ordeal by battle, we feel profoundly shocked by the effect of the malignant waves of destruction which have been let loose upon our capital, but full of admiration for the way in which Londoners as a whole are standing up to the ordeal. .... The war has come very near to one part of the parish [*the bomb on Buttons Farm*] during the past few days. The deep sympathy of us all goes out to the two families which have suffered bereavement and loss. Tribute should be paid to those who rescued the children from the ruined house.

November 1940: A recent visitation, which befell one part of the parish [*for October 1940 bombs see p. 57*] and caused some material damage, affords a case in point. The predominant feeling amongst those who suffered seems to be that of thankfulness that the personal injuries were so few and that, compared with that, material damage just does not count.

January 1941: May I offer Mrs Carr and her son our deep sympathy in the grievous injury which she has sustained through enemy action [*she lost an arm as a result of a bomb falling on Edge Hill*], and express the hope that her recovery, even if slow, may be sure. Reference was made in last month's Magazine to the good work which she had carried on for the troops for several months [*organising dances*], and only on the evening before her house was bombed, she was in her place in the Commemoration Hall.

and It is a pleasure to be able to record the award of the George Medal to a Wadhurst girl. We all congratulate Miss Rose Ede [*for her rescue work at Buttons Farm*], and are glad to remember that not so very long ago she attended our Day School.

July 1944: The first Wadhurst soldier to give his life, as far as is yet known, in the invasion of Normandy is Roy Fazan, whose death in action has just been announced. Deep sympathy will be felt with Dr. and Mrs Fazan, and their family, so loved and honoured in our Wadhurst community.

September 1944: Quite rightly, there is still a ban on the immediate publication of details about the results of enemy action, but perhaps a word of sincere sympathy with the family of Mr and Mrs Blaylock, who lost their lives, may now be permitted, and also of Miss Boyd, and all who lost their homes or suffered damage at the end of July. The Green Square was an attractive addition to the amenities of Wadhurst, and it is to be hoped that at no very distant date it may be restored, and used for the purpose for which it was built.

Conclusion

Throughout these extracts, there is a clear sense of optimism even when things were going so wrong; the strain on the vicar must at times have been almost overwhelming as he tried valiantly to maintain morale among those left at home, worrying about their loved ones and their own futures. It is, perhaps, not surprising that the Revd. Ernest Mannering wrote in January 1946:

> I expect that most of you have already heard that Mrs Mannering and I will shortly be leaving Wadhurst, as I have been appointed Rector of Westonbirt, in Gloucestershire, and Chaplain of Westonbirt School. This offer came, quite unexpectedly, at a time when I had been told that I ought to seek a parish which would be less exacting physically than Wadhurst, which really needs a younger man to deal with the post-war situation.

To conclude, some things never change. The Parish magazine for January 1939 provided a foretaste of what was, in fact, to come; the vicar recorded:

> We have had a somewhat adventurous Christmas Day. On Thursday the Church boiler, which has given good service for thirteen years, sprang a leak, which made it impossible to keep the fire going. With heavy snow and several degrees of frost outside this made things distinctly awkward. A special wire was fixed up to take some small electric radiators, and oil stoves were lent, but you cannot really heat a church by such means, and all we can say is that they did take off the worst of the chill. But the additional current was too much for the fuses, and during the 7 am. Celebration, the lights and the organ current failed. At Mattins we had to manage without the organ, though the lights were on again. At Evensong the organ was working, but the lights again failed, so we had to carry on with the help of a few candles. Stronger fuses have now been put in, and we hope that in the future we shall be spared excitements of this kind.

CHAPTER 2: THE WOMEN'S WAR AT HOME
MAKE DO AND MEND
HEATHER WOODWARD

"Much is said about medals for troops,
but I'm sure most housewives have earned a row of 'em.
Theirs is a job and a half."

Ernie Britton October 1940

Roma Ogilvy Watson (née Patterson) remembers Wadhurst before the war as

a very different place to what it is now – far fewer cars and practically
no one commuting to London. As I recall, there were only two people
travelling to the City each day – my father and one other. On Christmas
Day, you heard the Salvation Army band proceeding down the main
street playing carols – they started quite early and it was a wonderful
start to the day. Occasionally a procession of horse-drawn carriages
would come through the town taking the inmates of Ticehurst House for
an outing.

The Bassett brothers and Rodney, their nephew, ran the forge at
Durgates where I used to take my pony to be shod. They did all the iron
work .... and you would find them all walking round a wagon wheel
pouring cans of water on to the iron tyre to shrink it on to the wheel,
lots of sizzling and spitting.

Tennis tournaments were run, all on grass courts, to support Tunbridge
Wells Hospital sited where the main Post Office is now at Five Ways.
Dances were held in the Commemoration Hall in aid of various causes
and, at that time, the only official alcohol allowed in the hall was cider
cup.

In 1939, everything changed. Black-out, rationing of petrol, food and
so forth – but life went on as normal as possible. We were rather
shocked when, about two or three weeks after war had been declared,
we were playing tennis and a German plane came over, quite low and
unmolested. It must have been on a reconnaissance flight ....

The Rôle of Women

The Home Front very much revolved round the women. Women were involved in almost every aspect of the War. Despite disrupted home lives and trying to keep the family going, they took in evacuees, cooked meals with remarkable ingenuity, did washing (without a machine to make things easier) and ironing, sometimes still with a flat iron, mended and altered clothes. They collected salvage, worked in canteens and for organisations like the WVS, dug for victory and often also worked to earn money to support the family. They were also being asked to fight, or at least actively resist by joining the ARP, WVS and other such organisations. Never was it more truly said: *A woman's work is never done!*

Thinking of Others

Over its history, Wadhurst has always seemed to be conscious of its duty towards and care for others. This was undoubtedly a good foundation for the restrictions and ingenuity which would have to be developed in the years of what would be called the Second World War. Generosity was much in evidence prior to those devastating 6 years of War.

On 16th December 1938, a meeting in the Commemoration Hall decided to go ahead with a scheme for housing a non-Aryan Christian refugee family in

Wadhurst as a communal effort to deal with a fraction of the wide-spread distress being caused. A suitable family and a house for them were to be found, an appeal raised the considerable sum of £283 plus promises of gifts of furniture. Weekly gifts of vegetables and groceries were also promised. The Girl Guides offered to get the garden ready and others who could speak German promised to meet the refugees.

As Ken Jones, however, remembers all too well:

> *The constraint on money-supply controlled family and commercial life.*
> *No pay rises. Prices had to be static and everyone was struggling to*
> *make a living whether employer or employee. My father was working*
> *eight-hour shifts for six days and alternate Sunday. Six and a half days*
> *for £2 10s 0d. Agricultural pay was less and for similar long hours.*
> *I remember our rent was 11/- a week for years and years and years*
> *without change.*

In the first War budget in late September 1939, the standard rate of income tax was increased from 5/6d to 7/-.

Pre-War Christmas Parcels

Giving continued and, in 1936, the Christmas parcel appeal was very generously supported and 77 families, 388 people altogether, had received a 'parcel of Christmas cheer'. Sixty-four parcels went out from Hill House to Spennymoor and Newcastle, and four to Wadhurst families. Fifty-seven iced cakes were sent and joints of meat to 57 of the 77 families but the Newcastle families were not able to receive either the cakes or the meat. Once all the parcels were packed, a trunk of useful clothing and blankets was sent to the Salvation Army Office at Spennymoor and a smaller trunk to the officer at Easington near Durham.

The Immediate Effects of the War

As War became increasingly imminent, one wonders how encouraged the women felt when they heard the January 1939 message of the Archbishop of Canterbury "*hope for the best and prepare for the worst*".

Sign-posts and finger-posts were removed making things awkward even for the locals; they were not replaced in these rural areas until mid-1943.

The Government leaflet, War Emergency Information and Instructions, told the population:

> All windows, skylights, glazed doors or other openings which could show a light at night must be screened with dark blinds, curtains, or blankets, or with brown paper fixed on to the glass so that no light is visible from outside. All lighted signs and advertisement lights and other outside lights must be turned out.
>
> All street lighting will be stopped till further notice.

As the spring months passed into summer, therefore, the priority for women had to be the creation of black-out which required all lights to be covered up after dark. Black material had to be bought to cover every window and outside door, and other advice was available about how to make them more attractive. The efficacy of the subsequent curtains was strictly monitored by the police and ARP wardens. Some people feared them more than they did the Germans!

The importance of women's magazines and other publications

Economise! Save! Re-cycle! Make-Do and Mend!

Keep the home going and bring up the children while the men are away fighting.

Do all the things previously done by the men-folk (decorating, gardening, do-it-yourself) as well as everything you used to do before the War.

During the War, it was so often the women who had to face up to the realities of daily life, feeding the family, often working outside the home to earn a bit of money whilst, at the same time, worrying about their relatives and friends at the Front, their children evacuated to other parts of the country or world – just living from day to day was a challenge.

It seemed that a multitude of practical tips and advice were being spawned daily to help women cope with all the various forms of rationing and restriction. These could be broadcast on the wireless, provided in an endless stream of leaflets from the Government, published in the newspapers even when paper was in relatively short supply and, of course, also in the women's magazines. Household hints and cookery columns appeared everywhere, not least in monthly or weekly journals such as Good Housekeeping, Woman and Home, Woman's Own, Woman, Home Notes, Home Front Fashions amongst others, and in our own Parish magazine.

A Handy Hint for the Black-out

If you have a number of Yale-type keys, why not mark them so that you don't need to try more than one to find the 'right' one?

A small saw can cut a v-nick in the round part of one key, and a piece cut right off will produce a flat on another. A drill can make one hole or two etc. Then the keys are all identified ready for immediate use, and can be 'found' in the dark without fumbling.   **from the Daily Mail**

The Government was particularly aware of the value of women's magazines because they were ideal channels for the communication of instructions, ideas and announcements. Because of restrictive publication resulting from the scarcity of paper, magazines changed hands often and became positive "*all-purpose household manuals and valued friends, ready with sympathetic sound advice*". The magazines focused on cheerful practicality and urged women to maintain their appearance though that was less and less possible as the War continued.

Fluffy Pillows

Have you any of Grandma's old feather cushions or pillows in the house, and do you feel like throwing them out when you try to 'fluff' them up?

Undo a small piece in the seam of the cover, just enough to insert the tube of a bicycle pump.

Use the pump in the ordinary way and the air will 'fluff' up the feathers.

Mrs E Allman in the Daily Mail

The Handy Hints which appear in this chapter come from a range of publications and give some indication of the diversity of advice around.

In every city, town and village of the kingdom, unless their men-folk were in reserved occupations and therefore exempt from military duty, the women were left responsible for more or less everything within the home, and their ageing parents and relatives, and the children plus also thinking about how to juggle reduced resources. The women of Wadhurst were no exception.

Let us therefore brace ourselves to our duties.

Winston Churchill

Recycling is not a new phenomenon

In the 21st Century, we are used to calls for a greater awareness of the need to bring back a greener environment through efficient recycling. Nothing is new, however. But the advertisement below was not really advertising recycling!

Your chemist can't **make** bottles . .

consequently, he relies on you to return your empty Ribena bottles promptly. He can't get new supplies without them. He's doing his best, dealing fairly with all "priorities" — young babies, expectant and nursing mothers, invalids, etc. You can help him — and yourself—to get Ribena, by returning your empties quickly.

Ribena
BLACKCURRANT SYRUP

H. W. CARTER & CO. LTD.; THE OLD REFINERY, BRISTOL. 2

The austerity and exigencies of the War years demanded similar or even greater awareness: cloth, paper, old pots and pans, metal railings and garden gates, all manner of scrap were all required to help the War effort.

Doreen Drury (née Hope) remembers that every scrap of cardboard was saved to make firelighters, and paper was also saved to be re-used. She still cannot bear to throw out envelopes and uses them for shopping lists.

Do not let us speak of darker days; let us rather speak of sterner days.

Winston Churchill

On top of so many other restrictions

Petrol Rationing was introduced in 1939. Cars were allowed to show the merest glimmer of light and had to have front and rear bumpers painted white and the running boards also. Most cars were put up on bricks for the duration of the conflict with, after 1942, only 'essential' cars being allowed coupons for fuel. Fuel rationing continued till May 1950. Admittedly, however, this was, perhaps, not the scale of problem that it would be today as fewer people had access to cars then, anyway, and public transport provided frequent services. The bus fare from Wadhurst Station to Tunbridge Wells was 1/- return.

In the light of comments made in the 21st Century, it is particularly interesting to read the vicar, the Revd. Ernest Mannering in October 1939 writing in the Parish magazine:

> Petrol rationing may make it difficult for some but a generation which
> has largely forgotten how to walk may learn to do so.

The Weather is a well-known British staple of conversation. During the War, Rationing replaced it.

Clothes rationing. Clothes were rationed so that clothing factories could be used to make parachutes and uniforms for the War effort. The general wartime scene was drab – all the frills and fripperies of the pre-War days were now considered bad taste and unpatriotic. Clothes were practical and restrained, and they had to be useful in all sorts of situations. Because every type of cloth was in short supply, the rationing system which was introduced on Whitsunday, 1st June 1941, was extremely strict. Clothing was 'on coupons' and coupons were issued in different colours to stop people using them all up at one go. The Government announced when a new colour could be used.

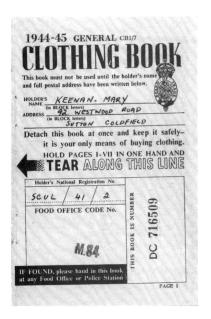

Each person was allowed a maximum of 66 coupons for 12 months with children being allowed 10 coupons more. This was reduced in the spring of 1942 to 60 for 15 months. This would mean that a man with the basic ration could buy one pair of socks every four months, a pair of shoes every eight months and a shirt every twenty months. When he had managed to buy everything else he needed, he would have about 3 points a year for items such as handkerchiefs.

The points needed for items included:

	Adult	Child
An unlined mackintosh	9 points	7 points
A coat, jacket or blazer	13	8
Trousers	8	6
Shirt	5	4
Pair of socks or stockings	3	1
Frock, gown or woollen dress	11	8
Skirt	7	5
Pyjamas	8	6
Nightdress	6	5

Mid-War, clothing coupons fell to 48 for a year and, by 1945, they were as low as 36 for a year.

It is not surprising, bearing all this in mind, that the women really did need advice more specific than just *"use the clothes you had before the War started"*. Inevitably they would wear out but the good bits were re-modelled into some other garment.

Besides having to save up the points, everyone found that clothes became increasingly expensive as the War went on, so women tried to raise extra money in whatever way they could. In 1941, Nora Skilton went hop-picking to make enough money to buy the clothes for her wedding.

Her wedding dress, veil, satin shoes and orange blossom for her head-dress were bought for £7 5s 4d and a great number of coupons in a bridal shop in Camden Road, Tunbridge Wells. Her bridesmaids wore second-hand dresses and her own outfit was worn by two other brides-to-be – Nora was the only one who wore a new dress when she married Fred 'Jock' Tweedley.

Her bouquet of red carnations was tied with a tartan ribbon which matched the tartan trews of her husband's dress uniform.

Nora Skilton and Fred 'Jock' Tweedley

By late 1944, 'Utility' gloves cost 11/- plus three points, 2 pairs of winter underwear 5/3d and 4/9d plus 6 points, and a length of dress material 8/9d. No paper was allowed for wrapping anything bought.

Hats were never rationed and so many Handy Hints were offered for modelling a hat out of whatever material might be available. Turbans and scarves became especially popular – they were handy devices to cover unkempt hair when women certainly had no spare time to attend to it.

Mrs Churchill clearly saw the advantage of a turban even though in her case perhaps it was not to disguise a poor hair day.

One thing that was not rationed or on points, of course, was the compulsory gas mask. Small babies were to be put into a claustrophobic 'cot'

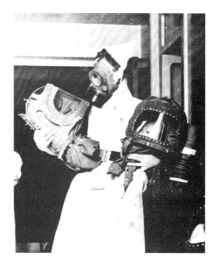

and toddlers had special Mickey Mouse masks. When they were issued, the fit and seal were tested by officials who covered the end with "*something which cut off the air supply which made you pull the mask off!*" Usually it was the women who would have had to sit pumping air into their baby's gas mask – if they stopped (and some did) the baby suffocated. This was not such a problem if they remained in Wadhurst but not all mothers and babies did, and so would have to learn the realities of life under the more regular bombing.

Clothes rationing did not end till March 1949. Even after the War, therefore, plenty of Handy Tips and advice were available for dealing with clothing shortages in a fashionable way!

Pillow cases could be turned into white shorts for the summer or, trimmed with lace, became blouses; the only way to have really feminine underwear was to make it yourself; skirts could be made from men's old plus-fours or trousers; cast-offs could be made into children's clothes, collars could be added and trims applied to eke out a limited wardrobe; blankets became coats. Nothing was wasted and women were very resourceful.

The Board of Trade published multitudes of leaflets, advising, admonishing,

Utility motif to guarantee that everyone could buy clothing or furniture of good quality.

explaining and generally making sure that the population was well aware of its responsibilities as regards helping the War effort. Whereas people living in the country fared better when it came to food, town dwellers had much greater choice when buying clothes.

There was a clothing exchange in the Wadhurst Institute, [*where the library is now*], where outgrown clothes were handed in and exchanged for points towards new clothes.

Mothers were encouraged to sell or exchange outgrown clothes and received plenty of instructions under headings like:

> Cutting down Grown-Ups Clothes for Children. (Leaflet No. 4)
> Looking after Shoes (slippers should be worn in the house for a start)
> How to Darn Holes and Tears by Mrs Sew and Sew. (Leaflet No 5)
> Your household linen has got to LAST! (Leaflet No 3)
> Every Woman Her Own Clothes' Doctor (Leaflet No 8)

Those hard-pressed mothers could certainly not claim ignorance about how to go about things.

Handy Hint for Buttons

When cutting buttons from discarded garments, string them on a safety pin and drop in a wide-necked jar. When you want a set of buttons, there they are, already sorted.   **Mrs M Roche in the Daily Mail**

Nora Tweedley (née Skilton) recalls Make-Do and Mend: sheets went sides to middle; shirt collars were turned; socks were darned again and again; and shoes could be repaired at one of the four shoe repairers in Wadhurst.

Fashion as such was no longer an issue. Shabbiness was now socially acceptable. Jumble sales became a major social occasion with tickets for admission at the door at some of them. Cup hooks and bottle tops could be made into jewellery, burnt-out cork used as mascara. Women applied gravy-browning with an eyebrow pencil to draw the line down the back of their legs for a 'seam'. Old stockings were cut into strips and made into rugs; silk scarves became children's frocks; cats and dogs were combed for their fur.

MAKE DO AND MEND LEAFLET. No. 14

CHILDREN'S UNDERWEAR BUYING AND REPAIR HINTS

"Keep them tidy underneath!"

says Mrs. SEW-and-SEW

It's quite a problem to keep children in underclothes. They give them such hard wear and grow out of them so quickly. Here are some practical hints which may help you keep them tidy underneath !

BUYING TIPS

★Never forget to allow for rapid growth. When buying ready-made underwear, always buy a size or more larger than needed.

When buying judge quality and workmanship by (*a*) well reinforced knicker forks and under-arms of vests. (*b*) good finish at edges of seams. These should be strong but soft to stand frequent washing and keep in shape, neither fraying nor chafing the skin. (*c*) Good button-hole finish and well-sewn seams.

ISSUED BY THE BOARD OF TRADE

And Mrs Sew and Sew kept popping up!

38

Chart Leaflet No. 5
ISSUED BY THE BOARD OF TRADE

HOW TO DARN HOLES
AND TEARS

by Mrs. SEW-and-SEW

● Do not wait for holes to develop. It is better to darn as soon as garments begin to wear thin. Imitate, as well as possible, the texture of the fabric being darned. When darning a big hole, tack a piece of net at the back and darn across it, and this will give an extra support for the stitches. A tear should be tacked round on to a piece of paper, to hold the edges in position.

If clothes did have to be bought, Marks and Spencer in Tunbridge Wells was a regular source and some items could be purchased at Baldwin and Watt in Wadhurst [*now Celia Hammond's*] or at Gardners in St James's Square. Most shoes were bought from a shop called the Leather Market which gave good value.

A National Pastime

Knitting became a national pastime. Whenever women stood or sat still for a minute, they picked up the knitting needles. Jumpers and pullovers were carefully unpicked starting at the seams, wound round trays and then into  skeins, washed and rinsed thoroughly to remove all the kinks, and then knitted up into some other useful garment. Mittens, scarves, socks, gloves tumbled off those needles. Really expert knitters created jumpers in open lacy patterns because that stretched yarn even further. Fair Isle short waist cardigans or V-neck sleeveless waistcoats for either men or women became the fashion because their random colours made use of shorter lengths of wool when it was being unravelled. "*Knitting Pays!*" was the heading on one of the Government's advice leaflets: "*Even an amateur can knit a child's vest, and you can always make a hand-knitted garment bigger by knitting on to it*". 'Knitting Bs' flourished and provided much–needed social contacts for the women with their contemporaries, as well as heaps of 'woollies' for the troops and the civilians who had been bombed out of their homes.

A Handy Hint for Knitting

If you have a small teapot with a broken lid – use the teapot as a holder for knitting wool.

Place the wool in the pot and draw the wool through the spout. This way, it keeps perfectly clean, never tangles and is easily carried by the handle.
Mrs Kirkham in the Daily Mail

In September 1939, the Kent and Sussex Hospital Linen League put out an appeal for help with knitting and needlework with volunteers receiving cut-out garments and the wool for the knitting. Things most needed were night-gowns, pyjamas for men and children, vests for children of 6 – 10 years, operation stockings and operation vests.

A Handy Tip for Knitting Children's Dresses

sent into the Wadhurst Parish magazine by Mrs Smith:

Cast off at the waist and cast on again for yoke and join together when making up the garment. When the child grows and the yoke becomes too small or the dress needs lengthening, the waist can easily be unpicked and the yoke re-knitted or the skirt made longer by knitting more on at the top.

Wadhurst was helping a much wider community than itself as can be seen clearly from extracts from the Parish magazine. In September 1939, a letter was received from the vicar of St Thomas's in Bethnal Green, thanking the Needlework Guild for the gifts sent to poor families.

> We do especially appreciate the generous gift of the new household linen and the socks and boys' jerseys. The latter are just exactly treasures for two little lads from a long family just going off on a country holiday, and the sheets will be a most valuable help.

In February 1940, Mrs Miller of Uplands (House) was collecting knitted garments and odd furs to send to Finland. She also had white, grey or buff-coloured wool which she would give to any good knitter for the same purpose. Meanwhile the Girls' Club had already completed one patch-work knitted blanket which had been sent to Finland and another blanket was nearly ready. When the Club sent off their third blanket to the Finnish Relief Fund, they received a letter of acknowledgement from the Crafts Council Secretary:

> It really is extremely nicely made, and very firm; and this time you have been particularly successful with your colour scheme.

A year later, the Guides were appealing for any old clothes which they could mend or alter because they wanted to make and mend for people from bombed areas. They were also asking for odd pieces of wool or material. By the April of 1941, 80 garments had been sent off including 4 knitted pullovers, a knitted frock and knickers, 3 blouses and 5 pairs of small boys' knickers.

Very soon after the beginning of the War, comforts were being sent all over the world for the Wadhurst men serving in the Forces and by June 1940 the first 50 parcels had been dispatched. There was an urgent request for more socks and sweets in tins. As the War progressed, more information meant that the knitters of Wadhurst were told that

> All socks have to be completed by November so that packing can be done early. The socks have to be 11" long in the foot. Some socks received have been rather on the small size and the Services like them long in case of shrinking!

The Wadhurst Comforts' Fund added that "*if funds allow, parcels will be sent to Wadhurst girls serving, as well as to the men. Comforts for them, scarves and gloves, will be welcomed.*"

In January 1941, 121 Christmas parcels were sent to the Forces: 88 to the Army, 21 to the RAF and 12 to the Navy and Marines. By September of the same year, 143 were sent out and women serving in the Forces were to get parcels for Christmas. Particularly needed were still the socks but the Navy and Air Force personnel also needed 'woollies'.

The time and effort being put into this sewing and knitting must have been tremendous because, in February 1942, the Carnleigh Working Party had received the following message from the Navy League Seafarers' Comforts Supply:

> *How splendid to get 91 pairs of mitten gloves all at once. We wish to thank all knitters, who very kindly helped to achieve this good result so quickly.*

The mittens had gone to Russia.

Handy Hint for Wrapping Parcels

Ever tied up a parcel and found the string too loose?

Do it this way. Wet the string first and then tie up the parcel.

It will stay securely tied up, as the string shrinks as it dries.

Mrs Kenny in the Daily Mail

By that December, the Cousley Wood War Working Party (usually around 30 knitters) had completed 767 garments, 332 sewn and 435 woollies. These had been sent to HM Forces, War Nurseries, Russia, SSAFA and the Parish Church Comforts' Fund. 680 garments were completed the following year. By the end of the War, 3987 garments had been dispatched and the Working Party continued to meet after the War, now for 'Clothing Europe' and SSAFA.

Nora Tweedley was delighted to receive a parachute from her friend and it was made into underwear, pants and slips by Nellie Gibb, a seamstress who lived with her parents at Brick Kiln Cottages, Wallcrouch.

Jennifer Hawkins (née Tunbridge) remembers that her Mum acquired a huge yellow parachute. She unpicked it all and then made several pairs of pyjamas from it. Her mother was a good seamstress because Jennifer also remembers that, for the George Street street-party to celebrate the end of the War, her Mum made her a dress in red, white and blue check. It must have inspired Jennifer because in the races afterwards she won 3d for being the first to reach Daddy Heasman's garage.

Handy Hint when Ironing

sent in to the Parish magazine by Miss M.E. Rees

To remove a scorch mark:
rub the mark immediately with a cut onion, then soak in cold water and wash in the usual way.

Later in the War, one Ministry of Trade Leaflet was entitled

NYLON NEWS

from Mrs Sew-and-Sew

How To Look after Parachute Silk.

The nylon appearing in the shops at the moment is parachute nylon so don't expect all the advantages next year's nylon will offer.

This is how to wash nylon.

Use warm water and dissolve the soap thoroughly. Rinse repeatedly to remove all traces of suds. You may rub or wring the fabric but it is not advisable to twist it. As nylon fabric dries very quickly, it is an advantage to iron it as soon as possible after washing.

In the case of coloured goods, be sure that the colours are fast. If they are inclined to run, wash the garment by itself.

Too hot an iron is dangerous.

After washing, nylon should be dried by laying it out flat. If this is done, you will find little need to iron it at all. If you do decide the garment needs pressing, make this test: stand your iron on a newspaper for 15 – 20 seconds. If the paper scorches, the iron is too hot. Give it time to cool.

Dressmaking with nylon:

Allow ample material so as not to strain the seams and never make the garment too close-fitting. This nylon is rather apt to slip at the seams. So make liberal turnings at seams and hems, and always tack very carefully before you start to sew. By machining with a loose, easy stitch, you will avoid puckering at the seams.

FACTS TO REMEMBER

Nylon is exceptionally strong material.

Nylon is moth-proof.

Normal spot-removing liquids may safely be used on nylon.

Domestic Fuel was allocated according to the size of the house and many were the strictures to house-wives about avoiding waste:

> Use a three-tiered steamer to cook a complete meal.
>
> Cover a cake with double layers of grease-proof paper and steam for an hour.
>
> Put a baking sheet over a gas ring to spread the heat across the base of two saucepans.

Being economical with resources was vitally important to help the War effort. In London, one Times' correspondent suggested that during daylight hours traffic lights should not be used: *"The present day volume of traffic could quite well be controlled by the police"*. This was not of much value as a suggestion for Wadhurst, of course.

The furring of kettles was, however, a problem for many and one retired Indian Navy Officer calculated that in Greater London alone a minimum of 375,000 hours of gas and electricity was being wasted daily through kettles taking longer to boil because of the fur on them. He could not understand why scientists could not find the same liquid as did *"a wandering pedlar who, many years ago, for a small fee, would clean one's kettles, removing all trace of fur"*.

One Sussex reader, address unknown, was much more draconian in attitude:

> the BBC should cut their 17-hour programme by at least a half; shops throughout the country should be shut for at least two whole days a week; offices and business places not engaged on essential War work should cut down their days or hours of work; cinemas and other places of entertainment should have their opening hours further restricted.

Some of these suggestions if implemented would certainly have had an impact on people in Wadhurst.

Then on top of all the other restrictions:

in July 1941	coal was rationed because so many miners were called up into the Services.
in February 1942	soap was rationed so that oils and fats could be saved for food (this ended September 1950).
and in March 1942	gas and electricity were rationed.

One 1943 advertisement was headed

Don't Waste Fuel.
Keep warmer on BOVRIL.

Gillian Briggs of Durgates remembers times being hard in the War *"but we knew nothing different and made the best of them"*. Her mother mended their saucepans and kettles with 'pot-menders', small metal discs which you placed over the hole and screwed on, keeping the screw on the inside of the pan. Everything was saved for further use, of course, especially string, thread and wool.

Morale Boosting

It was still important to look good and sometimes morale did need boosting. Handy hints included suggestions for personal care:

Kill Freckles

To make freckles less conspicuous, soak cotton wool in lemon juice, then rub gently over the freckles. Do this for 5 – 10 minutes daily until the freckles fade. **Miss Fletcher in the Daily Mail**

Wart Killer

To clear warts, boil some potatoes, and with the water in which they are boiled, bathe the warts.

At the end of a week, they will have nearly, if not quite gone.

This remedy I have proved successful when all others had failed.
Mrs G W in the Daily Mail

Smooth Complexion

No need to spend money on an 'improved' complexion.

After using eggs in cooking, just smear the white remaining in the shell on your face, let it dry, then rinse off with cold water and pat dry.

Your skin will glow! **R M in the Daily Mail**

To Cure Chilblains

sent in to the Parish magazine by M L Jones.

Rub well with the juice of an onion, then rub cooking salt well in. This acts like magic and one dressing is usually sufficient.

Perhaps they do not all appeal to 21st Century taste but some seem extremely sensible even today.

Things which were more and more difficult to find as the War progressed included anything connected with hairdressing: setting lotion, hair nets and pins, Kirby grips, permanent waving products.

It must have been quite a relief, therefore, that in 1942 Miss Rofe installed in her new salon in Middle House an *Ical* Waving Machine which was the latest system of Permanent Waving. She reassured potential customers *"comfort for the client being one of the great features of the machine"*.

Victory?

Victory in 1945 was not the cause of great celebratory euphoria as it had been after the First World War. Technically Britain won the War but impoverished herself in so doing. The austerity of the War years did not cease and Britain was increasingly unsure of her place in the world. The Empire was shrinking and the economy was more and more dependent on American loans. There was also the need to feed a starving Europe and this fact ensured that domestic rationing pinched just as hard after as it had during the War. Even cricket balls were rationed in June 1946.

The next greatest misfortune to losing a battle is to win such a victory as this.
Arthur Wellesley, Duke of Wellington

SOURCES

The People's War: Calder, Angus [1969], Jonathan Cape
Our Hidden Lives: Garfield, Simon [2005], Ebury Press
Voices from the Home Front: Goodall, Felicity [ed] [2004], David & Charles
Despatches from the Home Front: McCooey, Chris [ed] [1994], JAK Books
The Wartime Scrapbook: Opie, Robert [2005], pi global publishing
Wadhurst Parish magazine 1936 - 1947: ESRO PAR 498/7/4

The personal memories of people of Wadhurst including:
Gillian Briggs, Doreen Drury, Jennifer Hawkins,
Ken Jones, Roma Ogilvy Watson and Nora Tweedley.

CHAPTER 3: THE WAR ABOVE WADHURST PLANES, BOMBS AND DOODLEBUGS

ARTHUR DEWAR

Introduction

During the First World War, the British civilian population only came under limited attack and no major battles were fought on or above British soil. The Second World War was very different with much of the civilian population suffering repeated and often devastating onslaughts from aerial bombing. Moreover, Southern England also witnessed the Battle of Britain and later in the War was in the forefront of the preparations for the D-Day invasion. Sussex was very much in the firing line. According to official wartime records [1] 103,985 bombs fell on the county. These included over 11,000 high explosive bombs, over 90,000 incendiary bombs, 907 flying bombs and 1,405 anti-personnel bombs. As a result of these assaults 1,015 Sussex civilians were killed and 3,895 were injured. 152 enemy aircraft were brought down in Sussex with the death of 220 enemy aircrew. 715 allied aircraft were also lost over Sussex with the death of 533 aircrew.

In the War years East and West Sussex were subdivided for administrative purposes into a number of districts. The main towns in East Sussex such as Brighton, Hove, Eastbourne, Lewes, Rye, Bexhill and Hastings were all Municipal Boroughs. The more rural parts of East Sussex were allocated to one of five Rural Districts: Chailey, Hailsham, Battle and Uckfield. The border between Uckfield and Battle Rural Districts lay between Wadhurst and Ticehurst. Wadhurst, Tidebrook, Frant and Mayfield lay within Uckfield RD whereas Ticehurst, Stonegate and Burwash were in Battle RD.

It is unfortunate that many of the published statistics relate to these administrative groupings since this sometimes makes it difficult to derive figures for the wider 'Wadhurst area'. This chapter is based on published statistics, contemporary newspaper reports [in particular, those in the Kent and East Sussex Courier], accounts in the Parish magazine and a series of invaluable interviews, letters, notes and research provided by those living in Wadhurst during the period. Inevitably there are some disagreements and inconsistencies between the various sources and what follows makes no claims to be exhaustive or definitive. It merely aims to give a broad overview of Wadhurst's experience of aerial warfare during the Second World War and to record some of the more dramatic incidents and examples of personal courage that occurred during those turbulent years.

Aircraft crashes

In August 1940 Hermann Goering, Head of the Luftwaffe, launched an operation to eliminate the RAF south of a line from Chelmsford to Gloucester. This was designed to clear the way for Hitler to order a large scale invasion of Britain in September 1940. However, thanks to the bravery and endurance of RAF Fighter Command during what came to be known as the 'Battle of Britain', this attempt failed. Much of the battle was fought in the skies above East Sussex and during this period as many as 67 planes crashed within the boundaries of Battle RD and as many as 30 within Uckfield RD [2]. Some of these fell in Wadhurst and its immediate environs.

Enemy aircraft crashing in Wadhurst

Between 4th September and 25th October 1940 five enemy planes were shot down and crashed in the Wadhurst area.

Table 1: Enemy aircraft that crashed [2, 3, 4]

Date	Location	Aircraft type
4.9.40	Little Butts, Cousley Wood	Messerschmitt Bf 110C (3602)
11.9.40	Foxhole Lane	Messerschmitt Bf 109E-1 (6293)
6.10.40	Snape Wood	Dornier 17
15.10.40	Owls Castle, Cousley Wood	Messerschmitt Bf 109E-1 (3535)
25.10.40	Church Settle Farm	Messerschmitt Bf 109E-4 (3724)

Little Butts Farm

At 1.30 pm. on Wednesday 4th September 1940, at the height of the 'Battle of Britain', Mr and Mrs Rex Brissenden of Little Butts Farm, were alarmed to see a German twin-engined fighter aircraft, with a menacing shark's mouth motif painted on its fuselage, careering towards them before slithering to a halt on their lawn a few feet from the side of their house. The plane, a Messerschmitt 110, had just passed over the heads of men gathering plums in an adjacent orchard. As it roared towards them belching smoke, they had dived for cover convinced that they were about to be attacked. However the pilot and his gunner were more intent on trying to land safely. As the men rushed up towards the crashed plane the pilot, Oberleutnant (Lieutenant) Herman Weber, emerged and in broken English warned them to extinguish any naked flames to prevent the danger of the aviation fuel igniting. The gunner, Unteroffizier (Corporal) Max Michael, had two wounds in the chest and one in the throat and had to be lifted from the bullet-peppered fuselage. He was placed on a garden seat and a doctor was summoned. [2,3,4,5.]

The Messerschmitt 110 fighter bomber that crash-landed on the lawn at Little Butts Farm [2]

Shortly afterwards the military arrived to take charge of the wrecked plane and Unteroffizier Michael was taken to the Kent and Sussex Hospital in Tunbridge Wells for treatment. In the following year both crew members were transferred to a prisoner of war camp in Canada (Camp W). Both lived to a ripe old age: Weber died in 2004 at the age of 92 and Michael in 2002 at the age of 83 [3].

According to the most authoritative sources [3,4], the reason that the aircraft crashed was that its tail had been seriously damaged by fire from RAF fighters. However, the RAF records at Kew credit no named pilot for downing the plane although there were several claims. Two fighter squadrons were engaged in combat with Me 110s at that time: No. 72 Squadron from RAF Croydon and No. 79 from RAF Biggin Hill. The latter, comprising nine Spitfires, was engaging enemy bombers and fighters in the Tenterden-Tunbridge Wells area and claimed that it had destroyed six Me 110s, possibly destroyed two and damaged one. Probably the plane that landed so dramatically at Little Butts was a victim of that squadron [3].

Soldiers guarding the wreckage of the Messerschmitt.

The wreck of the crashed Messerschmitt 110 under guard

Nevertheless, at the time, there were several others who wished to take the credit. For example the Ticehurst Searchlight Platoon claimed to have shot the plane down by machine gun fire [6]. There was also a considerably more speculative claim by members of a partridge shoot on the Whiligh estate who had taken a couple of shots at what they described as *"rather a high bird"*. Their entry in the Whiligh game book for that day listed 10 brace of partridges, two hares and a Messerschmitt 110!

A future High Sheriff of Sussex, Michael Reid, of Coopers Farm, Stonegate, was a 15-year-old schoolboy who participated in that eventful partridge shoot. In 1980 he wrote to the Courier with his memories of the day [7]. His witty account has a distinct flavour of 'Dad's Army' in its combination of bravery, noble intentions, local rivalries and unconscious comedy:

> *On that day my father had taken me partridge shooting at Chessons Farm. There were one or two young lads who were on leave with us, in particular, Tommy Hussey, who had recently returned from three days on the beaches of Dunkirk. He was killed some four years later in Normandy. I remember vividly that in the party were Admiral Henley of Lamberhurst, the late Sir George Jessel of Goudhurst, his son Charles and his two cousins.*

> *We had just broken for lunch in the stackyard at Chessons. Beer and sandwiches were being extricated from the game bags. Suddenly there was an awful clatter of machine-gun fire and a Me 110 flew low over the farm. It was either being shot at or it was strafing the local countryside. It was obviously in difficulties. Everyone was taking shelter behind the haystacks and buildings except for Tommy Hussey, who loaded his gun, took a right and left, and observed 'Rather a high bird, I fear'. Sir George Jessel grasped his pint of beer in one hand, his son and heir Charles in the other, and with authority commanded Charles to 'Take cover, boy'.*

> *Sir George, who took the role of Captain Mainwaring, and his band set course at the double and arrived at the scene of the disaster armed with their 12-bore guns, puffing and blowing. They beat the police by two minutes and the Ticehurst searchlight platoon by four. The latter were claiming to have shot down the aircraft by machine-gun fire and later arrived in the Chestnut Laundry van which they had commandeered to get to the scene of triumph.*

> *When the captors arrived on the scene, the pilot had extricated himself from the wreckage and was already bartering a camera with Miss*

Brissenden in return for his safe conduct to the authorities and medical aid for his stricken air gunner. Sir George was the only one in the party who had even the faintest smattering of German. He marched up to the tall Aryan pilot and demanded, somewhat inaccurately 'Zind zie die Fahrer?' There was some doubt as to whether he had said 'Fuhrer'. He concluded: 'I am Sir George Jessel of Ladham, and I arrest you in the name of the King'. History does not relate what happened after that, because the Ticehurst searchlight platoon arrived on the scene, and no way were they going to allow the quarry to be removed by a bunch of partridge shooters.

Foxhole Farm

One week after the crash at Little Butts Farm, on 11th September another Messerschmitt crashed, this time at Foxhole Farm. It had been shot down by Acting Squadron Leader Flight Lieutenant G R Edge of No. 253 Squadron during combat over Tunbridge Wells. The aircraft crashed at 3.40 pm. The pilot was unable to escape from the burning and exploding wreck and died.

That afternoon Ken Jones, then a fifteen-year old schoolboy living in Old Station Road in Wadhurst, was working with his mother and two sisters in the hop fields at Great Pell Farm and remembers hearing the sudden 'whoosh' of pursuing aircraft with machine guns firing at a very low level. Later in the day he cycled over to Foxhole Farm to find the still smouldering remains of the burnt-out Messerschmitt. Here he smelt the unmistakable odour of burning flesh for the first time. The unfortunate pilot was buried in Wadhurst churchyard. The Revd. E Mannering, the vicar of Wadhurst at that time, recorded the burial in the Parish Burial Register on 16th September 1940 as a 'German airman Disc no 5329-15'. Later research, conducted by Ken Jones, revealed that the pilot was Feldwebel (Flight Sergeant) Herman Siemer, aged 23. He had commenced pilot training in 1939 and belonged to Unit 2 J Geschwader 20. Unit records have not survived and it is not known from which airfield he set out on his ill-fated last sortie. On 26th September 1962, Herman Siemer's remains were exhumed and re-interred at the German Military Cemetery, Cannock Chase, Staffordshire.

In contrast, a study of the RAF records held at the National Archives at Kew gives a clear picture of the events leading up to Siemer's death. He was part of a group of 50 Messerschmitt 109 and other fighters escorting a formation of some 30 Heinkel 11 and Dornier 215 bombers heading in a NW direction from Dover. The formation was first intercepted in the Maidstone area and attacked by a group of 10 Hurricanes based at RAF Kenley, Surrey. Squadron Leader Edge was flying as 'red leader'. His personal combat report shows that, after making a second pass at the bomber formation, he saw hits on a Heinkel 11 which spiralled away. He then pursued and attacked Siemer's Messerschmitt over Tunbridge Wells. His combat report gives this brief, but dramatic account of the ensuing dogfight:

> *Observed Me 109 at 6,000 feet heading S.E. As I approached he dived and endeavoured to take evasive action by flying very low and then pulling up, doing a half roll, and then diving in another direction.*
>
> *This latter made it easy to overtake and, as he was diving out of his fifth roll, he crossed in front of me at 50 yards. I gave about a half second burst and as he pulled out smoke was coming out. Few moments later he crashed in flames by the side of a farmhouse in Wadhurst. Circling round ammo could be seen exploding on the ground.*

A few days after this action Squadron Leader Edge was awarded the Distinguished Flying Cross. However, sixteen days later, he himself was shot down after combat but, fortunately, he was able to abandon his plane over the sea and survived. [3, 4]

Others

Rather less is known about the Dornier bomber that crashed near Wadhurst Hall on Sunday 6th October 1940. Walter Hodder, then a schoolboy living in the Tidebrook schoolhouse (see p. 74), remembers hearing machine-gun fire followed by a crash as he was about to enter Tidebrook Church to sing in the choir. Apparently only one airman survived, one died at the site of the crash and one died later in the Kent and Sussex Hospital at Tunbridge Wells. One, Hans Wagner, was buried in Tidebrook Churchyard but both are now thought to have been removed for re-burial in the German Military Cemetery at Cannock Chase [6].

At 8.35 on the morning of 15th October another Messerschmitt 109 crashed, this time at Owls Castle Farm near Cousley Wood. This followed a combat with RAF fighters over Kent. The pilot, Unteroffizier Hoehn, bailed out and was captured unwounded [4].

The last German plane to come down in Wadhurst was yet another Messerschmitt 109. This was shot down by a Hurricane of No. 501 Squadron and crashed on land owned by Church Settle Farm. The pilot, Oberleutnant Eichstaedt, baled out but his parachute failed to open and he died smashing through the roof of the garage/outhouse of a house on the south east corner of the Shovers Green turning [3,4, 8].

British planes crashing in Wadhurst

As indicated earlier, many more British planes fell in Sussex than enemy ones but for understandable reasons - not least the need to maintain civilian morale - downed RAF aircraft received far less publicity than enemy planes and were very rarely photographed.

At 4.12 pm. on 11th September 1940 a British Hurricane (P3534) crashed at Lake Street Farm between Tidebrook and Mayfield. According to one source the aircraft had been shot down during a German attack above Tunbridge Wells. The pilot, Flying Officer T B Little, despite being wounded in the leg and suffering from burns to his face and side, was able to bail out and landed at Rotherfield. From here he was taken to the Kent and Sussex Hospital. His plane was a complete write-off [4]. Tidebrook residents recall a Spitfire crashing at Lake Street with the death of its Polish pilot [6].

On 28th September 1940 another Hurricane (P3415) crashed near Wadhurst. It was hit over Ticehurst and crashed at Hook Farm [*on ground now under Bewl Water*] at 2.20 pm. The pilot, Flying Officer R Hope, baled out and landed unhurt at Ticehurst. His plane, however, was irreparably damaged [4].

Although the Battle of Britain was essentially over by late 1940, sporadic German air attacks continued, as did the loss of British fighters. On 26th March 1943 a Spitfire crashed on Great Shoesmiths Farm and four Piper Cubs crashed near Wadhurst on 24th October 1944 [1].

High explosive and incendiary bombs

It has been estimated that over 2,000 high explosive and incendiary bombs were dropped on Wadhurst parish, most of these during the first half of the War. However, it is highly unlikely, given the haphazard distribution of the bombs, that Wadhurst (with the possible exception of the railway) was being specifically targeted. It is more probable that the majority of these bombs were jettisoned by enemy bombers returning to their continental bases. Nevertheless, despite their haphazard pattern of distribution, some resulted in considerable damage and, in one case, two civilian fatalities.

A list of some of the more significant bomb incidents is shown below. This table does not include those associated specifically with the Hastings railway line nor does it include the explosions caused by crashing flying bombs that occurred later in the War. These will be discussed later.

Table 2: Bomb incidents in Wadhurst [2, 3, 9,12]

Date	Location
18.9.40	Jonas Lane and Stonebridge (incendiary bombs)
19.9.40	Buttons Farm (a series of bombs fell on the farm around 9 pm.; one made a direct hit on the farmhouse causing two fatalities)
20.9.40	Tapsell's Lane and Windmill Farm (bombs landed at 4.30 am.)
20.9.40	Woods Green and Balaclava Lane (incendiary bombs)
23.9.40	Wadhurst Park (several bombs)
1.10.40	Whiligh, Puttick's Farm and Shant (several bombs)
18.10.40	Monk's Lane, Cousley Wood (two bombs in cottage garden opposite Old Monks; three houses were damaged)
9.3.41	Sparrows Green (four heavy bombs caused extensive damage and two casualties)
15.3.41	Junction of Darby's Lane and Wadhurst-Ticehurst Road (two bombs)
25.2.44	Pell Green (bomb exploded in hop field, resulting in blast damage in adjoining houses)
28.2.44	Cousley Wood (parachute mine explosion damaged a large number of houses and caused one serious and two minor casualties)
22.7.44	Wadhurst Castle land (the blast from a high explosive bomb removed one side of the Market Hall from its brick support)

The bombing of Buttons Farm

Undoubtedly one of the most tragic episodes in Wadhurst's War was the destruction of Buttons Farm on the evening of 19th September 1940. At around 9 pm. a series of bombs fell on the farm and its surroundings. Although remote and down a quiet country lane, Buttons was quite close to the railway line and this led some to suspect that a German bomber had been attempting to destroy a train and the track. One of the bombs landed directly on the picturesque farmhouse and reduced it to rubble, a large crater being created where the kitchen used to be. The farmer's wife, 32 year old Mrs Florence Topp, and a friend, Mrs Parfitt, who were thought to be sitting in the kitchen when the bomb struck, were killed instantly. Ironically, Mrs Parfitt had only recently moved to Buttons from Croydon to escape bombing raids.

. A farmhouse which was destroyed by a bomb in a peaceful Sussex hamlet. Two women lost their lives.

The destruction of Buttons Farmhouse [Kent & Sussex Courier]

The destruction of Buttons Farmhouse [Bocking Collection]

The ruins of Buttons Farm, Wadhurst after an air raid on September 19, 1940. A girl of 14 earned the George Medal for her rescue of a baby from the ruins at great personal risk

The destruction of Buttons Farmhouse [Courier]

At the time of the incident Mr and Mrs Topp's three small children, Valerie aged 5, Sylvia aged 2½ and Heather, a baby of 14 months, were sleeping upstairs but miraculously survived with only scratches and bruises despite the

Another scene of the farmhouse as some of the wrecked furniture is brought away on a waggon. The ladder indicates the room where the baby was found unhurt.

Furniture being removed from the wreckage of Buttons Farmhouse [Courier]

total destruction of their bedrooms. One of them was actually flung out through the wall on to a pile of debris in the garden. A jagged piece of wooden roof structure was protecting her when rescuers heard her cries in the darkness. The two others were buried in the wreckage. That they survived was due in large measure to the heroism of Rose Ede, the teenage daughter of a local farm worker. While bombs were still falling, Rose rushed across the field from her cottage to the devastated farmhouse. She heard the trapped children crying and, regardless of her own safety, began crawling into the wreckage in the direction of the sound to try to effect a rescue. Soon several other neighbours, ARP workers and policemen arrived on the scene and started to dig through the debris. Rose continued to work her way forward on her stomach, her hands seeking to make contact with the trapped children. Suddenly she called out that she could feel a foot and the two policemen, PC Clemmence and Special Constable Charles Bloomfield, rushed over and started to dig feverishly. Rose edged closer and comforted the child while the two men struggled to lift a stout beam that was impeding progress. Eventually the beam was lifted sufficiently to allow Rose, by this time covered in dust and plaster, to crawl further under the rubble and pull the child clear [9].

Mr Topp and a young farm student, Barry Stiles, were out on Home Guard duty when the bomb struck and this saved their lives. Mr and Mrs Topp's maid, Gladys Beeney, also had a lucky escape. She had been due back from a holiday on the day of the bombing but at the last minute had been granted permission to return a day later. The next morning the farm, the adjoining lane and orchards presented a very sorry sight. The contents of the former farmhouse including clothes, bedding, shattered furniture, crockery and children's toys were strewn everywhere; dead chickens littered the grass and the other farm buildings were pitted with holes. There was also evidence of more than seven other bombs: one had fallen on a stream and created a new pond in the crater, five had landed in nearby fields and one had buried itself in the garden of some cottages further up the lane. According to the Courier coverage of the incident, the locality was visited by another raider the following night and further bombs wrecked an empty cottage and damaged a second, fortunately without causing serious injury to its inhabitant.

One of the rescuing party attending the incident commented to the Courier that he hoped that Rose's exceptional pluck would be recognised. It was.

In December 1941 she was awarded the George Medal for her bravery. Later, Rose was summoned to Buckingham Palace to receive her medal in person from King George VI. On 17th May 1941 she travelled up to London by an early train accompanied by her sister Violet and a local representative of the WVS to attend a special ceremony for the presentation of George Crosses and George Medals. After the ceremony, during which she was warmly congratulated by the King, the small party lunched at the Headquarters of the WVS. Here she received the congratulations of the current Head of the WVS in England, Lady Reading, on being the first member of the WVS to receive a George Medal.

The contemporary Courier report of the incident [9] states that Rose Ede was 14 when she made her heroic rescue. However, this is incorrect. A letter from Sylvia Manning (née Topp) and her husband Richard to the Wadhurst History Society Newsletter in 2004 refers to her as being 17. This is consistent with a report from the Daily Telegraph of 10th November 2003 which describes Rose, under her married name of Rose Taylor, walking past the Cenotaph at the age of 81 [10]. Rose was one of a number of George Medal winners traced by Betty Boothroyd in connection with the unveiling of a new Monument to the Women of World War Two in Whitehall. Rose was asked to appear with her on Channel 4 television on 25th January 2005. The Queen unveiled the Monument on 9th July 2000 [11].

The bombing of Sparrows Green
The nearest that Wadhurst got to being blitzed was when, on the evening of Sunday 9th March 1941, four large bombs struck Sparrows Green in quick succession. One of the bombs fell on the site now occupied by Costcutters and its car park. It fell between some cottages and the rear of the shop premises of Fred Newington and caused considerable damage to the surrounding property. Given the scale of the destruction there were remarkably few casualties. Mr and Mrs Barham, an elderly couple occupying one of the cottages, were admitted to hospital suffering from shock and, in the case of Mrs Barham, also a suspected back injury. Miraculously, four children sleeping at the rear of the shattered shop survived unharmed. Fortunately they were sleeping in a Morrison shelter and this saved their lives although their beds were damaged.

Damage to the rear of Newingtons and a pair of adjoining cottages [Courier]

A second bomb fell at the rear of what is now the primary school. Construction of the school had commenced in the late 1930s but had been halted at the outbreak of war. The explosion severely damaged the partially built wing nearest to the War Memorial, hurling lumps of clay and building materials across adjoining fields and left a crater several feet deep. The old fire station adjacent to the school suffered only minor damage although its siren was put out of action.

The third bomb fell on the garden of a cottage near Cockmount Lane belonging to Mrs Whitten. Luckily the ground was soft and the bomb penetrated some way before exploding. The blast, therefore, had extended upwards and had left the cottage largely unscathed. If the ground had been harder the outcome would have been very different [3]. The fourth bomb also landed on soft ground, this time near Green Square. It gave some newly built cottages a shaking and temporarily cut off electricity and water supplies.

At this time the Salvation Army was running a canteen at its hall [*now demolished*] at Sparrows Green to entertain the soldiers stationed in Wadhurst.

When the bombs fell, the hall was packed with people. The blast from the bombs split the roof and many fell or were thrown to the ground. Fortunately, however, no one was seriously hurt although a young woman working in the canteen had to be treated for cuts. The soldiers acted promptly to extinguish all lights to maintain the black-out and then joined local fire crews and Civil Defence staff in the task of rescuing and caring for those in the damaged buildings [3,12]. The Salvation Army said that it was determined to serve refreshments as normal on the following day!

The Pell Green bomb
During a night in February 1944 a bomb landed in a hop field near Pell Green while the occupants of the nearby houses were asleep. Some were awakened by being flung out of their beds and one unfortunate woman, Mrs Halliday, was severely injured by a piece of the bomb which had hurtled through the timbered part of her house. She was seriously wounded in the thigh, and it was only through the presence of mind of Charlie Bocking, one of the local ARP wardens who had arrived promptly at the scene, that her life was saved. With alacrity he applied pressure to the femoral artery to stem the copious bleeding and maintained this until medical aid arrived and she could be rushed to hospital. Mrs Halliday's invalid husband who was sleeping downstairs was unhurt.

The bomb blast caused extensive damage to many houses near and along the Cousley Wood road. The roof and windows of Pell House were damaged and an adjoining house had its tiling torn away and its windows and frames reduced to wreckage. The windows of the Rehoboth Chapel were shattered and on the opposite side of the road the gable end of one house was blown away. However, two semi-detached cottages had taken the full force of the blast. One was occupied by a 70 year old lady, Mrs Hammond. At that time her granddaughter, Mrs Vosden, was also staying in the cottage together with her 18-month-old baby and her 10-year-old brother. Mrs Vosden provided a Courier reporter with the following graphic account of the night's events [13]:

> *The baby seemed to stir, and I got out of bed to tuck him up. At the same time I heard the drone of a 'plane, and then suddenly there was a terrible noise. I put my arms round the baby and then there was an*

64

explosion. I felt that baby was breathing and was really asleep. As the explosion came everything came tumbling down on me, and when I had collected my senses I heard my young brother calling. I went to him and found that he had been blown half out of the bed, and he wanted to know what was the matter. I then hurried downstairs where Grannie had been sleeping. I found her lying on the floor pinned down by a door. I managed to lift this off her, and although shaken and bleeding from a cut forehead, she did not appear to have suffered much ill effects. Several kind friends have been in to see us and help us out of our muddle, and we have been advised that it would be best for us to leave the house, but Grannie says she won't be 'druv' from the house which she has lived in for well over 30 years.

The reporter was clearly much affected by the old lady's stoicism and described how she resolutely refused all offers of more secure and comfortable accommodation and how she set about preparing a much delayed breakfast over a simple oil stove in her wrecked kitchen surrounded by debris.

Bombs on the Hastings railway
One of the objectives of the Luftwaffe was to destroy Britain's infrastructure and consequently railway lines and stations were one of the principal targets for enemy attack. The lines in and out of London were particularly affected and passengers to and from Wadhurst often had their journeys disrupted due to bombing. Although the lines north of Orpington bore the brunt of the damage, the Hastings branch from Tonbridge to Hastings also suffered considerably. The air raid log books kept by the Southern Railway give a graphic impression of the extent of the disruption and the efforts made to effect repairs and keep the trains running. Table 3 summarises some of the incidents reported in the log books that related to the sections of the Hastings line from Frant to Wadhurst and from Wadhurst to Stonegate [*then known as Ticehurst Road*] [14].

One of the most bizarre incidents occurred on the afternoon of 24th February 1942 when a schoolboy passenger, on a Charing Cross-bound train leaving Tunbridge Wells, presented the guard with a missile that had crashed through the roof of a carriage between Wadhurst and Tunbridge Wells. It was handed to the police at Tonbridge who declared it to be an unexploded British Trench

Table 3: Bomb-related incidents on the railway between Frant and Ticehurst Road (Stonegate) stations 1940-1944

Date	Details
16.9.40	At 1.50 pm. both railway lines between Frant and Wadhurst were blocked as a result of bomb explosion which caused a crater under the track. The down line was cleared by 8.30 pm. and single line working was introduced at 5.35 the next morning. By 8.46 am. both lines had been cleared.
29.9.40	A suspected delayed action bomb was discovered between Wadhurst and Ticehurst Road at 8.45 pm. and both lines were closed as a precaution. After full investigation the lines were re-opened at 8.45 the next morning.
28.11.40	At 5 am. a high explosive bomb landed 15 feet from boundary fence adjoining the up siding at Wadhurst station causing a ten-foot wide crater. The track appeared undamaged but trains proceeded over the line under caution. The line was blocked for just under two hours for examination.
11.12.40	At 8.15 pm. a bomb dropped 15 feet from railway property between Wadhurst and Ticehurst Road causing the destruction of telephone lines and three trees to fall across and block the down line. The trees were cleared by 9.45 pm. and all telephone communications were restored by 5.30 the following morning.
12.12.40	At 8.40 am. 500-lb delayed action bomb was discovered between Wadhurst and Ticehurst Road. It was lying 30 feet from the down line. Both lines were blocked. A bomb disposal squad commenced work the following Monday. Single line working was introduced on the up line railway until 23rd December but for goods trains only. The bomb was finally rendered safe at 8.30 pm. on 2/1/41.
24.2.42	A missile crashed through the roof of a train between Wadhurst and Tunbridge Wells.
22.2.44	At 3.10 am. bomb exploded near the line near Frant. The track was examined but proved to be undamaged.
12.7.44	At 4.35 pm. a flying bomb fell 150 yards from the down line near Ticehurst Road station. The blast caused damage to the station.
6.8.44	A flying bomb exploded at 1.25 pm. on the track near Wadhurst on the Frant side of the Faircrouch Lane road bridge. There were no casualties but six lengths of rail were blown out of both lines and all communications down the line were destroyed. Nevertheless, by 8.22 pm. repairs were sufficiently advanced to introduce single line working on the down line, albeit with a speed restriction of 15 m.p.h. The up line was fully reinstated the following day.

Mortar bomb. The damaged coach was detached from the train before it continued its journey to London. The log merely notes laconically that this incident caused the train to be delayed for four minutes! Later, bomb disposal experts reported that the offending missile was a practice bomb filled with sand but how it happened to crash through the carriage roof was not explained.

If anything, the log appears to understate the efforts made by railwaymen to ensure the safe running of trains. For example, the record for 19th September 1940 notes that the line between Ticehurst Road and Etchingham had returned to normal working following a bomb incident but it makes no reference to the bombs that fell on Buttons Farm. Ken Jones's father was on duty at the Wadhurst station signal box that evening and saw the bomb flashes in the distance. Fearing that the railway line had been damaged and that trains would have to slow to walking pace in the black-out to avoid derailment, he set out to check that all was well. Ken clearly remembers [3] his mother's anxiety when his father failed to return from his shift at the expected hour of midnight and had still not returned by 2 am. It took a long time before it was safe to declare the line clear and Mr Jones was able to return home only in the early hours of the morning.

V1 Flying Bombs 1944-1945

The last two incidents recorded in Table 3 relate to the German flying bombs , known as Vergeltungswaffe 1 (Vengeance weapons 1) or V1s. The Germans first unleashed their vengeance weapons on 13th June 1944, in the aftermath of the D-Day landings. V1s were pilotless aircraft powered by a pulse jet engine whose direction was governed automatically by a gyroscope. They were over 25ft long, with a wing span of 17ft 6in and the nose contained 850 kg of high explosive. They were designed to fall to the ground after they had travelled a pre-set distance and therefore functioned as a flying bomb.

The V1s were promptly nicknamed buzzbombs or, more disparagingly, 'doodlebugs' by those unlucky enough to lie in their path. They were aimed at London and the position of their launching sites in France meant that most of them passed over what became known as 'Doodlebug Alley'. This comprised Kent and Sussex although Essex was also affected especially after September 1944 when some V1s were launched from the air.

67

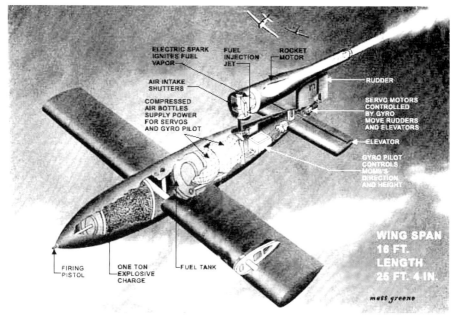

ELECTRIC SPARK
IGNITES FUEL
VAPOR

FUEL
INJECTION
JET

ROCKET
MOTOR

AIR INTAKE
SHUTTERS

RUDDER

COMPRESSED
AIR BOTTLES
SUPPLY POWER
FOR SERVOS
AND GYRO PILOT

SERVO MOTORS
CONTROLLED
BY GYRO
MOVE RUDDERS
AND ELEVATORS

ELEVATOR

GYRO PILOT
CONTROLS
BOMB'S
DIRECTION
AND HEIGHT

FIRING
PISTOL

ONE TON
EXPLOSIVE
CHARGE

FUEL TANK

WING SPAN
16 FT.
LENGTH
25 FT. 4 IN.

matt greene

The anatomy of a V1   [Matt Greene]

Many V1s, however, either fell short, were shot down or were deliberately made to crash by fighter aircraft before they reached London. Between June 1944 and March 1945, 1,422 fell on Kent and 412 on Essex. 907 fell on Sussex, of which over 85% (775) landed in East Sussex [15, 16]. These figures do not include the thousand or so V1s known to have crashed off the coast. Approximately 3,700 were destroyed by fighter aircraft and anti-aircraft defences.

A V1 rocket in flight   [www.atlanticwallbelgiumboulogne.110mb.com]

As this illustration from a contemporary advertisement shows, Wadhurst was well and truly in 'Doodlebug Alley'.

The directors of Croydon's three great departmental stores, ALLDERS, GRANTS and KENNARDS, invite the inhabitants of all towns, villages and districts contained within this area map of "Doodle Bug Alley" to take lunch and tea free on any one day at their stores during the remainder of this month of September.

Indeed a study of the statistics shows that Wadhurst and surrounding parishes suffered a relatively high incidence of V1 hits when compared with other Sussex towns and villages. A total of 18 fell on Wadhurst parish, 31 on

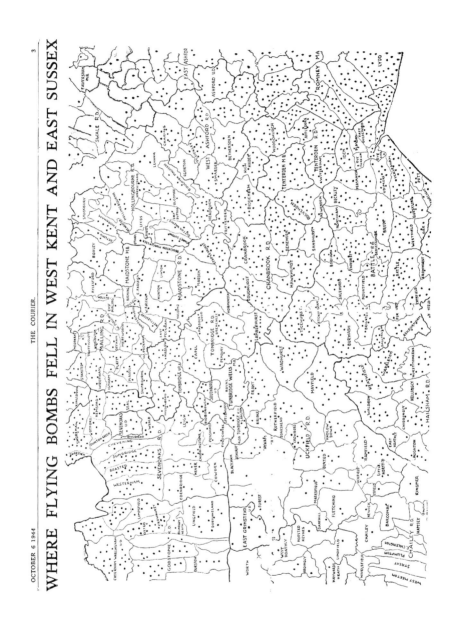

*The first official map of where flying bombs fell
in West Kent and East Sussex* [Courier 6 Oct 1944]

Table 4 Doodlebug incidents in Wadhurst parish during 1944 [15, 21]

Location	Outcome
Wood beside Frankham Dene	Malfunctioning bomb flew into the wood causing extensive damage
Garden at Lodge Hill Farm	Bomb only partly exploded causing minor damage
Green Square, Wadhurst	Explosion resulted in two deaths, one serious injury, and seven minor injuries; eight houses were rendered uninhabitable
Towngate Farm	Bombs crashed into the same field on the farm on two separate occasions causing minor damage
Bassetts	Bomb crashed on bridle path causing some damage to main house
Upper Walland Farmhouse	Bomb badly damaged the farmhouse and the adjoining cottage. Both buildings were later demolished
Railway line just beyond the Faircrouch Lane road bridge in the direction of Frant	Railway track lifted and parts blown across a field, demolishing part of the wall that surrounded the Dewhurst estate (*see also Table 3*)
Tidebrook School	School extensively damaged but there were no deaths or serious injuries and only 6 minor injuries.
Manor Farm, Tidebrook	Two bombs fell on the farm, one of which damaged the farmhouse
Wadhurst Hall lake	A bomb falling beside the lake damaged Flattenden farmhouse
Woodland behind Dewhurst House	No damage to property
Woodland near Dens Farm	No damage to property
Wickhurst Farm	Damage to farmhouse and out buildings
Wadhurst Castle grounds	A bomb landing on a Saturday afternoon interrupted bowls and cricket matches but there were no casualties
Woodland near Merryworth cottages	No damage to property
Woodland near Frankham House	No damage to property

Ticehurst, 19 on Burwash, 17 on Mayfield, 16 on Frant and 12 on Rotherfield. This compared with, for example, 14 on Hastings, 14 on Eastbourne, 10 on Robertsbridge, 6 on Rye, 1 on Lewes and none on Brighton. Over the border in Kent, Tunbridge Wells received 6 hits, Tonbridge UD 10 and Tonbridge RD 95 [17]. The first official map of where V1s fell was published by the Courier in early October 1944 [18]. This slightly underestimates the totals in some regions.

Given the large numbers of V1s that crashed and exploded in the rural districts of Kent and Sussex, it is remarkable that there were so few fatal casualties amongst the civilian population. Fortunately, many of the bombs fell harmlessly in open country and resulted in no human casualties or major damage. Indeed one of the V1s that fell on Ticehurst failed to explode at all and this enabled technical experts to remove and examine the warhead for the first time. However, although the number of casualties were relatively few, this does not diminish the fear they induced. There are many accounts of how the V1s flew very noisily overhead often emitting flames, and how they plunged terrifyingly to the ground when their engines cut out.

The first sighting of a V1 in Wadhurst was on 13th June 1944 when one was spotted roaring across Great Butts belching fire and heading in the direction of Crowborough. Shortly afterwards they started to fall in Wadhurst itself. The locations and impacts of the eighteen V1s that landed in the parish are summarised in Table 4. Although some caused relatively minor damage several had considerably more serious consequences. Two of the most dramatic incidents occurred within one week of each other near the beginning of August 1944: the wrecking of Green Square and the destruction of Tidebrook school.

The Green Square incident
On 29th July 1944 a flying bomb was brought down over Wadhurst and landed in a field immediately behind Green Square. The resulting explosion destroyed eight cottages in the square. The effects of the blast were also felt in the main street where many shop windows were shattered and several ceilings collapsed. The church also suffered some damage. Given the scale of the explosion and the extent of the damage caused, it was remarkable that

there were so few casualties. Nevertheless, two Green Square residents, Mr and Mrs Robert Blaylock, a couple in their late fifties, were very severely injured and, sadly, later died in the Kent and Sussex Hospital. Another householder, Mrs Styles, had to be taken to hospital suffering from severe shock.

Others in the square had very lucky escapes. Mr J White had just left his cottage when the bomb struck. Although he was cut in the head by flying glass, he sustained no other injury. His wife and son Charles also avoided serious injury by taking rapid refuge in a cupboard under the stairs. Nevertheless their cottage was ruined and Charles lost his entire wardrobe apart from one suit and his army cadet uniform. In another house the West family heard the approach of the bomb. However, whereas Mrs West, her sister and her three boys managed to take shelter in time, Mrs West's 76-year old mother, who was lame, was unable to take cover sufficiently quickly and consequently was exposed as the building collapsed around her. Miraculously, however, although covered in debris, she suffered nothing worse than a black eye. Her daughters attributed her avoidance of serious head injuries to their mother's "*wonderful head of hair*"! Mrs West's sister had only recently joined the household as a refugee from bombing in another district.

In addition to being rendered homeless by the destruction of Green Square, some residents suffered major disruption to their means of livelihood. A toy-maker, Mr G E Smith, lost his workshop and a large proportion of his stock and was forced to seek new accommodation to enable him to carry on his business [18].

The funeral of Mr and Mrs Blaylock took place in the Methodist church and was reported in the 11th August edition of the Courier [19]. The Methodist minister, the Revd. G H Crossland, officiated and was assisted by the vicar, the Revd. E Mannering. There was an extensive list of attendees including members of the rescue party who responded to the incident and representatives from many village organisations, local service units and the Salvation Army. Two of the Blaylock's three sons, Lance Corporal R Blaylock and Lance Corporal J Blaylock, were on military service abroad and were unable to attend. The younger daughter, Miss Lotte Blaylock, also could not attend for reasons unspecified. However, she was sent 'expressions of sympathy' plus 'generous gifts' from the Wadhurst Methodist church, the Wadhurst Sisterhood, the Wadhurst Village Relief Fund and from individual residents.

The Tidebrook School incident

In 1944 there were about 36 pupils attending Tidebrook School. Virtually all of these were the children of tenant farmers and farm labourers or of domestic staff in the local large houses. Earlier in the War the school had seen a major change in staff. The former headmistress had left to take over a large girls' school in Seaford and had been succeeded by Mrs Hunter who had recently returned from Canada. She was joined by Mrs Guest, a teacher who had come out of retirement and who travelled from Rotherfield each day on an auto-cycle.

Tidebrook School after the V1 had struck   [Bocking Collection]

The school building had two main rooms: one for the infants and a larger room – subdivided by a curtain – which housed the junior and seniors. Adjacent to the school was Tidebrook School House. This was originally built to accommodate the headteacher but, because it was no longer required for this purpose, had been let to the Hodder family. Walter and Colin Hodder both attended Tidebrook School. In 1941 Walter left to go to Skinners' in Tunbridge Wells but his younger brother was still a pupil in 1944.

74

On the morning of 3rd August, when Walter and his father were working at Mark Cross, they spotted a doodlebug being shot down by a fighter overhead. To their alarm they saw that it was likely to land in the direction of Tidebrook and decided to return home immediately. On passing the Best Beech Hotel, they were informed by the landlord that a flying bomb had hit Tidebrook school [20].

On that day 32 children were attending school and first became aware of the approaching bomb at approximately 11.05 am. The infants (seven in number) were doing drill in the school playground at the time. One of the older pupils, believed to be Derek Hemsley, had been issued with a special whistle to blow whenever he heard a doodlebug approaching and raised the alarm. The infant teacher, Mrs Guest, also saw the oncoming bomb and, having first given a loud blast on her whistle as an additional warning to those inside, rapidly marched her charges to the safety of dugouts in the playground. Meanwhile, Mrs Hunter briskly shepherded the older children inside the building to the two Morrison shelters.

Colin Hodder has a vivid recollection of the bomb's approach:

> *we could hear it coming and, what was worse, we could hear the RAF in hot pursuit, and the ear-splitting cannon fire getting closer. Then, worst of all, the motor of the doodlebug stopped and we knew what was coming next* [21].

The bomb exploded on the road 25-30 yards from the school with devastating effect [1]. The blast shattered all the windows and seriously damaged the fabric of the building. The account of the incident in the Courier [22] commented on some bizarre effects of the blast. A few pictures were still hanging on walls that had been wrenched from their foundations and a rocking horse in the infant room was still rocking but minus its tail.

After it was considered safe to do so, the children emerged from their shelters, picking their way through the debris and, after reassembling, they were sent home. Apparently, most were surprisingly unfazed by their experience – indeed many were excited and eager to explore the wreckage and inspect the remains of the bomb.

Within a short time the various emergency services were on the scene and the work of salvage and clearing-up commenced. As the realisation of what had happened spread, fathers of the pupils raced to the scene desperate to rescue their children and were immensely relieved to find that this was not necessary. Walter Hodder arrived to find his home wrecked. However, his mother had escaped serious injury by sheltering under the stairs. The only organisation apparently unaware of the dramatic events at Tidebrook was the school dinner delivery service whose van duly turned up at lunchtime to be confronted with a shattered school building and workmen clearing the rubble, instead of the expected 32 hungry children. Fortunately, the workmen were able to make short work of the lunches.

At the beginning of the next term the dispossessed Tidebrook children were bussed to Mark Cross School. At a later date they were transferred to Wadhurst School. The Hodder family was rendered homeless and spent the next six months living in the basement of Tidebrook Vicarage.

The remarkable fact that, despite the severe damage to the school, none of the children or teachers sustained even the slightest injury speaks volumes for the standards of contingency planning and discipline prevailing in the school at that time. Undoubtedly the cool headedness and efficiency of the staff averted what could have been a major tragedy on the scale of the contemporary Petworth school incident which resulted in the death of many children. A commemorative plaque in Tidebrook church records this deliverance:

> *With thanksgiving to God for the preservation of the teachers and the scholars of Tidebrook Church School on 4th* [sic] *August 1944, when an enemy flying bomb shattered the school buildings. Honour and discipline.*

Curiously, the date carved on the plaque gives the incorrect date.

V2 Rockets 1944-1945

The successor to the V1 was the almost invincible long-range rocket known as the V2. This was first deployed in September 1944. Four landed in Sussex but fortunately none hit Wadhurst. However, on 28th November 1944, one exploded above nearby Burwash causing extensive damage to Southover Hall [1].

BIBLIOGRAPHY

[1] Burgess, P. and Saunders, A. (1995) "Bombers over Sussex"
      Middleton Press
[2] Burgess, P. and Saunders, A. (1990) "Battle over Sussex"
      Middleton Press
[3] Jones, K. Letters, diary and research notes sent to Editors (2007/2008)
[4] Ramsey, W.G. (1980) "The Battle of Britain: Then and Now"
      After the Battle Publications
[5] Kent and East Sussex Courier 4.9.40
[6] Savidge, A. and Mason, O. (1988) "Wadhurst Town of the High Weald"
      Meresborough Books
[7] Reid, M.C. (1980) Letter to Kent and East Sussex Courier 12.9.80
[8] Interview with W. Hodder by Mary Offord (2007)
[9] Kent and East Sussex Courier 27.9.40
[10] Wadhurst History Society Newsletter no 2 (March 2004)
[11] WW2 People's War – An archive of World War Two Memories (2005).
      www.bbc.co.uk/ww2peopleswar /stories /34
[12] Kent and East Sussex Courier 14.3.41
[13] Kent and East Sussex Courier 25.2.44
[14] Southern Region Air Raid Log Books 1940-1945 SOU4 (or Rail 648)
      in The National Archives, Kew (abstracted by N. Rose)
[15] Ogley, B. (1992) "Doodlebugs and Rockets – The Battle of the Flying
      Bombs" Froglets Publications
[16] Rootes, A. (1980) "Front Line County : Kent at War, 1939-45"
      Robert Hale Ltd
[17] No.12 South–East Region Report, October 1944
[18] Kent and East Sussex Courier 6.10.44
[19] Kent and East Sussex Courier 4.8.44
[20] Hodder, W. Letter to editors, September 2007
[21] Hodder, C. Letter to editors, 2007.
[22] Kent and East Sussex Courier 11.8.44

Constructing an Anderson shelter

Chapter 4: Local Defence
Rachel Ring

This chapter describes how Wadhurst set about defending itself in the face of impending invasion and aerial attack. It covers such topics as the Home Guard, the Women's Voluntary Services, Air Raid Wardens, Fire Watchers, fundraising for the war effort and pillboxes.

The Home Guard

Very early on in the research for this chapter the realisation hit home that there were virtually no men now alive and still living in Wadhurst who could give first-hand accounts of their time in the defence units of the local Home Guard, or indeed any of the other defence groups within the community. Enquiries revealed that most of the young men who volunteered were awaiting their call-up papers and after the war they either married and then moved away, or started jobs that took them from the community never to return. Furthermore, many volunteers were former WW1 veterans or middle-aged men in 1940 so, by the start of this research in 2007, few were still alive.

Nevertheless, those few HG veterans who were found were able to give fascinating accounts of the units they served in. However, before presenting their memories it is useful to have an overview of the national Home Guard to set the scene. It is clear that one could examine the Home Guard units in almost any corner of England and find that their stories would be broadly similar, albeit with some regional differences.

The national Home Guard

At the outset it has to be said that most people in England nowadays associate the HG defence with their comic portrayal in the BBC's 'Dad's Army' series set in fictional Walmington-on-Sea. The reality, however, was somewhat different and it was only in the early months after their formation that the HG had resembled their fictional counterparts. Once uniforms and weapons were issued to the units they became a disciplined home force for the defence of the country.

On 14ᵗʰ May 1940, one of the darkest days in the early stages of the war when the Germans were entering France almost unchallenged, Anthony Eden, the Secretary of State for War, in a historic broadcast to the nation, warned of a very real threat of invasion by German parachutists and how such an event would require a real fighting force ready to deal with them.

His rallying message was to all male civilians, between the ages of 17 and 65 (although the ages were not strictly adhered to) and who had not been drafted into the Services for whatever reason, to come forward for their country and become part of a new fighting force to be called the Local Defence Volunteers, or shortened to LDV. According to our interviewees, many at the time irreverently took the abbreviation LDV to mean "*look, duck and vanish*".

Eden told the nation that no medical would be required and as long as you were male, "*capable of free movement*" and the right age, all you needed to do was enrol locally, usually at the police station. Within 24 hours as many as a quarter of a million men had volunteered, coming from every walk of life, and by the end of the month, a staggering three quarters of a million men had come forward.

Shortly afterwards Winston Churchill came up with the more inspiring name 'Home Guard' and the LDV was renamed barely two months after its inception. This did not, however, help with the limited supply of uniforms and weapons. Initially the so-called 'uniforms' consisted of a simple denim battledress and armband made by the WVS, with the initials LDV on them.

The HG were encouraged in these early months to improvise and make their own weapons, apparently from scraps and litter. Much has been written about Molotov Cocktail anti-tank grenades being made from beer bottles, and pieces of cast iron drainpipes being transformed into 3-inch mortars. Some units patrolled with such items as truncheons, pickaxes, broom handles and even packets of pepper! However, by July 1941 the United States had provided the HG with half a million WW1 .300 rifles as well as revolvers and ammunition.

A great deal was expected from the volunteers and their tasks were not easy, especially as the vast majority were working a full day in their normal occupations and by evening were expected to take on a totally different rôle with their HG duties. Their work was often dangerous and many hundreds lost their lives whilst on duty and almost half as many more were seriously wounded.

The HG coped with the hard manual work of clearing up the debris following air attacks and the harrowing job of searching for survivors. They erected anti-tank barriers, were known to lay barbed wire along the seashore and at checkpoints placed all types of farm implements to block the roads. Further obstacles were put in fields to prevent enemy aircraft from landing and, as if this were not enough, they were also expected, if necessary, to assist the army in fighting.

The removal, or blacking-out, of signposts was another, albeit less strenuous, assignment. The HG also patrolled railway stations, aerodromes, factories and other strategic locations. Myth has it they were constantly on the look out for German parachutists landing on British soil disguised as nuns!

In addition, the men had to drill each week and undertake target practice. Under the National Service (No. 2) Act of December 1941 male civilians were to be called up, ordered to join the HG and complete up to 48 hours' training per month. Apparently this call-up was a surprise since the HG numbers never fell lower than one million and, by the end of HG's first year, its strength was said to be at one and half million. To recognise this, a celebration parade was held at Buckingham Palace.

Winston Churchill spoke often about the HG and one of his speeches in 1940 included the following tribute:

> *If the enemy had descended suddenly in large numbers from the sky in different parts of the country, they would have found only little clusters of men mostly armed with shotguns, gathered around our searchlight positions. But now, whenever he comes, if he comes, he will find wherever he should place his foot, that he will be immediately attacked by resolute, determined men who have a perfectly clear intention and resolve to namely put him to death.*

The HG was eventually disbanded in December 1944 once the real threat of an invasion had diminished. A stand-down parade involving 7,000 men was held in London on 3rd December. After this the national HG ceased to operate. King George VI paid a fitting tribute when he said "*you have earned in full measure your country's gratitude*".

The local Home Guard

Our own few local members of the HG provide some vivid recollections of how the HG operated in Wadhurst. For example, Frank Bishop, a Wadhurst carpenter and builder, offered these memories of his time with the HG prior to his RAF call-up:

I joined the Local Defence Volunteers after a 6 o'clock news broadcast asking for volunteers to join at the local police station .... in Cousley Wood .... I think I got there about one minute after 6pm, and already a number had arrived to sign on, about 20 men.

At the outset we never had any weapons or uniform. We made Molotov Cocktails with a wine bottle filled with petrol and with a fuse taped to the bottle. The fuse would be lighted and the bottle thrown at tank tracks which, when the bottle broke, would catch the rubber mountings alight. In fact this was used by the Russians with good results but we never had to throw any in anger.

We had a number of 12-bore shotguns and we would take the wads out of the cartridge, remove the shot and mix with melted candle grease, then refill the cartridge. This made quite a lethal mixture but, again, we never had to use them.

After a while we were issued with army type gas masks and denim uniforms followed by standard uniforms. Later we received rifles which were Canadian ex-WW1 design .300 bore, and a very good weapon.

We were formed into units under a HG Sergeant, usually a WW1 trained ex-serviceman. We would do a duty usually once a week and at first we met in a very large old chicken hut near Bartley Mill hill. Six of us were on duty each night (three outside, three on make-shift beds inside) to watch out for German parachutists. We had to do drill once or twice a week, I think, and we had weapon training too.

There was one Sunday morning when we were called out at first light after being told that parachutists were being dropped. We quickly formed up and started our patrol to look for the Germans with only one or two shotguns. Jack Casterton, one of our patrol, the son of the local postmaster, had a real pistol. When he was asked if he had fired it, his reply was to the negative. We then told him he should do so and someone pointed out a rabbit sitting in the next field. Jack took careful aim, pulled the trigger and there was a loud bang and lots of smoke - however, the rabbit still carried on having his breakfast! Shortly after this we were stood down as the powers had decided it was all a false alarm.

About this time we moved up to Cousley Wood to a much better hut and received real rifles with a magazine for five bullets. All of us had a uniform and service issue gas masks. Just as I was called up we were getting machine guns.

One moonlit night I was on duty and German bombers were going overhead on their way to bomb London so I had picked up a rifle from our hut but unfortunately it was the wrong one. My own had no cartridges but the one I had taken had five in the magazine. I made out that I was pointing at the German aircraft and pulled the trigger. The gun went off with such a big bang that we all fell to the ground thinking that we were being attacked until I realised that I was the cause of the loud bang. I had to go before our CO and be reprimanded.

By this time I had volunteered for the RAF as aircrew even though I was aware of the high loss of life of aircrew. I was soon called up and became a wireless operator air gunner and serviced for the rest of the war years as a WOP/AG.

In a second interview Frank further recalled:

Men joined their local area unit, even if it was only a hamlet. I joined the Cousley Wood one as I was living in Benge's Cottage but I was born at the Old Vine; however, I cannot remember a lot about my time of living there. I knew of the other units in and around Wadhurst.

I was an apprentice carpenter at the time and this was a reserved occupation. I was later drafted to Crowborough Camp. Next I reported at the local Labour Exchange and went to Cowley, Oxford.

I told the foreman I wanted the sack so as I could go back home; he did not seem to think that that was a problem! I next went to Detling aerodrome for a time. After this I 'was at Horseferry Road, Westminster, where I worked to build the underground Cabinet shelter - it was from here that I was called up in 1941.

Whilst I was in London I caught the 7.30 pm. train home from Charing Cross then would bike to Cousley Wood to be on duty. Those nights I would be on the 6.20 am. train back to London the following morning. I wanted to be with the Home Guard.

The hut we moved to in Cousley Wood was in Windmill Lane (there used to be a windmill in the field and there were the foundations). Turn left opposite the Old Vine into Newbury Lane and after 100 yards there is a road to the right and up there and in a field was our hut - owned by Dr. Wilkins. It was a good site and look-out so we could see aeroplanes coming over quite low. There were searchlights to try and pick them out - it was a night fighter area.

The point about each area of the parish, regardless of its size, having its own unit was borne out by the recollections of Don Henderson, who was a Brockley schoolboy evacuated to Wadhurst. He joined the HG (one must assume a little under the age of 17) and was based in Brinkers Lane. He had a bicycle, brought down to him in Wadhurst by his father. Don was one of the seven young men in the unit and became a messenger taking notes between units and to the Drill Hall where Lt. Walter Usherwood, the leader of the Wadhurst Home Guard, was stationed. He remembered that:

The hut in Brinkers Lane was on the right hand side, it was a little look-out hut. It has long since gone but I know where it was. It was a dusk to dawn shift and we were looking out for anything suspicious like headlights or flashing torches. In this platoon was my headmaster, Dr Sinclair.

Peter Wicker was another 'Brinkers Laner' who recalled wryly that, had German paratroopers landed, "*we'd have had no chance in hell*". He described their hut as having an old charcoal burner in it. Laughingly, he also spoke of the lack of equipment and its poor quality. He said you could never hit very much with the American .300s and recalled practice shooting sessions in the old quarry down past the station (Three Oaks Lane). They were on duty from 6 pm. for a 12-hour shift, then relieved by someone in the morning. He worked during the day and told us that men did as many nights on duty as they could but said he never did get a uniform!

Others interviewed confirmed the initial lack of equipment. Some spoke of broom handles being taken for drill practice in lieu of a rifle and "*young men joining the HG before call-up having one rifle between them with which to exercise*". Nora Manktelow (née Usherwood) told of how, early on after the formation of the HG, her father, Lt. Usherwood, stored loads of tin hats and a stack of rifles in the front room of their house until he handed them out. It seems that one hat must have been left behind since she recalls her mother putting it on when there was any aerial activity.

Some recall the HG participating in exercises in Cousley Wood and how the troops had to to tie leaves on to old tin hats to act as camouflage. The Wadhurst HG units also took part in manoeuvres with the Canadian troops stationed in the parish.

Nellie Thompsett (née Newington) remembers that the field to the right of Whitegates Farm was a good vantage point for looking for enemy aircraft and described guns being down at Moon's at the bottom of the lane, near Shoesmiths. Her recollections were of guns "*rattling around and seeing flak where they were often after 'planes*". The other site she remembered was at Step Stile [at the bottom of the path behind the church], near Pell Bridge.

In 1944, V1 flying bombs started coming over Wadhurst. One lady interviewee clearly recalled "*the frightful noise and flames*" as they came over at regular intervals and remembers there was "*a unit stationed nearby (army and home guard) trying to shoot them down as they came over*". She added "*they must have been under canvas as they came to us for baths*".

John Turley served in the Rotherfield HG, which he joined in 1944 at the age of 17. Many of his memories were very similar to those of those who served in Wadhurst and some throw further light on the activities of the HG units in the Wadhurst area. For example, he described rifle leagues and shooting competitions between HG units and he remembered a pub in Tidebrook that had a rifle range in its cellar.

He also recalled going on guard duty overnight at Kings Standing on the Ashdown Forest. This was where the secret bunker was in our part of the world and where the HG would guard beneath one of the pylons making sure no-one came along. He spoke of words being relayed, Morse-tapping tones and possibly a foreign language heard coming up deep from within the earth. John went there three or four times, standing on guard all night, but never saw a soul. Duty here was done in rotation with other HG units including those from Wadhurst.

Like the Wadhurst HG units, John's unit participated in manoeuvres with Canadian troops who would attempt to reach a point that his unit was guarding. He gave the following account of one of these skirmishes:

> *One Sunday, when we were defending the (Eridge) road, we formed an ambush their side. One officer had the brainwave to put dinner plates on the road. They stopped and got out to inspect what was on the road and we threw thunder flashes. We won that particular exercise.* [The outcome was decided by umpires who wore white arm bands.]

Training

In addition to on-the-spot training, some members of HG units attended Home Guard training schools. One such school was the Home Guard Fieldcraft School on Bowmans Farm in Burwash, through which some 3,000 men passed. This was set up in March 1941 by Major John Langton-Davis, a journalist who had reported for the News Chronicle newspaper on the Spanish civil war. The major had lectured throughout the country to HG units and realised the importance of proper training for the men, so, with the backing of a newspaper, the Sunday Pictorial – but not initially with the authorities – he established the school.

Due also to the expertise of his local staff team, including the local baker whom he appointed Quartermaster-Sergeant, along with '*a carpenter and mechanic who became Corporals*', he soon had a school able to offer every aspect of guerrilla warfare - topics such as unarmed combat and stalking, surviving in the open and how to live off the land with limited supplies of food and, most importantly, the care and maintenance of weapons. It was not long therefore before SE Command gave official recognition of the importance of the major's training establishment; it became the training school for the command area.

Courses ran from a Friday evening to Sunday and from the moment the men entered the farm they were expected to consider themselves under fire from nearby Burwash and they also, after sleeping for the first night in a barn, had to bivouac:

> *the course involved sleeping out in the open under a hedge and although I had a sweater, there was only a groundsheet cape between me and the ground. An April frost added to the pleasure. It was very hard and very cold.*

Lt. Gen. B L Montgomery watching training at Burwash 31 Dec 1941
[Imperial War Museum]

Women and the Home Guard

On 10th April 2007 a photograph and editorial appeared on page 7 of the Daily Telegraph with the heading "*Mums with guns ready to take on Nazi storm troopers*". The photograph depicted women doing target practice as members of the Home Guard. This raises the question: did women serve in the Wadhurst HG units?

It was not until 1943 that the War Office allowed women officially to join the HG but, even then, only then to drive, cook or type. This was not taken very well by the women because throughout the War there had been significant pockets of them serving in areas of Great Britain alongside the men, even though their commanding officers had disobeyed orders from the War Office in allowing them to do so. The tireless and outspoken Labour MP, Dr. Edith Summerskill, campaigned for their formal recognition and for their right to have weapons, a uniform and, if necessary, to fight alongside the men. To this end she founded the Women's Home Defence organisation.

It would appear, however, that no women served in the Wadhurst HG units. None of those interviewed remembered seeing any women participating in manoeuvres or rifle shooting competitions. Nevertheless, some undertook secretarial duties for the unit officers. One such person was Jennet Hemsley (née Pilbeam). She was at secretarial college in Tonbridge but in the evenings became secretary/typist at the old Drill Hall in the Lower High Street [*now Kingsley Court*] to Lt. Walter Usherwood. She said her work held little of real interest as she mostly typed up lists of HG names and their platoons, details of men going off on activities, the drills, rotas and some letters. All of this was done "*on a horrible old typewriter at the Drill Hall every evening, but not on a Saturday*". For this she earned £6 a month. She said that Lt. Usherwood had an office upstairs in the Hall.

On the other hand, Roma Ogilvy Watson was secretary to Colonel Donald, commanding the HG Company, at Downgate in Tidebrook. Consequently her work covered a wider range of issues.

Stand down of the local Home Guard

In common with all other HG units, the Wadhurst HG units were stood down in December 1944. Lt. Walter Usherwood received a personal, handwritten letter of thanks from Colonel W Donald (a testimonial really) for all he had done for the Wadhurst Home Guard throughout the war, quoted here with the kind permission of his daughter:

Downgate,
Tidebrook, Sx.
Decr. 8th 1944

Dear Usherwood,

I cannot let the H.G. fade away without letting you know how much I valued your work in Command of No 3 Platoon while I was in command of the Company.

You were one of the hardest workers in the Battalion. You were prompt & capable in your handling of "Q" and administrative affairs. Above all, however, you were zealous in the training of your men along the best lines and you attained a good standard throughout. The work of your patrols was particularly meritorious.

Although you commanded a Platoon at least twice the size of any other you had the good will and confidence of your men and that is what would have counted had you been called upon to lead them into action.

I wish you well.

Yours sincerely,   W. Donald

Lt. Usherwood was also presented with an engraved barometer from his fellow officers, NCOs and men who served under him, in recognition of his dedicated service throughout the war within the HG.

Air raid warnings, air raid precautions and fire watchers

How Wadhurst residents coped with air raids is best told in the words and writings of some of those who lived through that time.

Peggy Bartholomew (née Sinden), who was a child during the War, said at the sound of an air raid warning:

We had to file out of school in strict order. Mr Mould's class first followed by Mrs Newington's, Mr Keast's, Miss Mould's and Miss Larcombe's. We went through the cutting by the girls' playground into the adjacent field where trenches had been dug out. We all had to get down into the trenches and stay there; everybody just about fitted in.

Ruth Skilton (née Yeoman), also a child at the time, recalled:

My father was an air raid warden and he often went out to ensure German pilots had been gathered up from crash sites. There were a number of 'planes shot down around Lamberhurst. We had many air raid warnings and we all were terrified. We had a Morrison air raid shelter in our sitting room. It had an enormous iron top with caging around the sides. We children were always put inside the shelter but there was not enough room for Mum and Dad as well, so they slept outside in the living room. My father was out on duty most nights as he was a 'foot warden'. He wore a tin hat and an armband to prove his identity.

A Morrison shelter introduced in March 1941, for people without gardens. The shelter, made from heavy steel, could also be used as a table. It was named after the Minister for Home Security, Mr. Herbert Morrison, and was approximately 6 feet 6 inches (2m) long, 4 feet (1.2m) wide and 2 feet 6 inches (0.75m) high.

The Parish magazine in December 1938 made the following announcement relating to Air Raid Precautions:

About 40 volunteers are needed immediately in connection with ARP in Wadhurst. Their duties will be to act as messengers in case of emergency, and they will be required to undergo a short course of training. Motor cyclists or cyclists are specially wanted and anyone over 17 years of age can volunteer. Enrolment forms can be obtained at Col. Cheale's office in the High Street, or application may be made to any of the wardens of sectors - Mr W Fisher-Barham, Col. Cheale, Mr Kemp, Mr A R E Kelsey, Mr Grant MacLean, Rev G T Maw, Rev E Mannering, Mr F Radcliffe, Dr Wilson.

According to Peter Wicker, ARP wardens checked that the black-out was observed but he also noted that a "*special constable used to march around every now and then as well*". According to documents in the Bocking Collection a First Aid post and fireguard and warden centre was situated in the end-cottage of a block situated behind Benge's shop in Cousley Wood. This has subsequently been demolished.

In April 1940 the Parish magazine made the following request for stirrup pumps:

The Wadhurst ARP Committee is anxious to compile a list of those householders who own stirrup pumps and would be willing for them to be used elsewhere than on their own premises in case of emergency. Would any such please notify the Hon. Secretary to the Committee, the Rev G H Crossland, Wesley Lodge, and also the Senior Section Warden or nearest warden. It will clearly be of great advantage to those who might have to deal with our emergency, if they could have exact knowledge of the location of all stirrup pumps and whether they would be available in case of necessity.

An entry in the Parish magazine in March 1941 provides information about the Fire Watchers' Service in the community:

As many already know bands of fire watchers have been organised at Wadhurst, Durgates and Sparrows Green to be on the look-out for incendiary bombs and to give the alarm by blowing whistles should they fall in the immediate neighbourhood. When no alert is on, the time must be spent at HQ which in two cases is a hut, and in the other a small, rather draughty room. Those who watch are entitled, it is felt, to heating and lighting and some provision for refreshments. Some have already helped in different ways but should a request be made to you, do not dismiss it as one more troublesome appeal, but give such help as you are able. But it should be remembered that it is an entirely voluntary matter, and only a member of one of the Fire Watchers' Committee, or someone authorised by them, is entitled to ask for your help.

Then, two months later in May 1941, there was an entry entitled 'Fire Watching Scheme - High Street Sector', which reported that there were 62 voluntary watchers who manned the post in relays from dusk to dawn, taking a turn once in every ten days, and, during an alert, patrol the High Street from Hill House to Black Barn, Brinkers Lane. The entry notes the following donations to support the volunteers in their work:

£1	Westminster Bank and Lloyds Bank
1s 0d	Mrs Eastman, Messrs Ansell, Goble, Howell and Watts
5 cts coal	Miss Taylor, Mr E Gardner, Messrs Cheeseman and Newington, Messrs Baldwin and Watts
Tins of coffee	Miss Taylor (2) Mrs Gardner (6)
Kettle	Mr Gardner

Further contributions, which should be sent to Mr M Watts, will be very gratefully received.

The last mention for the Wadhurst Fire Guard was in February 1945:

The Committee which has been responsible for the Fire Guard desires to express its appreciation of the wholehearted cooperation of the Fire Watchers and to thank them for carrying out their duties so willingly and cheerfully. E A Bloomfield Hon Sec.

The Women's Voluntary Service

Nationally the WVS was formed in 1938 primarily to assist in ARP. However its rôle expanded considerably and it engaged in many different activities to aid the War effort. In Wadhurst it played a major part in supporting the many

British, Canadian and American troops that came to the parish in the course of the War. They were billeted in requisitioned large houses in the district and local canteens were set up and run for them by volunteers and the WVS in St. George's Hall along with many other 'messes' in various areas of the parish. The volunteers manning the canteens served up *"endless fried eggs, bacon, sausages, tea and coffee"* - all, we suppose, before severe rationing became the norm.

Peggy Bartholomew recalled that her mother was in the WVS and that there was a clothing exchange at the Institute where outgrown clothes were handed in and exchanged for points towards new clothes. The Misses Briggs bore this out and said their mother also helped in the WVS for the War effort. One fund-raising event she was involved in took place at Horsegrove, down Osmers Hill, the home of Brian Nicholls, who at that time worked for the BBC. The event was said to be a mime.

WADHURST'S SALVAGE QUEEN
Woman's Unusual War Effort

Mrs B C Nicholls and her fellow collectors   [Courier]

This article in the Tunbridge Wells Courier, of 25th August 1942, provided a further example of the work undertaken by the WVS within the community. The local WVS had asked Mrs Nicholls of Horsegrove to undertake the work of Salvage Officer - a job she obviously undertook with great diligence. The same editorial gave details of a mime, entitled *The Dustman's Dream*, written by Mrs Nicholls, and performed in her garden.

'Home Front' edicts from the Government

During the War the local defence organisations and the local population were issued with countless guidelines and edicts from the Government on how best to cope with almost every aspect of life. The bulk of these came from the Ministry of Information. A good example was a leaflet sent to all homes in Great Britain advising in detail what to do in the event of a German invasion. This is reproduced in the Annex to this chapter. Thankfully, none of the measures recommended was required to be implemented.

Fund-raising for the War effort

The local defence organisations made an important contribution to local fund-raising events in support of the War effort. Documents in the Bocking Collection indicate that there were three major national fund-raising initiatives to which Wadhurst responded.

The first was 'War Weapons Week'. Wadhurst's 'War Weapons Week' was held in the week of 19th April 1941 and, according to the accounts, made a profit of £215 17s 4d.

Raffles and Collections brought in a substantial £9 0s 5d and the fun fair £67 2s 10d. The community supported a wide range of events during the week. These included five gardens open to the public and two card evenings. There was also a large military parade. This formed up in Durgates and marched to the High Street via Sparrows Green accompanied by brass and pipe bands. Also represented were Home Guardsmen, ARP wardens, local detachments of the Red Cross, WVS, Fire Brigade and Auxiliary Fire Service, along with Scouts, Guides and Wolf Cubs. Field Marshall Lord Milne took the salute.

APRIL 19 - 2L 1941

Wadhurst War Weapons Week

INCOME.

	£	s.	d.
Dances—Mrs. Cheale £7 : 18 : 7½ ; Mr. Still £10 ; Mrs. Wildy £5 ...	22	18	7½
Gardens—Miss Boyd, Mrs. Edwards, Mrs. Nicolls, Miss Previté, Miss Watson	1	14	11
Sale of Programmes	10	14	2
Military Entertainment	24	6	5
Fire Brigade Demonstration	2	9	6
Fun Fair	67	12	10
Whist Drives—Mr. Greig £7 : 6 : 6 ; Mrs. Bocking £3 : 12 : 6 ; The Rangers £9 : 3 : 0	20	2	0
Collections—Mrs. Bulteel (cats, dogs and tortoise) £5 : 6 : 5 ; Mr. J. Ratcliffe 10/-	5	16	5
Gifts—Mr. and Mrs. Gardner £10 ; Mr. Rivington £5 : 5 ; Anon. 12/6	15	17	6
Exhibition in the Institute	13	1	3
Bridge Drives	26	2	2
Sale of Flowers—Miss Moutray Reed	10	6	9
Raffles and Competitions—The Vine Inn £4 : 10 ; Best Beech Hotel £12 : 19 : 11 ; E. Gardner's Stores £18 : 19 : 6 ; Wellington Stores £3 : 0 : 6 ; Miss Malpass £5 : 0 : 6 ; F. Gadd's Stores £1 : 17 : 6 ; Mrs. Bocking £13 : 10 ; Mrs. Hemsley £12 : 15 ; Mrs. Pritchard £6 : 4 : 0 ; Mrs. Baldwin £4 : 13 : 6 ; Mrs. Kennaird £2 : 10 ; Mrs. Newington £3 ; Mr. Barham £3 ; Mr. Juson £1 : 10 : 0	93	0	5
	£314	2	11½

EXPENSES.

	£	s.	d.
Printing	4	11	6
Fun Fair—Equipment, Lights and damage in Hall	5	13	1
Programme Prizes for No.'s 59, 198, 296, 409, 779, 992, 1148, 1329	6	0	0
School Children's Prizes	2	2	0
Certificates and Stamps at Military Entertainment	5	0	8
Stamps at Fun Fair	52	19	0
Stamps at Exhibition	9	15	0
Certificates for Bridge Drives	8	9	6
The Banks	1	0	9
Haulage	1	10	0
Petrol, 'Phone calls, postages	1	4	1
	98	5	7
Balance	**215**	**17**	**4½**
	£314	2	11½

[Bocking Collection]

The Wadhurst effort was part of a larger effort, the Uckfield Rural District 'War Weapons Week'. This was formally declared open at the Regent Cinema in Crowborough, by General Sir Cecil Romer who commanded the Home Guard for Surrey, Kent and Sussex.

No. 3 Platoon A Compy 18th Bn Home Guard

The Kent and East Sussex Courier of Friday 25th April 1941 reported that the target for the week was £150,000, sufficient to purchase fifteen light tanks.

In the following year, Wadhurst 'Warship Week' was held in the week beginning 14th March. Proceeds of £510 8s 4d were raised but, because of hefty expenses totalling £383 5s 3d, the profit was a more modest sum of £127 3s 8d. However, in total, the towns and villages in the Uckfield RD area raised £27,371.

The programme, detailing the events organised for the week, had a message from H C de J du Vallon [*Wadhurst Parish Council Chairman*] who urged people to 'lend' whatever they could since it would be going to the cost of the ship; and whatever expenditure people made, it would provide comforts for the crew. A vast range of entertainments and events were on offer and the week commenced on the Saturday with the parade of Civil Defence Forces. The salute was taken by Cdr. N Crozier RN in the High Street and the Rt. Hon. Sir George Courthope, Bt, MC, MP, delivered the opening address.

One of the many events was a local HG platoon shooting-competition. In her scrapbook, Nora Manktelow has press cuttings and photographs of her father, Lt. Walter Usherwood, the leader of the Wadhurst Home Guard, together with the Wadhurst HG No. 2 Section receiving the cup (which she still possesses) for the winning team from Cdr. Crozier.

WADHURST CUP WINNERS

Members of the Wadhurst Home Guard who have won the local platoon shooting cup

[The newspaper identifies those in the photograph as Sgt O'Malley, H Reed, F Watson, L Barham, Webster, Hollis, E Lavender, Goldsmith and J Francis.]

*Wadhurst Home Guard at the opening of 'Salute the Soldier' week;
the salute was taken by Col. Eric Gore-Brown* [T. W. Advertiser]

The last major War effort fund-raising event was 'Salute The Soldier Week', which took place between 6th and 13th May 1944. The Tunbridge Wells Advertiser carried a picture of Sir George Courthope as he introduced Colonel Eric Gore-Brown, a photograph of the Colonel inspecting the Wadhurst Home Guard and a picture of an ATC contingent marching past the saluting base at the opening ceremony.

An editorial from another newspaper gives the following account of the opening ceremony under the heading 'Wadhurst on Parade, Salute taken by Colonel Gore-Brown':

> *On Saturday the Salute the Soldier Week opened at Wadhurst with a parade of the various services which assembled at Durgates and marched through the town headed by the Tunbridge Wells Home Guard*

band under Sgt V Usherwood. The procession consisted of the Wadhurst Home Guard (Lt. W. Usherwood); Cadet Force (Lt. C G Foote); ATC (Flying Officer W Goble); Wardens (Deputy Warden Connolly); First Aid Parade Party (Leader H Sinden); Red Cross, Sussex 134 (Commandant Miss A Collier); Red Cross Youth Detachment 570,(Miss Rowcliffe); WVS (Mrs Wildy); lst Wadhurst Rangers (Miss B Courthope); lst Wadhurst Girl Guides (Lt Pam Edney); 2nd Wadhurst Girl Guides (Capt. G Clements) and Brownies (Miss E Avis).

COLONEL ERIC GORE-BROWN, D.S.O., O.B.E., T.D., A.D.C., inspecting the Wadhurst Home Guard.

Col. Eric Gore-Brown inspecting the Wadhurst Home Guard
'Salute the Soldier' Week 1944   [T. W. Advertiser]

In the High Street Colonel Eric Gore-Brown took the salute supported by Colonel Sir George Courthope and Mr M Watts (vice-chairman of the Parish Council). Col. Gore-Brown, who is chairman of the Southern Railway, in an address said his railway had already given £500 to their Week, but he promised that if they reached their target of £25,000, they would give another £500. He urged them to invest every penny they could spare. It would all be repaid one day and not only in terms of money. He reminded them of the misquotation 'Nothing succeeds like Sussex' and hoped they would make it come true.

Colonel Gore-Brown afterwards inspected the personnel of the local Civil Defence at Sparrows Green.

Pillboxes

Pillboxes are defensive structures, round or polygonal in shape. The circular type was primarily associated with the First World War and was built infrequently during the Second. They can be dated as far back as to the Romans and the Martello Towers, built to ward off a possible French invasion by Napoleon's armies, were the grander versions of the smaller Second World War pillboxes. The Russians were the first to use the more commonly known style of concrete structure in the 1904 Russo-Japanese war. From 1914 on, the Germans made great use of them. After Dunkirk, Britain embarked on a massive pillbox-building programme in South East England where the threat of invasion was felt to be the greatest. They were built at sites with a good field of fire, covering areas considered vulnerable. These included the coast and key parts of the infrastructure such as railway lines, level crossings, crossroads or junctions and airfields.

Construction was undertaken by military RE Field Companies or the Pioneer Corps, aided by civilian contractors such as, in the case of Sussex pill boxes, the Ringmer Building Works. A first gang would dig and lay the foundations and the next construct the shuttering, then another group came for the pouring of the concrete. If there was a shortage of wood for shuttering, brick was used. This was not normally removed after the concrete was set; this gave the appearance of the pillbox being built of brick. Only when the bricks fall away can the concrete 'case' be seen.

Few pillboxes remain despite the numbers quickly erected during the early days of the War. The exact number is not known. Indeed Chris Butler, an authority on the archaeology of the defences of East Sussex, had no record of the two in our community. However, there are two pillboxes one and half miles from the centre of Wadhurst, in the parish of Frant but effectively in 'our area', since they lie in the fields either side of the B2099 from Wadhurst to

Tunbridge Wells, on the stretch known as Riverhall Hill. Both are visible from the road, one to the south west and the other to the north east.

The reasons for building the two pillboxes in this position are not known. Certainly they command unrestricted views of the railway line, one closer than the other. The one to the south west could also cover the Partridges Lane junction with the B2099 [*during the Second World War, this road was the A266*]. The north eastern structure has views of the upper part of Riverhall Hill, as well as fair all-round vision of the railway line and the present B2099, east and west. This latter pillbox is constructed into the rising slope of the field and is now shielded by mature vegetation, but it is unlikely to have had such camouflage seventy years ago.

PILLBOX DESIGNS - A COMPARISON

Both pillboxes are 'thick walled' Type 24 - six-sided, with an embrasure in each main wall plus an anti-ricochet wall inside. This type of pillbox could hold a garrison of up to eight men.

The two pillboxes are almost identical in size and external appearance; the external dimensions in metres are:

	SW	NE
Wall 1 - rear	5.63	5.95
Wall 2 (going clockwise)	2.75	2.70
Wall 3	2.92	2.88
Wall 4	2.95	2.98
Wall 5	2.85	2.86
Wall 6	2.75	2.72

The SW box is 2.11 m high above ground level; the NE box is sunk into the ground at the rear and is 2.29 m high above ground level at maximum. Construction is of stretcher bond brickwork externally and internally up to the level of the embrasures; these are 0.67 m wide and 0.18 m high. The door to the SW box is at ground level with hinges set well inside the opening and a steel door; the NE box is approached down a ramp to a similar steel door.

Both boxes have found a peacetime use as sheep shelters and there is now much mire and rubble that makes access difficult, but not impossible. Inside, the two boxes are very similar: above the brickwork, the embrasures are finished with reinforced concrete and each has a shelf 1.5 m deep to the opening to the outside; the wall at that point is 0.67 m thick. In the centre of both boxes is a reinforced concrete roof support 0.24 m thick and roughly Y-shaped. Headroom is 6' 2" – enough for most men to wear a steel helmet and still stand upright; in the NE box it is possible to walk all round the central pillar but in the SW box, the leg of the Y extends into the centre embrasure, dividing the internal space in two. Around the inside walls are small brick pillars, presumably as supports for some sort of shelving in front of each embrasure.

There is no evidence to suggest that any shots were fired from either pillbox.

SW pillbox from the N.

Inside the NE pillbox.

NE pillbox from the E.

SOURCES

Home Guard Manual (1941): Tempus edition [2006]
British Anti-Invasion Defences 1940-1945: Ruddy, A. J.
    Historic Military Press
Our Longest Days - A People's History of the Second World War:
    Koa Wing, S. [2008], Profile Books
Sussex Home Guard: Crook, P. [2004], Middleton Press
**Contesting Home Defence - Men, Women and The Home Guard
    in The Second World War:** Summerfield, P. and Peniston-Bird, C.
    [2007], Manchester University Press
The War in East Sussex: Sussex Express and County Herald [1985]
Wadhurst Parish magazine 1936 - 1947: ESRO PAR 498/7/4
The Bocking Collection - archive material and photographs
Newspapers: Kent and Sussex Courier
            Tunbridge Wells Advertiser
            Sussex Express and County Herald
Keep Military Museum, Dorchester - various posters and archive records
    www.homesweethomefront.co.uk
Imperial War Museum - photographs
Wadhurst Primary School Log Book
www.historylearningsite.co.uk/home_front.htm

The personal memories of local residents including:
    Peggy Bartholomew, Frank Bishop, Gillian Briggs, Jenn Hemsley, Don
    Henderson, Walter Hodder, Nora Manktelow, Des Mansfield, Roma
    Ogilvy Watson, Rosemary Pope, Ruth Skilton, Nellie Thompsett, John
    Turley, Nora Tweedley and Peter Wicker.

Our thanks also go to John Lamplugh and William Whitehorn for allowing
pillbox inspection on their land.

MINISTRY OF INFORMATION LEAFLET
"IF THE INVADER COMES:
WHAT TO DO - AND HOW TO DO IT"

The Germans threaten to invade Great Britain. If they do so they will be driven out by our Navy, our Army and our Air Force. Yet the ordinary men and women of the civilian population will also have their part to play. Hitler's invasions of Poland, Holland and Belgium were greatly helped by the fact that the civilian population was taken by surprise. They did not know what to do when the moment came. **You must not be taken by surprise.** This leaflet tells you what general line you should take. More detailed instructions will be given you when the danger comes nearer. Meanwhile, read these instructions carefully and be prepared to carry them out.

I

When Holland and Belgium were invaded, the civilian population fled from their homes. They crowded on the roads, in cars, in carts, on bicycles and on foot, and so helped the enemy by preventing their own armies from advancing against the invaders. You must not allow that to happen here. Your **first rule** therefore is:

1   **If the Germans come by parachute, aeroplane or ship, you must remain where you are**. The order is "stay put". If the commander-in-chief decides that the place where you live must be evacuated, he will tell you when and how to leave. Until you receive such order you must remain where you are. If you run away, you will be exposed to far greater danger because you will be machine-gunned from the air as were civilians in Holland and Belgium, and you will block the roads by which our own armies will advance to turn the Germans out.

II

There is another method which the Germans adopt in their invasion. They make use of the civilian population in order to create confusion and panic.

They spread false rumours and issue false instructions. In order to prevent this, you should obey the **second rule** which is as follows:

2 **Do not believe rumours and do not spread them**. When you receive an order, make sure that it is a true order and not a faked order. Most of you know your policemen and your ARP wardens by sight, you can trust them. If you keep your heads you can also tell whether a military officer is really British or only pretending to be so. If in doubt, ask the policeman or ARP warden. Use your common sense.

III

The Army, the Air Force and the Local Defence Volunteers cannot be everywhere at once. The ordinary man and woman must be on the watch. If you see anything suspicious do not rush round telling your neighbours about it. Go at once to the nearest policeman, police station or military officer and tell them exactly what you saw. Train yourself to notice the exact time and place where you saw anything suspicious, and try to give exact information. Try to check your facts. The sort of report which a military or police officer wants from you is something like this:

> 'At 5.30pm tonight I saw twenty cyclists come into Little Squashborough from the direction of Great Mudtown. They carried some sort of automatic rifle or gun. I did not see anything like artillery. They were in grey uniforms'.

Be calm, quick and exact. The **third rule** therefore is as follows:

3 **Keep watch.** If you see anything suspicious, note it carefully and go at once to the nearest police officer or station, or to the nearest military officer. Do not rush around spreading vague rumours. Go quickly to the nearest authority and give him the facts.

IV

Remember that if parachutists come down near your home they will not be feeling at all brave. They will not know where they are, they will have no food, they will not know where their companions are. They will want you to give them food, means of transport and maps. They will want you to tell them

106

where they have landed, where their comrades are and where our own soldiers are. The **fourth rule** therefore is as follows:

4   **Do not give any German anything**. Do not tell him anything. Hide your food and your bicycles. Hide your maps. See that the enemy gets no maps. See that the enemy gets no petrol. If you have a car or motor bicycle put it out of action when not in use. It is not enough to remove the ignition key, you must make it useless to anyone except yourself.

If you are a garage proprietor, you must work out a plan to protect your stock of petrol and your customers' cars. Remember that transport and petrol will be the invaders' main difficulties. Make sure that no invaders will be able to get hold of your cars, petrol, maps or bicycles.

V

You may be asked by Army and Air Force officers to help in many ways. For instance, the time may come when you will receive orders to block roads or streets in order to prevent the enemy from advancing. Never block a road unless you are told which one to block. Then you can help by felling trees, wiring them together or blocking the roads with cars. Here, therefore is the **fifth rule**:

5   **Be ready to help the military in any way**. But do not block roads until ordered to do so by the military or LDV authorities.

VI

If you are in charge of a factory, store or other workplace, organise the defence at once. If you are a worker, make sure that you understand the system of defence that has been organised and know what part you have to play in it. Remember that parachutists and the fifth column men are powerless against any organised resistance. They can only succeed if they can create disorganisation. Make certain that no suspicious strangers enter your premises.

You must know in advance who is to take command, who is to be second in command, and how orders are to be transmitted. This chain of command must be built up and you will probably find that ex-officers or NCOs, who have been in emergencies before, are the best people to undertake such command.

The **sixth rule** is therefore as follows:

6   **In factories and shops, all managers and workmen should organise some system now by which a sudden attack can be resisted.**

VII

The six rules which you have now read give you a general idea of what to do in the event of invasion. More detailed instructions may, when the time comes, be given you by the Military and Police Authorities and by the Local Defence Volunteers; they will not be given over the wireless as they might convey information to the enemy. These instructions must be obeyed at once.

Remember always that the best defence of Great Britain is the courage of her men and women. Here is your **seventh rule**:

7   **Think before you act**. But think always of your country before you think of yourself.

CHAPTER 5: TIDEBROOK EXPERIENCES
DAVID JAMES

Background

As 1937 drew to a close the people of Tidebrook naturally were very conscious of the developing international uncertainty. Their newspapers and the wireless over the past two years had reported Mussolini's invasion of Abyssinia, Hitler's advance into the demilitarised Rhineland and the onset of the Spanish Civil War. In Tidebrook, however, life continued very much as normal.

Tidebrook School 1938 [Bocking Collection]
l to r: Dorothy Warren - John Lancaster - ?? - John Knight - ?? - Bert Bassett - Miss Davies
front: Bill Eaton - Lucy Eaton - ?? - Marjory Everden - Nancy Hemsley - Jessie Everden - Peter Brown

After his class on Religious Instruction to the children of Tidebrook School the Revd. G T Maw called in on the Headmistress, Miss Wadeson, to congratulate her on the recent report by His Majesty's Inspector, which had concluded that "*this rural school is successfully and pleasantly conducted*". They agreed to press the County Council to tackle the recommendation to improve electric lighting since "*the main classroom is unusually dark*". A year later the school closed for its installation. The vicar was also pleased to hear that the new teacher of the infants, Miss Mai Davies, was settling well both into the school and into her lodgings with the Hodder family in School House, even if her affections lay principally with a chapel minister in Wales whom she was to marry in 1939. Together with Miss Pike, the teacher of the junior children, they had the care of just 44 pupils.

The vicar himself had become the incumbent three years previously and was in his final parish, planning to retire at the end of 1944. A graduate of Trinity College, Cambridge, Mr Maw had served as a chaplain in the First World War when he had the distinction of baptising his admiral.

Tidebrook parish contained 670 souls, who lived in an agricultural community where the land was devoted mainly to pasture, with some corn and hops. Much was in the control of a few estates, especially Tidebrook Manor, where John Budd enjoyed touring his property in a donkey cart controlled by Charlie Lancaster, and where John Sands was the farm bailiff. John's son, Horace, was the manager for Mr E A Thompson, who owned Towngate and Chittinghurst Farms and the many cottages that went with them. Grant McLean at Wadhurst Hall [*now Park*] was another principal landowner. The Kelsey family owned Riseden Farm. As their main interest was in the brewing industry the farm was managed by Bob Ballard, but they took much interest in local affairs. Eileen Kelsey was the wolf cub Akela and was reputed to climb trees faster than any boy.

Such estates employed many people from Tidebrook as farm workers, in domestic service, or as gardeners like Mr Lavender at Riseden or Albert Winzer at Brocks Ghyll. There were also several small family dairy farms where a dozen or so cows were milked by hand, and the churns stood at the roadside awaiting the Matthews' milk lorry from Heathfield to take them to Tunbridge Wells. Others were employed in the building industry, on the railway or in local shops. Several, of course, had careers beyond Tidebrook. Cecil Slowe had been a merchant in Shanghai but now grew carnations at Tabley for the London market, and his son Edward was training as a chartered accountant in London.

Wadhurst Hall - c.1920

Tidebrook was a community. Alfred Taylor was the local police constable and Florence Powell the district nurse, while William Riles offered carpentry skills at Chittinghurst. Kate Weston looked after the little post office and shop near the bridge at the bottom of the hill. Other sustenance was provided by Nathaniel Newman at the Fountain Inn [*by the junction of the main road and the lane leading to Mousehall*], with alternative public houses nearby at the Best Beech and the Miners' Arms. Not far away too at Best Beech was petrol from Alfred Dodman's garage at Fair Glen, Reg Hodder's grocery business and the Gallup brothers' forge which provided shoes for the shire horses so crucial to the farmers, and which sharpened the families' shears.

Florence Powell

Walter and Colin Hodder remember their childhood when several families had their milk delivered by 'Creamy' Barden from Stone Cross Farm, who dipped a measure from his churn to fill the jugs which had been left on the doorstep. Twice a week a horse and high-wheeled van would deliver crusty bread from

111

Lesters of Mayfield. On Fridays, Malpass would make the meat delivery from Wadhurst, receiving the following week's order in return, and Pedro would arrive from Tunbridge Wells with his motorcycle and sidecar to provide fresh fish. Reg Hodder's van was another frequent sight, delivering groceries. Other needs had local solutions. Bean poles were provided by Mr Ellis, honey by Mr Manwaring, and shoes were repaired by Mr Ireland.

Reg Hodder's grocery van and car   [Walter Hodder]

The approach of war

The Tidebrook School Log Book shows normality continuing during the spring and summer of 1938. The annual egg collection and pound day in April for the Tunbridge Wells Hospital found the children bringing 267 eggs, 22 lb of sugar and 16 lb of other goods to school. There were the usual closure days at the end of the summer term for the Wadhurst Sunday School outing, for the Women's Institute treat and for the outings of the choir and of Tidebrook Sunday School. The most significant changes seemed to be the introduction of the school milk service and the farewell to Miss Pike at the end of term on 12th August when she was presented with a fountain pen and pencil.

However, life in this idyllic community was about to be challenged. While Miss Pike left because the falling numbers in the school could not justify the number of staff, it is significant that she was soon to have a new post, in the WRNS. Shortly after the new term opened the Log Book recorded on 30th September how "*most of the children were fitted with gas masks this morning*", a task completed the following day. International tensions had escalated since Hitler's annexation of Austria in the spring and his clear ambitions in Czechoslovakia. On 27th September Tidebrook wirelesses relayed the address to the nation by the Prime Minister, Neville Chamberlain:

> *How horrible, fantastic and incredible it is that we should be digging trenches and trying on gas masks here because of a quarrel in a far away country between people of whom we know nothing.*

Tidebrook School 1939 [Bocking Collection]
l to r: back: Eileen Springett - Lucy Eaton - Joy Latter - Walter Hodder - Bill Eaton - Jim Everdell - Ted Knight - John Lancaster - Muriel Ross - Derek Hemsley - Mrs Guest
centre: Eric Beeney - Alistair Ross - Mary Warren - Rosemary Jones - Angela Reeves - Vic Ellis - Dennis Farmer - Stanley Everdell - Alan Dodman - Marjory Eaton - Gwen Lancaster
front: Joan Ward - Joy Ballard - Nan Hunter - Pat Latter - Edwina Ballard - Peter Ross - Colin Hodder

While the Munich agreement three days later seemed to have brought 'Peace in our time' by discarding Czech interests in ceding the Sudetenland to Hitler, life in England and in Tidebrook was about to change. The children at the school were a miniscule percentage of the recipients of the 38 million gas masks that were issued at the time. Plans were made to expand the army from five to thirty-two divisions, and expenditure on the RAF accelerated. Men flooded to join the Territorial Army and investment in the ARP service tripled. A strategy was established for the evacuation of 2 million people from the capital.

The talk at the Fountain Inn during the early months of 1939 was increasingly foreboding. Hitler's invasion of what remained of Czechoslovakia in March was followed by guarantees to Poland and military conscription for the first occasion at a time of peace. During August London had a trial run for black-out, followed by the Nazi/Soviet Pact, the Emergency Powers Act and the call-up of military reservists. After Hitler had invaded Poland on Friday 1st September people, returning from Tidebrook Church the following Sunday morning, turned their wireless sets on to hear the Prime Minister querulously informing the nation at 11.15 am. that his work for peace had failed, and that Britain was at war with Germany.

The first years of War

While the early months were called the 'Phoney War', there were immediate implications for the people of Tidebrook. Several enlisted. Patrick Slowe of Tabley was among those called up at the end of August to serve in the Royal Sussex Regiment. Others joined the Civil Defence, like Frank Hodder as an air raid warden. Several of the large houses were requisitioned for army use, including Tidebrook Place, Gill Wood End, Wadhurst Hall and Cinder Hill.

Alice Wadeson - headmistress of Tidebrook School [Bocking Collection]

The Beech Hill hall was turned into a canteen where members of the WI served tea and sandwiches.

At school Colin Hodder recalls how the children had to practise putting on gas masks and how "*they were uncomfortable and smelled of rubber and we didn't like them*". It was now a more congested school. The thirty Tidebrook children were joined by forty five evacuees and three teachers from London. Chittinghurst Lane, for example, had welcomed Mrs Ward and her three children from Balham. East Sussex responded with a delivery of tables and chairs, but the situation only eased in November when the junior girls from Elfrida School transferred to Frant and others drifted back to Lewisham. By the end of term just 14 evacuees were still at the school to enjoy the normality of the Christmas tree and the chocolates and oranges provided by the managers. It was also Alice Wadeson's last day in school before taking up an appointment in Seaford and she was presented with a cut-glass bowl of anemones. She was succeeded eventually in March by Frances Hunter.

Older evacuee students staying in Tidebrook were from Brockley Grammar School and had their classes at Whiligh and Oakover. Similarly a little later, after the 1941 School Log entry had announced that "*Walter Hodder has been awarded a special place at Skinners' School*", he found his afternoons devoted to sport and cadet corps activities since evacuees from Corfe Grammar School then took over the buildings.

The evacuees were not solely children and their mothers. In the same way as some businesses relocated from London, such as the Hearts of Oak Benefit Society when it moved to Herstmonceux Castle, Tidebrook welcomed a group of men. They were members of the Embankment Fellowship, wounded veterans of the First World War, who were evacuated to Downgate. Several became enthusiastic members of the Home Guard, and seventeen were to be buried in the churchyard.

The war changed dramatically in 1940. After Hitler's invasion of Norway in April, his blitzkrieg turned to the Low Countries and France in May. Editha Blaikley's diary records "*the nerve-racking, almost continuous murmur* .... *which came over land and sea to us.*" Sad news followed. As the British Expeditionary Force withdrew towards Dunkirk, Lieutenant Patrick Slowe was killed near Wortegem on 23ʳᵈ May. Four days later, Albert Baldock, also of the Royal Sussex Regiment, fell while defending Caestre. He was a former pupil of Tidebrook School, whose parents worked at Wadhurst Hall.

Editha Blaikley records how after Dunkirk *"the rest got safe to England (in such a very English way, in every kind of craft) .... It must be because we were not to be beaten."* The south-east of England was overwhelmed by the evacuation. The station-master and two porters at Headcorn station enlisted the support of local ladies to help to feed the 145,000 troops who suddenly arrived. Then there was the spectre of invasion after France fell in June. The Sussex coast and its hinterland became a 'Defence Area' and a permit was required to visit the region.

The people of Tidebrook were only too aware of the 'Battle of Britain' which followed that summer as the Luftwaffe attacked the airfields and radar stations in preparation for invasion, before it unwisely shifted its attention to London.

Editha Blaikley's diary recorded that

> *Processions of aeroplanes passed nightly overhead to bomb London, or circled around us in a nerve-wracking jug-jug way .... And during the day there were unknown aeroplanes by ones and twos, and later by scores, and dog fights leaving cotton-wool tracks in the summer skies .... We heard that a hundred bombs were dropped in this parish, but mercifully no lives were lost.*

She herself lay on the floor when she heard a *"swishing sound"* and found four craters *"up the road"* the following day. There was a fifth close to Sharnden House, blamed on a soldier who had been negligent over the black-out, for, as a Luftwaffe prisoner had revealed: *"we have orders to drop them on any light we see"*.

The diary also records in August that while a group of ladies were in the canteen at the diminutive village reading room

> *a dreadful booming filled the air .... and we presently saw an immense fleet of planes very high up .... We found sixty of them but there were probably many more. 'They've gone too far to dive-bomb now,' said Frank Hodder, who was clipping his garden hedge next door to the*

*canteen. His wife and boys were outside with him and no doubt he felt
much less indifferent than he sounded. North of us the attackers were
met by what fighters were available. We heard bombs dropped and saw
a parachute descend, and the smoke from a crashed plane. Before long
the enemy returned, helter-skelter, at a much lower altitude, a little to
the south west of where we were standing. Our wardens appeared from
I don't quite know where and reported on events. In September another
massed attack came over when we were doing some choral practice at
a house at Beech Hill. On the way home by car there were soldiers at
their action stations and civilians obediently sheltering under hedges.*

During these days the village was conscious of the presence of the Military
Police, of despatch riders looking for parachutists and of engineers dealing
with unexploded bombs. The autumn presentation of prizes at the school was
postponed because a time bomb had to be exploded. A huge crater was left in
December after another time bomb was dealt with by the Royal Engineers,
who reported that there would have been devastation had it gone off as the
Luftwaffe had intended. Villagers would have had some sympathy with the
1st August 1940 entry in the Hampstead ARP Warden's Bulletin: "*It may be a
privilege to see history in the making, but we have a feeling that it is being
overdone at the present time*".

Further sad news came through on 26th August. The Blenheim aircraft
carrying Sergeant John Fletcher as its rear gunner crashed while returning
from a night patrol. He had been married to Joyce Corrie for just a month.

These were exciting weeks for youngsters. Walter Hodder remembers how

*on Saturdays us lads cycled miles to view crashed aircraft, Dornier 17
at Argos Hill, Spitfire at Lake Street, Me 110 at Little Butts, Me 109 at
Upper Wallands, Hurricane at Hook Farm.*

His brother records how

*enemy bombers came directly over us and some preferred to empty
their bombs on to us rather than risk London, and it did get a bit lively
at times. One Sunday I watched a German bomber come down in
flames. It fell on to the reservoir which served Wadhurst Hall.*

Its pilot, Hans Wagner, was buried in Tidebrook churchyard.

The people's reaction to the War

As in London so in Tidebrook, the people reflected the spirit which led Queen Elizabeth to write to Queen Mary on 10th October:

> *I feel quite exhausted after seeing and hearing so much sadness, sorrow, heroism and magnificent spirit. The destruction is so awful and the people so wonderful - they deserve a better world..*

For people had responded to the emergency. On 14th May, Anthony Eden [*Secretary of State for War and Foreign Secretary*] had broadcast:

> *We want large numbers of men in Great Britain who are British subjects to come forward and offer their services in order to make assurance doubly sure. The name of the force will be the Local Defence Volunteers.*

Within 24 hours, a quarter of a million had come forward. A Tidebrook nucleus developed around such men as Messrs Wildy, Reade, Ives, Whitbread, Haffenden, Guy, Stonard and Newman, supplemented by veterans of the Embankment Fellowship, and under the leadership of their warden, Colonel Donald.

There were 'Dad's Army' parallels initially when the issue of British .303 bullets were not suitable for their Canadian Ross rifles with a .300 bore. They soon became trained and well-equipped and filled a vital rôle in relieving the regular army of routine guard duties and in preparing young men for the call-up. They used the rifle range at Pennybridge Farm, and Sunday morning services were often disturbed by explosions from practices just half a mile away. On Saturday evenings Mrs Hodder senior enjoyed watching the gun flashes from her bedroom window.

At times there were major manoeuvres, as in June 1942, when the group joined with the sections from Mark Cross, Wadhurst and Mayfield to be put through their paces by the Canadians. The womenfolk prepared 780 sandwiches on 14th June to serve from the mobile canteen provided by the Stonards' trailer, which was on Ted Thompson's fields. The Mark Cross commander wrote subsequently to express his thanks.

The Home Guard were particularly alert in September 1940 after the Chiefs of Staff had issued the codeword Cromwell, indicating the likelihood of imminent invasion. The valued rôle overall of the Home Guard was recognised two years later when churches across Sussex held special services on 12th April in appreciation of their work. It was reflected by J B Priestley when he wrote in *Out of the People*:

> *In order to protect and defend their island, not only against possible invasion but against all the disasters of aerial bombardment, it has been found necessary to bring into existence a new network of voluntary associations such as the Home Guard, the Observer Corps, all the ARP and fire-fighting services and the like. They are a new type, what might be called the organised militant citizen. Men and women with a gift for leadership turn up in unexpected places.*

Colin Hodder recalls his father as an air raid warden:

> *and it was part of his job to find unexploded bombs, not an easy task in the fields and woods, but he did find one on the Riseden property and another, much larger, on the land behind the church. This was let off one afternoon by the bomb disposal team who warned us to keep away from windows.*

The Tidebrook fire crew had a practice on 6th November 1942, based on the school being supposedly ablaze, and a subsequent letter declared that "*the village would be safe in the care of such ladies*". Editha Blaikley and her brother Gilbert were in the equivalent crew at Rushers Cross, complete with helmets and Fire Guard handbook, and "*have been promised armlets*". She modestly said that "*of course I should not be the slightest use at the pump if a fire occurred as I am not strong enough to force the spray any height*".

Others had different responsibilities. The vicarage was the centre for distributing emergency food rations should the need arise. Annie Sandeman was among those who received training at the Mayfield First Aid Point so that they could respond in an emergency. More significant incidents would be covered at the Mayfield First Aid Post, where a doctor, two fully trained nurses, a VAD staff and two men would be available and St Leonard's had been prepared to be converted into a hospital with 200 beds if the need arose.

Local doctors were requested to give priority to patients who were on national service.

Throughout Sussex the WVS, clad in green tweed skirts with grey woven into them, red jumpers and schoolgirl hats, was organised in the summer of 1940 to be a service of 'messengers on bicycles' who would maintain communications if roads were blocked and telephone lines were cut. It was they too who were entrusted to co-ordinate the response to Lord Beaverbrook's appeal of 10th July for aluminium: "*We will turn your pots and pans into Spitfires and Hurricanes....*"

Much of Tidebrook's response to the pressures on 'Fortress Britain' was as a farming community. There was an urgent need to increase food production. In the first winter of the War the Government offered farmers a £2 subsidy for each acre of farmland that was brought under the plough, and, further south, the Downs soon carried their first crops since the days of the Saxons. The Women's Land Army with their uniform of green jerseys and brown breeches was recruited since so many farm labourers had joined the armed services. In June 1944 their numbers had reached 80,000. The local fields heard the WLA song:

Back to the land with its clay and its sand,
Its granite and gravel and grit.
You grow barley and wheat
And potatoes to eat
To make sure that the nation keeps fit.

Editha Blaikley observed that the son of the Connells, who farmed most of Sharnden, "*galloped home with a land girl on a large cart-horse .... Lucky land girl, I thought.*"

Each section of the community responded to the War effort in different ways. The school held a 'Salute the Soldier' week in May 1942, with the children giving a drill display. The ladies knitted comforts for the Forces: scarves, mittens, socks and balaclava helmets. It became something of a local competition. They vied with the Wadhurst knitters, who received a letter of thanks in 1942 from the Navy League Seafarers' Comforts Supply saying *"How splendid to get 91 pairs of gloves all at once."* In the same year the Cousley Wood Working Party provided 767 garments. There was a further rallying of support when the Ministry of Supply appealed in April 1943 for books and periodicals for the Red Cross, the Forces and war-damaged libraries.

Similarly the WIs happily became centres for fruit preserving after the Ministry of Food had established the Co-operative Fruit Preservation Scheme in 1941, releasing the necessary amount of sugar to enable it to happen. Later in the year the Vitamin Welfare Scheme was launched to provide all children under two years old with a free issue of blackcurrant juice and cod liver oil. The following September Tidebrook women scoured their rose bushes to take hips to the rosehip collection centre in Mayfield to be converted into vitamin syrup.

Fund-raising was a permanent theme. By February 1945 the Wadhurst War Savings Committee had accumulated £467,489. Bensfield was the centre for the Tidebrook and Best Beech Savings Group helpers, and Fillery, Mrs Leete's chauffeur and handyman, was often out and about delivering collecting tins, whether for 'War Weapons Week' or 'District Nursing Flag Day'. In March 1942 the postmistress rallied support for a campaign which, in Tidebrook, raised £600 for the Warship fund, and people were a little irked that their sum became submerged in the overall total which Wadhurst forwarded to Uckfield District Council. The following month collectors were at work for the Nursing Association and on behalf of St John Ambulance.

The Red Cross Sale at Tidebrook School in March 1942 found six-year old Michael Sands declaring *"I've got a book about Henry V"*, a pocket edition of Shakespeare, and Mrs Hunter proudly pasted into the Log Book the letter of thanks from the Duke of Gloucester for the *"truly handsome donation"* which followed the sale. Another occasion at the school provided £21 7s 8d for Tunbridge Wells Hospital, after a sale of cards, calendars and needlework.

The danger of invasion had diminished in 1941 after Adolf Hitler diverted his attention towards Russia in Operation Barbarossa, and after Pearl Harbour had brought the United States into the war. Nevertheless awareness of military activity was ever present as the following extracts from Editha Blaikley's diary show for 1942.

> *Squadrons of fighters and fighter bombers going towards the Channel (17th April) .... I pulled up my bedroom blind and saw a very pink moon .... and on either side of her two or three distant searchlights (3rd May). Mrs Hodder senior was disturbed by the low flying aeroplanes which went over during the service (21st June) .... Much military traffic passed this house during the night .... all sorts of mechanised vehicles, some caterpillar-wheeled, guns and infantry. (29th July) .... My walk was rather spoilt by a large convoy .... vans and despatch riders making the road very noisy and awkward (7th August).*

Daily, Canadian sentries were posted outside Tidebrook Place and Sharnden. From time to time too there were major military manoeuvres involving trench mortars and tanks. In late May Miss Weston at the post office felt as if her house was being lifted up when the Tidebrook bridge was destroyed during one of the exercises, and repairs to Cinderhill Lane, where a derelict tank remained for days, cost over £200. In August many of the Canadians were involved in the raid on Dieppe, and people listened to the reverberations of the attack. Walter Hodder recalls that "*many didn't return, including one who was courting a land girl who lodged with us*". She was Maeve Horsfall who was a milkmaid at Towngate.

Tidebrook had developed a good relationship with its Canadians. Although Miss Mathewick felt that they had an "*embarrassing way of becoming sentimental after a spell of friendship*", most developed good relationships, referring to 'our' Canadians and exchanging hospitality for peppermints, cigarettes and magazines. When the Hodders found hens and eggs missing after the June 1942 manoeuvres, they were relieved when it was discovered that troops on special training had been responsible and not Tidebrook's Canadians. Colin considers that "*It wouldn't have been so bad except that we had borrowed a fine cockerel from Mr Everdale to ensure that the eggs were fertile. I just hope it was a tough old bird.*"

It was, of course, a time of much personal anxiety. The tragedy of war was evident on 19th September 1942 as people heard a plane crash at Coggins Mill as it returned from action. The pilot was later identified as a Pole. The previous month, wives waited anxiously for news of their husbands after the fall of Singapore. In July Mrs Wickenden, who lived in the cottage next to the Fountain Inn, had heard that a newspaper had listed her son as having been taken prisoner in the Middle East. Mrs Jones waited anxiously for six months until December before a letter came through saying that her son was well and in Egypt. For others the news was tragic. Harry Day, who had become a trainee pilot after serving with the Metropolitan Police, died in a flying accident in South Africa. George Forsyth had perished in February 1941 when the Whitley 5 aircraft of which he was second pilot crashed on returning from a night bombing raid on Cologne. He was buried in Tidebrook churchyard. The Hodder boys lost their cousin in 1943 while he was serving as a wireless operator on a Halifax bomber near Arnhem.

'Hayden' Lane had been a gardener at Sharnden before joining the army in May 1940. He had first taken up a defensive position behind the Military Canal, before serving in Iraq and North Africa, where he saw the fall of Tunis. After time in Malta and Sicily he fought northwards from the Salerno bridgehead towards Monte Cassino. He heard that he was named to receive the North Africa Star with 8th Army clasp before he died defending a train at Anzio. A few months after D-Day the vicarage itself was in mourning. Denys Coote, whose parents were its housekeepers and who was a Sergeant Bomb Aimer, died on a mission while based in North Italy.

Life was dangerous and the people of Tidebrook willingly took precautions. All signposts had been removed in June 1940. People were careful to carry their gas masks, and there was a little flurry after morning service at the end of June 1942 when one belonging to a lady on Beech Hill was left behind on the pew. People were meticulous over black-out. In the winter Mr Maw delayed the 8 am. service for half an hour to accommodate 'unblack' time. It was frustrating. *"Oh for the time"*, wrote Editha Blaikley, *"when we can light up when and where we like, and let cosy lamps shine through the darkness to cheer passers-by."* It was, however, a necessity which everyone respected, especially after a light at Sharnden had led to five bombs falling at Rushers Cross in 1940. Such good caution extended to the school, where a police officer called to talk to the children about incendiary bombs and explosive materials in September 1941.

The village rallied to the emergency in various ways. Petrol was in short supply, so the vicar walked to his pastoral commitments whenever possible. Coal was in short supply, so the children were sent searching for twigs and branches and the men felled trees until Government decreed a limit in August 1942. The women sprinkled paraffin on to coal dust to bind it together and to help it to burn. They also made 'hay boxes' to keep water warm, insulating kettles or saucepans with hay, on the modern hot water tank principle. They were sufficient to cook boiled bacon. Food was in short supply, so the boys were sent hunting for rabbits.

Tidebrook School gardeners
l to r: Bert Eaton - George Spicer - Bob Knight - Miss Alice Wadeson -
Charlie Wickenden - Bill Spicer - ??
on ground: ?? - Jim Fairweather   [Bocking Collection]

Vegetable patches were extended. The encouragement to 'Dig for Victory' led Mr Manwaring of Pennyfields to listen to the guidelines broadcast on the wireless and to prepare his bean trenches accordingly. He was adept at making clothes pegs for the Red Cross jumble sales. He and his sister had a cow, much to the delight of visitors who could have cream in their coffee and bread with butter. Similarly the Stonards of Mousehall Hill kept goats and the Smiths and Roy Lavender were often seen with jugs carrying 'milk from Nanny'. Several households kept small numbers of poultry, and the postmistress was worried by reports in June 1942 that would limit permission to one bird a person because of feed shortages.

Everyone felt the squeeze. Rationing had been introduced in June 1940, and a weekly limit of 4 ounces of bacon or ham, 4 ounces of butter and 12 ounces of sugar per person was restricting. Even the House of Commons' dinner menus were affected. One in 1943 proclaimed 'Canapé cheval', while the celebratory feast after VE Day in 1945 centred on 'Chicken Ancienne'. Late summer brought some excitement to Tidebrook in anticipation of the apple harvest and cider-making, of plums and jam-making, and with the prospect of bottling blackberries. The WI became busy at the Fruit Preservation Centre at Bensfield after putting fruit by for the needs of their own families over the winter.

From time to time there were other additions. In November 1942 the Government launched the Rural Pie Scheme, enabling every person to have two fourpenny meat pies every week without affecting the ration card. Initial enthusiasm was soon blunted since the local pies were baked by the Wadhurst postmaster, who declared himself too busy as Christmas neared.

People thought wistfully of better times. *"When the war is over,"* Editha Blaikley mused in June 1942,

> *I should like to lie on top of the South Downs again, in some spot where no-one knows me, and see all the little villages and the distant Weald lying below while larks sing above. .... When I was on the Downs last it was July 1939 and the searchlights were already practising and I had a gas mask secreted in my trunk. The weather was in keeping with the international outlook, thunderous and menacing.*

Yet people continued to enjoy as much normality as possible. Mrs Fuller of Sharnden Farm kept puffing away on her briar pipe as she helped with little odd jobs around the farm. Families gathered around the horse and hay cart with their wooden rakes at harvest time as they always had. As usual at harvest time Mrs Haffenden would take a basket of mixed flowers to the Harvest Festival, and meet Miss Manwaring with her box of gourds and pears. Mrs Stonard still enjoyed the crossword, and people gathered at the little library at the school to exchange books.

They had fun where they could. At a little presentation by the drama section of the WI in February, Mrs Gallup, the blacksmith's wife, acted as Churchill, complete with cigar and felt hat, reviewing ARP personnel in their gas masks. The vicarage garden party in August saw little Rosie Brown and Edna Knight performing a folk dance, Michael Sands providing a monologue on rainbows, and a 'Brer Rabbit' play. The fête at Bensfield the following month included a baby show, where Mr Wildy caused much amusement as, dressed as a nurse, he pushed an enormous pram containing his son, a young medical student. The October meeting of the WI had a percussion band demonstration, and Freda James of Towngate House played the triangle with aplomb.

There was special joy in November when the church's bell responded to Churchill's request to lift the bell ban across Britain to celebrate success in the North Africa campaign. The school continued to enjoy such traditions as a day's holiday for Mrs Leete's party at Bensfield in 1941, and a performance of *A Pageant of Flowers* at the vicarage garden party. Christmas celebrations included carols, two plays (appropriately *Safety First* and *One Christmas Eve*), and a gift from the tree that Mrs Kemp kindly had provided.

The wireless entertained people with *Music while you Work*, Tommy Handley's *ITMA*, and *The Brains Trust*. Each week some 30 million cinema seats were sold in Britain, and there were jaunts from Tidebrook to the Ritz to see Laurence Olivier as Henry V or his wife, Vivien Leigh, in *Gone with the Wind*. The more ambitious attended Dame Myra Hess's concerts in London in the National Gallery, adjourning to its basement during air raids. More locally there were musical evenings, lantern-slide shows or whist drives in the Reading Room run by Billy Bourne. As well as being the NAAFI staffed by WVS volunteers and the centre for the WI, the village hall held dances most Saturdays and was where the youth group and drama group met.

Tidebrook's sports enthusiasts found things a little dislocated. Arsenal's Highbury had become a Civil Defence fortress. Twickenham was converted into allotments. The Oval was a prisoner of war camp. The playing area at Wimbledon was used for Home Guard drills. The RAF had taken over its practice ground and the pavilion but Lords still welcomed a quarter of a million spectators in 1943, although Sir Pelham Warner wrote to Bill Edrich that "*it was a bit close the other night .... a few incendiary bombs on the ground and an oil bomb at deepish mid-on*". The Brighton and Hove Albion side had to recruit additional footballers on the spot when they arrived with only five players to play Norwich City. They lost 18 - 0. More immediately, youngsters like Stan Goodhew, son of the verger and school caretaker, would walk over the fields to see Best Beech United play on their pitch behind Pennybridge Farm.

As the war progressed things were stabilising in Tidebrook, although at times the Revd. G T Maw found that the paucity of men available encouraged him reluctantly to add women to the collection team for the early service. Such were the origins of the gradual recognition by the established church of an increasing rôle for women.

Tidebrook School [Bocking Collection]

The closing months of the War

During the summer of 1944 the requisitioned houses found themselves emptying of the British troops who had moved there in preparation for the landings in Normandy on D-Day, and who were engaged in battling across France after 6th June. In their place Wadhurst Hall became a prisoner of war camp and Tidebrook farmers and builders welcomed a new source of labour. Hitler's response to the Normandy landings, the V1 rockets, provided a new menace for Tidebrook which lay firmly in 'Doodlebug Alley'. Whereas at the end of June the School Log Book suggests that the chief concern had been that

"Derek Hemsley was bitten by a dog", within a fortnight the County was making arrangements to deliver two Morrison shelters for the infants and the School Managers had drawn up emergency plans. Attendance plummeted, partly due to whooping cough, but *"in part due to the refusal of parents to send children while rocket planes are being sent over"*.

Families dreaded the noise of the rockets' roar and deafening rattle and the sight of their flaming tails, and of the RAF in hot pursuit, sometimes tipping their wings to make them crash. One fell at Sharnden on 20th July. At the end of the month the school closed for half a day to enable the headmistress to evacuate her daughter, and altogether five East Sussex children were evacuated. Such prudence was timely. In the matter of fact way with which the troubled crew of Apollo 13 later calmly reported: *"Houston, we have a problem"*, so too the Log for 3rd August simply records that

> *A flying bomb fell 30 yards from the school at 11 am. 32 were present; 7 infants sheltered with Mrs Guest in the playground trench. 22 children in the school sheltered in the 2 Morrison tables, 3 big children sheltered in the corner of the room. There were no casualties.*

The incident has been covered more fully in Chapter 3. The church was packed at the following Sunday's thanksgiving service, with many standing at the back and at the door, only too aware of how tragic it could have been.

The children's education continued, first as they crammed into Mrs Hunter's own home at Rushers Cross, then in October at Mark Cross. That school was clearly not large enough and the January term saw 34 seniors and 22 infants, and Mrs Hunter herself, welcomed by Mr Mould at Wadhurst School, inevitably creating congestion there.

By September the Germans had introduced V2 rockets and the more dangerous zones had shifted eastwards of London. Tidebrook could share in the sense of buoyancy as the Allies moved ever more closely towards Berlin. After Germany's surrender on 7th May, VE Day brought crowds to London, thronging the Mall, Piccadilly and Trafalgar Square, and at night the statues and public buildings were floodlit and searchlights danced a ballet in the sky. As the royal family appeared on the balcony of Buckingham Palace, a young Guards officer, Humphrey Lyttelton, had trumpet in hand and *"I dimly remember blasting a chorus of 'For he's a jolly good fellow' in the direction of His Majesty".* There were similar celebrations among those who remained in Tidebrook. A huge bonfire was lit at the tennis court near the church and someone produced fireworks. There was dancing in the road, and by 9 pm. the Best Beech Hotel was dry and had to close.

The aftermath

Gradually people adjusted to peace. The servicemen returned in their 'demob suits', as each received £12 worth of civilian clothing. The local Home Guard sections kept their camaraderie by re-forming into rifle clubs in the Argos Hill League. Tidebrook's team had a small-bore range at the Fountain Inn, with George Ives as warden, Ted Whitbread as president and Horace Sands as treasurer and secretary.

Much of the old system of large houses never quite returned. When Jane Lansdown was at Tidebrook Place in 1946 it was as a pupil of Fitzharries School. The Canadians were long gone. The most military item was a sword on the study wall of the headmistress, which Miss Burke proclaimed to have belonged to her ancestor, Captain Hardy, who had survived an earlier battle, at Trafalgar in 1805. Yet, with the exception of the school, much of Tidebrook remained unchanged, whereas in Wadhurst there was an immediate response to the acute housing shortage. Italian prisoners of war built the first houses in Bankside and soon a crash programme extended to Queens Cottages. Prefabs sprang up where Bayham Court now stands. Gill Wood End and Uplands were requisitioned and converted into flats.

Austerity continued as the new Attlee Government prepared to extend the welfare state. The bacon ration was reduced from four to three ounces, and bread also soon became rationed. The building programme put pressure on the availability of materials, with timber and cement becoming rationed. Yet life really was returning to normal. Before the end of May 1945 the ARP had called for those whose children had been issued with babies' gas masks to return them to collection centres like Buckhurst Lodge. It would be two years before petrol ceased to be rationed, and then it rose immediately in price from ten pence to a shilling a gallon. Yet in summer 1945 Tidebrook could bathe again in the natural normality of the harvest.

SOURCES

No Soldier: Diary of Editha Blaikley [1942]
The People's War: Calder, Angus [1969], Jonathan Cape
Log Book of Tidebrook Church of England School
Kelly's Directory for Tunbridge Wells, 1937 and 1939
Biographies of Tidebrook servicemen who died during the war: Ken Jones
Letter of Walter Hodder to the editors, September 2007
Letter of Colin Hodder to the editors, 2007

WLA girls taking a break   [PA]

CHAPTER 6: FARMING IN THE WAR YEARS
JOHN MILLETT AND MARTIN TURNER

"We rely on the farmers. We depend on the efforts they put forth in the fields of Britain .... Today .... the farms of Britain are the front line of freedom."

Winston Churchill in a speech to the National Farmers' Union
14th October 1940

Introduction

This account of farming in Wadhurst during the War years draws heavily on a very comprehensive farm survey completed by the Ministry of Agriculture and Fisheries (MAF) in 1941 and the publication 'The Working Countryside 1862-1945' by Hill and Stamper. It also incorporates several personal reminiscences related to the farming scene. A detailed interview with Mr Norman Gingell, whose father came to Earlye Farm at the north west of the parish in 1942, is added as an annex. This gives an insight into wartime life on an individual Wadhurst farm.

The lead up to the War

The lessons learnt so hard in the 1914-18 War stood the country in good stead when War threatened once more in the late 1930s. From 1937 stocks of tractors were built up and extra lime and basic slag were applied to the land. In September 1939 War Agriculture committees were set up. This was a revival of the practice of the First World War. These committees were powerful controlling bodies, which oversaw compliance with central Government policy.

The following two short excerpts from 'The Story of Towngate Farm, Tidebrook 1935-48' by Edward Thompson provide a local farm perspective of the years before the outbreak of War.

In 1935 farming was then at the lowest it had reached for years and apparently there was no prospect of recovery. An ungrateful country had forgotten the 1914-1918 war and the farmers' part in it. Shops even in the country were heavily stocked with imported eggs, bacon, chilled and frozen beef, lamb, pork, butter, cheese and fruit, much of it the surplus of other countries sold below cost. Potatoes except earlies and milk were the only items produced totally at home.

Ploughing was then done by a single furrow plough and a pair of horses. The ploughman (Geo. Wilson) rose at 5 am. He cleaned out the stalls, fed and watered the horses and went home for breakfast at 6 am. After breakfast he harnessed his horses and commenced ploughing at 7 am. He stopped at 9.30 for lunch break, then continued ploughing until 11.45, when he returned his horses to the stable, wiped them down and fed them, then went home to his dinner. Ploughing commenced again at 1.15 pm. and continued until 3.45. The horses were then returned to the stable, groomed, fed and bedded down. At 5 pm. the ploughman went home to his tea, having ploughed half an acre of this heavy land. At 7 pm. he turned out again, shook up the horses' bedding and saw them settled down for the night. For this he was paid 25 shillings [£1.25] per week, and a year or two later 29 shillings - less 3 shillings for his cottage.

In the interwar years, the pressures of life on the land remained essentially unchanged from those experienced at the end of the 19th century. The following excerpt, taken from 'Indoor Farm Service in the 19th Century' by M Reed, records the testimony of a maid-servant working at Earlye Farm in Wadhurst.

I'd be churning twice a week and cheesing twice a week and brewing twice a week, besides washing and baking: and six cows to milk every night and morning and sometimes a dozen pigs to feed. There were four men lived in the house and I'd all the billing to do - the cabbage and the peas and pork for their dinners besides all the beds to make .... one morning, I mind, I got up at four and worked till twelve at night then Missus wanted me to pluck a couple of ducks. 'No, Missus', I says, ' I really can't, I be quite tired'. 'Tired?' says she, 'if I was a young women like you I should be ashamed of myself'.

Harvesting - Ladymeads Farm - early 1930s
[Cosham Collection]

Wadhurst farms during the War

A clear picture of farming in the parish of Wadhurst emerges from the comprehensive survey conducted by MAF in June 1941. The records are held at the National Archives, Kew under reference MAF 32 followed by the parish number. The survey covered a total of 78 holdings in the parish. The details for each farm are given and include acreage, crops and grasses, livestock, labour, horses, machinery and buildings. There are also general comments made on the efficiency of the farm and problems of pests such as rabbits.

By far the majority (almost all) of the 78 farms were tenanted and most were of quite small acreages. The largest farm at that time, apart from Earls Place Farm at Mark Cross which was 355 acres, was Wickhurst Farm, near Bartley Mill, at 274 acres. A total of only 27 farms were 100 acres or more and 29 were of 50 acres or less. The amount of labour employed, in addition to the farmers themselves and their wives, was recorded as 121 men, 32 women and 25 youths. The Agricultural Wages Act, the legislation on which the Agricultural Minimum Wage is based, did not come into effect until 1948. Prior to that date, agricultural workers had to negotiate their pay independently with their employers. Many farms showed considerable diversity, both in the types of crops grown, and the types of livestock held. There was, of course, a connection between the two, with crops being grown for the farm's own livestock feed.

133

Livestock

Horses. While 14 farms were listed as having one or more riding horses, 49 farms were shown to have working horses, with numbers ranging from 1 to 5. Strangely, the number of horses did not correlate with the size of the farm, but this was probably because the larger farms were more likely to have a tractor as well. Tractors were obtainable, but a permit was needed to purchase and also for a ration of fuel. However, on the local Wealden clay, horses still had an important part to play. The working horses were usually of the Shire or Clydesdale type, and were valuable members of the farm team. They were used for carting, ploughing, tilling, mowing, sweeping, harvesting, and also for working equipment like hoists or elevators. Farms without horse power would sometimes borrow or hire one from a neighbour, but the carter would jealously guard his charges and would go with them. The large majority of farms that had horses grew an acreage of oats for feed.

The horses would, of course, need to be shod regularly. During the War there was Bassett's Forge in Durgates, the Forge at Best Beech and a forge at Cousley Wood, opposite the Old Vine. In those days a set of shoes cost six shillings and sixpence [32½ p] - today they cost over forty pounds! A ride or walk was necessary to get to one of the farriers. Sometimes this would mean going considerable distances. When the forge in Frant closed down, the horses from Frant would be taken to the Best Beech Forge, which meant a journey across Shernfold, across the main road at Knowle Lodge, down an old track to Lightlands, through the bottom of Earlye, across Buckhurst, finally arriving at Best Beech. This might have been reasonably enjoyable but only in fine weather!

Although the working horse was eventually replaced by the tractor, there was still a good number of horses around until the late 1950s.

Cows. 57 of the 78 holdings (73%) surveyed by MAF kept milking cows. 40% of these herds comprised less than 10 cows, and only 19% had more than 30 cows. The largest herd in the survey had 57 cows. Thus during the War years the majority of farms in the parish of Wadhurst possessed at least some milking cows.

By today's standards these herds were very small, but it must be remembered that most were hand milked. Although some progressive farmers had a milking machine, they did not come into general use until the late 1940s. Whereas today most milking cows in the country are Friesians or Holsteins, in the War years and until the 1960s there was a variety of breeds. Although the survey did not record the breed, they would have been Dairy Shorthorns, Red Polls, Ayrshires, and the Channel Island breeds - Jerseys and Guernseys, with the occasional small and pretty Dexter cow. The Friesian would have been in the minority, although one of the biggest herds in the survey consisted of pedigree Friesians. Another of the biggest herds was identified as being Guernseys.

When was the last time you saw a milking cow with horns? Nowadays cows have their horn buds painlessly removed as young calves, so that when they are herded together for milking in their large numbers, they do not injure themselves, or their handlers. This practice came in the late 1950s, and so in the War years the cow proudly displayed a fine pair of horns, particularly fine in the case of the Ayrshire cow.

An Ayrshire cow

Thirty of the holdings kept one or more bulls. The farms without a herd bull would have to take their cows to a neighbour who kept one. All bulls had to be inspected and licensed on behalf of the Ministry of Agriculture. Keeping a bull was not without risks and it is an animal to be treated with caution. Indeed a farmer in the parish, one with the largest herd, was killed by his herd bull.

Most of the milk produced would be sent off to the dairy in milk churns, collected by the milk lorry, but four farms in the district ran retail rounds. These were the Coleman brothers at Greenman Farm, under the railway bridge; at the other end of Wadhurst were the Boormans at Stone Cross Farm, then there was Pomfret at Hunters Hall, Cousley Wood and Pitts at Slade Farm on the way into Lamberhurst. The Boormans had two vans for their milk rounds in the village and outlying district. Over the War period, some of the owners of the retail rounds came into conflict with the authorities for over supplying a rationed commodity!

53 of the holdings also reared cows for beef. The milking herds would rear their bull calves, and many would also have some animals of the beef breeds like the beef Shorthorn, Sussex, Hereford, or Aberdeen Angus. Eight holdings in the survey reared beef alone, but five of these had under ten head. One interesting hazard of keeping cattle in the War years is described by Edward Thompson in his memoirs of Towngate Farm:

> *The explosions blasted the Doodlebugs into fragments and we had no end of trouble with pieces of steel in the binder at harvest, some pieces got into the sheaves and we had to be very careful when threshing. The power plant of the infernal machine was bound round with very fine high tensile steel wire, and this scattered in short lengths in all directions. We had some yearling heifers in the valley at the time of the explosions, and one died for no apparent cause, and then another, then we lost several more. The last one was cut open and a piece of wire was found in its heart. That was the only one I received compensation for. The animals had swallowed the wire while grazing, and this worked through the stomach into the heart. The rest of the stock on the farm were gone over by the vet with a mine detector, one cow gave a positive reaction and was opened up and a piece of wire removed from its stomach.*

David Hawken, whose father bought Beales Barn Farm in Bewl Bridge Lane, Cousley Wood in 1936/37, has memories of an early childhood spent on a dairy farm in Wadhurst during the war years. He recalls that on the farm there was a herd of pedigree milking Friesians and Sussex Blacks, with a great bull called Hilty. The milking was performed by Land Girls as somehow his father had got the farm an accreditation as a training farm for Land Girls. There was no mains electricity or mains water supply on the farm during the War (nor indeed was there any when David left in 1954). The lighting was 110v, powered by two Lister diesels feeding a huge line of batteries situated in separate rooms alongside the stables. The water came from a large concrete reservoir in the wood behind the old farmhouse. The water was never boiled but no one seemed to suffer any ill effects.

Women's Land Army at work

After the War the number of herds declined but they became much larger with milking machines and milking parlours, and the milk churn was replaced increasingly by bulk tanks and tanker lorries. Dairy farming in Wadhurst parish peaked in the 1960s and early 1970s but then, mainly due to the influence of the then EEC farming policy, local farmers gradually left milk production, until today there are only two milking herds left in the parish.

Pigs. 30 holdings kept pigs but all these farms also had other forms of livestock. 66% had under 10 pigs and 16 premises had only 1 to 3 pigs. There were 2 larger pig enterprises, one with 70 and the other with 106 pigs. These were serious commercial concerns and both also had milking cows.

Where there were only a few pigs, they were probably just to provide meat for the farmer's family, although this was controlled, and quarterly returns to the Agriculture committee had to show that the farmer was not over-indulging! In his memoirs of Towngate Farm, Mr Thompson wrote:

> *We kept a few pigs, and were allowed to kill two a year during the war for our own use, provided we sold half of each to the Ministry of Food. So at Christmas time we were able to provide the men with a good joint of pork for their dinner.*

Small numbers of pigs would be fed mainly on swill. This comprised boiled kitchen scraps plus home-grown cereals, where available. Many of the pigs kept would have been of breeds that are now rarities, such as the Saddleback pig (a black pig with a white stripe), the Tamworth (with gingery coat), the Gloucester Old Spot (white with black spots) and the Large and Middle Whites. Nowadays commercial pigs are mainly of the Swedish Landrace and Large White varieties, and of course it is now against the law, for disease prevention reasons, to feed pigs on swill.

Sheep. 18 holdings kept sheep, but only in one case were they the sole livestock enterprise; in every other case, cattle were kept as well. 50% of the flocks consisted of over 40 sheep. The largest flock was of 174 sheep at Wickhurst Farm, which also had the 70 pigs and a milking herd.

Poultry. There seemed to be a lot of poultry about in wartime Britain, which is hardly surprising as they were a ready source of meat and eggs. Rabbits were also a valuable source of meat. No doubt many households also had a few hens fed on various scraps. According to the MAF survey, 53 holdings in Wadhurst parish possessed poultry i.e. 67% of the total. All these holdings had chickens, ten also reared ducks, and 12 had geese. Eight holdings had over 100 chickens with the largest having 700 birds. Of the 10 holdings with ducks, five had over 15 birds; the largest number held was 40. Of the 12 holdings with geese, five had over 12 birds; the highest number held was 31.

Crops

Orchards. There were 16 farms with orchards of more than half an acre, 4 of these were more than five acres and the largest was 15 acres (Wickhurst Farm). The MAF records also show that 5 acres of soft fruit were grown at Great Shoesmiths.

Wheat, Oats, Maize and Barley. Oats were grown on 20 farms. The largest acreage, 26½ acres, was again at Wickhurst Farm. 12 farms grew maize, the largest acreage being at Hunters Hall in Lower Cousley Wood. Here the owner, Mr Pomfret, also had a milk round with a sizeable dairy herd - not to mention 100 sheep, 11 pigs and 4 working horses. He seems to have had the largest number of employees working on his 171 acre farm: eight men, one youth and three girls. Barley appears to have been grown only at Wickhurst Farm where an area of 14 acres is recorded.

Root crops. 24 farms had an acre or more of roots and 7 grew kale.

Hops. Hops were grown on 8 farms in the parish [*by mid 2008 this number had fallen to 2*]. Mr Fawkes at Great Butts, Cousley Wood, had 65 acres under hops and this was by far and away the largest hop enterprise. The only other farms with acreages in excess of 10 were Whitegates with 12 acres, and Mr Taylor at Cousley Wood Farm with 14 acres. Hopping during the War is discussed more fully in the next chapter.

Peas and Beans. There were 19 farms that grew more than an acre, with 4 having 10 acres or more. Mr Boorman at Stone Cross had 15 acres of peas.

Potatoes. During the War potato cultivation especially came to the fore. 31 Wadhurst farms grew potatoes, the majority with ¾ of an acre or less. However Wickhurst grew 12 acres of potatoes and 4 other farms had acreages of more than 2 acres.

Whereas the MAF survey gives an objective overview of the intensity of crop production during the war, the following extract from the 1942 diary of Editha Blaikley of Tidebrook provides a more subjective impression of the efforts made to maximise local crop production:

> *August 12th. A lovely day but not really hot. The ploughed fields are multiplying fast in this neighbourhood. From our bedroom windows we can see three or four that were simply grazing for cattle or sheep in previous years and indeed this year up to the present. Others are bearing wheat or oats for harvest.*

Similarly the experience of Norman Gingell, in the annex to this chapter, illustrates how in 1942 a lot of the land previously used for grazing was ploughed up for crop production.

Harvesting and farm machinery

It was not until the late 50s that combine harvesters came on the farming scene. During the War years the contractor would arrive with the threshing machine and its team of workers. Most of these machines would be driven by a steam traction engine, but later a Fordson tractor would do the job. In Wadhurst, Wm. Baldwin & Son had two threshing machines and teams of Land Girls manning them. Their premises were in Durgates where the Shell garage now stands. Their offices were in the building that was the dental laboratory. In the area where the petrol pumps now stand, there was a patch of grass with the machinery yard behind.

In his memoirs of Towngate Farm, Edward Thompson tells us more about harvesting in the War years:

> *With so much more corn grown, the local threshing contractor became very independent and would oblige when he thought he would. Therefore I joined with 19 other farmers under the chairmanship of Mr John Reid of Maplesden, and we all subscribed and bought a mill, a David Brown forestry tractor and a baler and did our own threshing, with a permanent man to look after the outfit, and I looked after the engineering side. This worked very well, and after the members' needs were satisfied, we were able to take on outside work as well.*

Sulphur spraying for pest and disease control
[Cosham Collection]

The 1941 MAF survey does not list those holdings with tractors, but it is known that there was a tractor at Earlye Farm and one at Stone Cross Farm. A new Fordson tractor cost £134 in 1942, a lot of money then, and probably beyond the means of many farmers. Nevertheless, Hill and Stamper comment:

> *By the onset of war in 1939 it is estimated that there were about 55,000 tractors in use in Great Britain. Over the next six years the need to increase home production of food led to an unprecedented rise in numbers. By 1945 about 175,000 machines were at work in the countryside, and ninety per cent of British built ones were Fordsons - still recognisable derivatives of the 1917 Fordson 'F' of the First World War.*

An important function of the War Agriculture committees was to run machinery depots where tractors and machinery could be hired at low rents. There was a local depot at Dewhurst where machinery could be collected or delivered. The depots were closed and auctioned off in October 1948.

Identification of problems

One of the purposes of the MAF survey was to identify how and where production could be improved in wartime Britain. It is clear from the comments on some local farms shown below that those conducting the survey did not hold any punches when it came to criticising the state of farms:

"Insufficiently stocked".

"More and better use should be made".

"Grassland rather poor and neglected".

"Inability to overcome difficulties, mainly labour".

"Old fashioned ideas, two hayracks unthatched".

"This farmer should be able to produce milk but unable to get landlord to make alterations or have accommodation for labour".

"Ill-health in middle age; landlord will not make cottage available for labour".

"Farmer in Navy, no one with farming knowledge, labour shortage".

"Land not being made the best use of, poor condition and neglected; hobby farmer".

However, it is clear that Wadhurst farmers rallied to the national emergency. With over 60% of Britain's food stuffs coming from abroad in the pre-war period, the country's agriculture faced a formidable task on the outbreak of War. However, despite the many problems, the need for rationing and the damage done by U-boats to merchant shipping, the country did not face the calamity it had in the dark days at the end of 1916.

SOURCES

No Soldier: The 1942 Diary of Miss Editha Blaikley
The Working Countryside 1862-1945: Hall, R. and Stamper P.
Ministry of Agriculture and Fisheries (1941) Farm Survey.
    The National Archives, Kew Ref MAF32 O32 Parish 41 E. Sussex
Indoor Farm Service in the 19th Century: Reid, M.
Memoirs of Towngate Farm, Tidebrook, 1935-1948: Thompson, E A.
    unpublished (in Bocking Collection).

Interviews with / research material from David Hawken and Norman Gingell.

ANNEX: A CONVERSATION WITH MR NORMAN GINGELL
OF EARLYE FARM

This interview was conducted on Saturday 19ᵗʰ January 2008.

What follows is a verbatim transcript of Norman Gingell's reminiscences on a number of topics. Earlye Farm is in the north west corner of Wadhurst parish. This ancient farm, known in olden times as Arligh, goes back to the 14ᵗʰ Century. In the 16ᵗʰ Century it was owned by the Fowle family.

The Start

When my father came to the farm in 1942, we moved over from Surrey where we had been farming. We brought all the equipment we wanted in five railway wagons for a cost of £6 10s. In addition to that, we brought our two big Shire horses with us in a separate wagon. They left the station in Surrey at 9.00 am. and were off loaded at Wadhurst at 4 pm. This all happened in June 1942. Earlye Farm at that time was 206 acres [*Authors' note: this, according to the 1941 MAF survey, made it the fourth largest farm in the area.*] Many farms were 50 acres or less with possibly two or three families living off that.

Norman Gingell on a Fordson tractor   [Norman Gingell]

143

Farm ownership

We were tenant farmers at that time as were nearly all farms in this area; it was not until after the Agricultural Act in 1947 that farms started to be sold off. Part of the reason for this was that the Labour Government introduced security of tenure for farmers. Landlords then found that it was more difficult to get farmers out as and when they liked, and they became happier to sell. Our landlord was Barry Williams from Cranbrook; he had three sons who in time wanted money to buy houses and so we were very, very lucky to buy the farm in 1967.

Rent

The rent when we started here was £1 10s an acre, I think.

Mechanical aids

At the farm in Surrey we had an elevator for lifting the hay but we did not bring that with us - in fact it was left as a road block against enemy invasion in Surrey. We had a horse fork as an aid to stacking hay. This consisted of a 30-foot pole which was secured with guys so that it angled slightly towards the haystack. Two thirds of the way up this pole a jib was rigged sticking out from the pole, over to where the stack was being built. A big rope was then led from the fork (hay grab) up to the jib back to the pole, down and to the bottom from where it was led out through a pulley and attached to a horse. The horse then pulled away so raising the fork and hay up to the desired height. We brought the pole over with us from Surrey.

We also had a horse sweep; this had a horse on either side of a big sweep which just pushed hay across the field in great lumps. It was effective but very strenuous for the horses, so we came to use the tractor to push the sweep. This very effectively moved the hay into great heaps across the field. It was possible to clear 12 acres in an evening. Sometimes we helped neighbouring farms with the sweep. We had the two original horses until 1955/56 and then bought one or two more after that.

We brought two big wagons and a cart with us from Surrey together with a harrow, disc harrow, roller, binder, mower and the ploughs. It wasn't until

1957 that we got a baler and then a combine in 1958. When my father arrived at Earlye he got a permit for a new Fordson tractor. You had to get a permit before you were allowed to have one. The Fordson came within a month of us arriving and cost £134. The fuel for the tractor was low flash point paraffin with a petrol start. There was no trouble getting the fuel, and lorries brought the fuel up to the farm. All cereals were threshed into hired sacks holding 4 bushels. These weighed 1½ cwt for oats, 2 cwt for barley and 2¼ cwt in the case of wheat. There were few lifting aids; as a result everyone over 50 wore a rupture truss.

Fertiliser

We could get sulphate of ammonia, super sulphate and lime; these were delivered by the merchant. We could also buy 'basic slag' which came by rail and was collected from the station.

What was grown

- *Roots.* We had five acres of roots which consisted of two different sorts: kale and mangolds grown to feed the cattle. All this land was initially ploughed mostly using the tractor with a two-furrow plough; a one-furrow plough was used with the horses. The horses were used for hoeing between the lines. If he kept at it, a man could turn an acre a day with a single furrow plough and would walk ten miles in the process. But, after, that the crop had to be hand-worked.

- *Maize.* The maize that was grown in these parts was purely for silage. Maize for other purposes did not ripen to a sufficient grade for harvesting.

- *Orchards.* There weren't any large orchards on the farm; we only grew a few apples, pears, greengages and cherries for the family. There were a lot of orchards at neighbouring Lightlands.

- *Hops.* No hops had been grown on the farm since 1921 when at that time they were dried at Riverhall.

- *Potatoes.* In 1942 only a quarter of an acre was grown here which would have been more than just for the family. In 1946 we took over an additional field from Riverhall and grew a lot of potatoes.

That was the wettest summer and worst winter we have ever had. However that winter we did have 6 acres of potatoes on a good dry field and this turned out to be very useful; since it was a very wet year and few spuds were lifted in the county, we got a good price.

- *Peas.* I am surprised that the record shows 11 acres of peas were grown, because my father certainly did not grow peas when we first came. But we did start growing peas and oats mixed in 1945.

- *Wheat, oats and barley.* We had 2 fields of wheat and 1 of spring oats, all grown for food for human consumption and for the 2 working horses as well. Our ground was not good for barley because barley needs lime. It is the easiest feeding cereal to combine, so barley did not get popular until ten years after the War, when combine harvesters came in. The best barley went for malting but virtually all ours went for food. Mostly we grew wheat for sale because that was what people wanted. We probably had 150 acres of wheat, with some oats.

Livestock.

- *Poultry.* The 1941 MAF survey shows that there had been 8 chickens and 5 ducks. I just remember a few poultry providing eggs for the house. I remember that foxes were a lot of trouble and took the poultry.

- *Cattle.* The survey shows 23 milking cows, 1 bull and a total of 45 cattle. I remember the shorthorn bull, but we only had a few beef cattle at that time which we had brought with us. The rest had been sold off before we took over. We did not get into milk until 1946. In 1942 we ploughed up a lot of the land previously used for grazing and grew corn. We did not bring any sheep or pigs with us.

- *Controls on selling.* There were very strong controls - you couldn't sell privately. I seem to remember that we used the Tonbridge market at that time.

Pay.

I remember a carter's wages being 12 shillings and 6 pence a week [62 ½ p] in the late 30s.

Labour.

The only labour we used was family labour but we did have three Land Girls to help at harvesting.

Social Life.

The Young Farmers' meetings did not start until 1945 so apart from the Home Guard dance there was very little else.

Changes in the farming scene.

There have been just so many changes: the increase in the size of farms, the fewer numbers of people employed in agriculture and the increased use of machinery. Looking from the top of the hill at Wessons, you could see 20 dairy farms when we came and now, in 2008, there are only 2 in the whole of the parish.

Milling of corn and iron smelting.

The valley below us must have been flooded for over half a mile. There was a large dam at the bottom, which is a scheduled site, and at least two more dams over that length. All would have been built by human labour. There was a corn mill at the top close to Riverhall and a foundry lower down. When the dams eventually went, the soil was found to be very productive and some fine hops were grown there. But that came later.

CHAPTER 7: FURTHER USES OF THE LAND HOPS AND CHESTNUT FENCING

MICHAEL BERKS

Wartime Hopping in the Weald

The annual September invasion of the Kent and Sussex countryside by Londoners (mostly East-enders) continued during the 1939-45 War. However, as with any activity which exposed large numbers of vulnerable people in a confined area to danger from the air, compliance with Government air raid precautions was necessary. Black-out was enforced not only on hopper huts, but also the communal cookhouses had screens fixed to prevent glare from fires being seen from above, and oast houses had sacks and blankets around the doors.

Every hop farm had to have an ARP Warden, who could be one of the regular farm workers trained for emergencies. Special equipment had to be provided: anti-gas clothing and masks, fire extinguishers and First Aid extending even to stretchers. Around some of the larger hop gardens, trenches were dug and roofed over with sheets of corrugated iron to provide shelter against what might fall from the sky. The greatest danger was not from bombs (destined for London) but from the deadly shards of anti-aircraft shrapnel and crashing or disintegrating aircraft. The fear that pickers might be strafed from the air was widespread, but this rarely happened. There was more danger from what is now termed 'friendly fire': an enemy victim of a dogfight, streaking for home, dropping to skim low to evade a pursuing Spitfire or Hurricane, would not be the sole recipient of the hail of bullets and cannon fire. Those that missed their target would spray indiscriminately but lethally downwards. The writer, as an eight-year old, has a vivid memory of just such an occurrence in Tonbridge on The Ridgeway. A stricken Junkers 88, heading for a crash landing in the marshland beyond Hadlow Road, was being raked by a Spitfire's 20mm cannon shells. Many of the houses and gardens received hits, not only from the scattered debris flying off the doomed plane but also from the cannon fire. Not all the shells exploded on impact. Out of six which landed in our house and garden, two were later found intact. One of these penetrated the garage roof and lay undetected for weeks between the bonnet and wing of my father's car, until revealed at a service inspection.

On some of the larger hop farms with groups of kilns and oast houses, attempts were made at camouflage because it was thought that enemy pilots might mistake such a concentration of buildings as being of military use; some of the white cowls were taken down after hop-picking, a few were even painted black. Despite all precautions, loss of life and damage to buildings occurred, occasionally an unpremeditated attack by an aircraft returning from a London raid with a few bombs to off-load on the way home. In some areas, to avoid the risk to pickers working out in the open hop gardens, hop bines were taken into the villages where 'bins' were set up in the High Street. This was not popular with the growers because it involved the hops being handled more often, to the detriment of quality.

Emergency ration cards were issued and pickers became eligible for extra cheese, tea, sugar and margarine; bread coupons were issued for exchange at the bakers. There was an enormous increase in paperwork as every family member had to have a railway warrant, usually paid for by the hop grower. Also, there was a huge increase in the amount of mail to be handed out from the men-folk and women in the Forces. The traditional weekend influx of boisterous friends and relations became more subdued, but even so, the customary 'Happy Hopper' element still prevailed; much missed were the evening sing-songs around an open camp fire, baking potatoes in the hot ashes.

Recollections of Hop-picking at Foxhole Farm by Noel Carley

I suppose I was about 3 or 4 years old when I was introduced to the hop garden, 1927-1928. My father worked for Sir George Courthope on the Whiligh estate. It was the yearly practice for all the wives and children to go into the hop garden to work if they wished to earn a little money for themselves.

The hop garden was at Foxhole Farm, at the top of Moseham Hill turning left into Foxhole Lane. We were transported by lorry which picked everyone up at about 7 in the morning, we would then pick the hops until about 6 pm. Normally, the season lasted from August to early October. Sometimes in the early morning it was very frosty and at other times it was pouring with rain and very windy making the job much harder. Still, we got used to all that and concentrated on 'scratching them off', the phrase used at that time.

I happened to say to my father as I got older that I could do with a bicycle as everyone seemed to have one except me. He suggested that I get a bin to myself and earn some money that way. I set about getting my act together. The rate of pay was 1½d [*less than 1p*] a bushel which meant that 8 bushels had to be picked to earn 1 shilling [*5p*]. A bushel was a large basket similar in size to a large log basket, with a capacity of 8 gallons. You can see that we did not make a fortune. A new single-speed bicycle at that time was priced at around £6 10s [*£6.50*]. Despite all my efforts, I did not earn enough for the bicycle. I took on two paper-rounds, one in the early morning and another in the evening. Eventually I saved enough to get the bike.

Unlike today, hop-picking then was quite hard graft. The pole-puller's job was to cut the bines at the foot of the pole and lump them up at the side of the bins. The women then lifted the bines on to the bins to pick. Most people seemed to like picking hops and enjoyed the company which went with it. Sometimes tempers would fly between the women as to who picked the most but generally it ended peacefully.

When the 'measure man' came to empty the bins some of the women tried to hold the basket themselves but that didn't work as the basket was taken and

[cont. over]

Recollections of Noel Carley: continued

snatched out of their hands. (The measure man would press the hops down in the basket thus ensuring they got more to the bushel.)

The hops were stacked in sacks, loaded on to a horse drawn wagon and taken to the oast house where they were dried and pressed into hop pockets. The hop pockets were collected and taken away by a huge lorry to the brewery for the process of making very good beer.

If we got behind with the picking in the hop garden we were helped by a coach load of Londoners. They thoroughly enjoyed their time in the countryside.

One thing to mention was the discipline in the hop garden. Most parents did make their children pick so many hops before they could leave the bin to go and play. The bailiff would come round and those children who were old enough had to pick up every hop on the ground and help mother to remove all the large leaves from the bin.

Ironically and sadly, stories were told of pickers, having had narrow escapes in the hop gardens, returning to London to find that the Blitz had claimed their home. Everyone who went hopping in those days had a tale to tell. They shared with the natives of Kent and Sussex a grandstand view of the 'Battle of Britain'. In those clear blue skies of September 1940 the deadly mile-high combat was enacted daily, as Spitfires and Hurricanes attempted to break up  the massed formations of Heinkels, Dorniers and Junkers, escorted by predatory Messerschmitts. In 1940 the number of families was down, but increased in 1941, 1942 and 1943. In June 1944, long after the conventional air raids had ceased, a new threat arose: the pilotless Flying Bomb or doodlebug, aimed at London, traversed the Wealden skies. Down below, watchers would wait for that ominous engine cut-out, or witness and cheer the underwing flip some brave pilots dared to use, directing the 'bug' away from its course and down into open country. Understandably, the number of pickers dropped again, although, by September 1944, the Allies had overrun most of the launching sites of doodlebugs and V2 rockets.

Memories of Hop-picking by Louise Skilton

Louise Skilton remembers hopping in the field opposite the Balaclava Inn [*now Dobbin's Inn*] on the road to Cousley Wood. This hop field was owned by Mr Vidler at Great Pell. Mrs Skilton recalls that pickers started at 7 am., had an hour for lunch and worked until 5 pm. Pickers earned one shilling (5p) for picking 5 bushels. Mrs Vidler reckoned that she earned enough to buy her three children new uniforms, winter coats and school shoes. Hop-picking was done to coincide with the six-week school holiday period. All local young people she recalls helped also with potato and fruit-picking during busy seasons.

For the children of those days, memories remain not just of the thrilling combats over the hop gardens, but of a method of harvesting hops that has vanished. These recollections of Noel Carley, who worked as a child in the hop garden at Foxhole Farm, and those of Louise Skilton illustrate this.

The War delayed the development of the hop-picking machines, first proposed in 1937, and even after the War there was opposition from those who believed hand-picking was more efficient and provided a welcome paid holiday for thousands. Whitbreads, in common with most other big hop growers, put in some picking machines in the mid-1950s. They kept hand-picking going, on a reducing scale for advertising purposes. Also, the London Education Authority clamped down on children missing school, which had been tolerated until 1948. Cheap holidays abroad drew thousands away from 'Hopping'. But on 15th September 1968, very heavy rainfall caused unprecedented flooding in the Medway valley, devastating hopper camps especially at Beltring and East Peckham, where pickers had to be evacuated. This disaster prompted Whitbread to decide that they could not accept responsibility for pickers in camps. Thus the incentive to mechanise and dispense with hand labour became imperative. In due course, other hop growers became reconciled to the fact that the annual invasion of 'Happy Hoppers' would never return. So, 400 years of hand-picking ended. As with any farming practice, 'progress' has inevitably brought about change in the farming year, but as long as hops are still grown (sadly in ever decreasing acreages), crisp September mornings may still conjure up memories of those 'hopping mornings' that now belong to another era.

Watching the Battle of Britain
[Margaret Lawrence]

From Wealden Coppice to the Battlefields of France

During the Second World War, the chestnut fencing industry, which drew its raw material from much of Kent, Sussex and Surrey, geared itself up to a huge demand from the Ministry of Defence. Prior to D-Day, problems were foreseen in maintaining transport links over rough terrain and roads made unusable by bomb or shell damage. In the First World War at the battle of Cambrai, where British tanks appeared for the first time, major obstacles were the massive German trenches which acted as 'tank traps'. To counter these, large bundles of brushwood were carried on the front of each tank, to be laid across the trenches to provide ersatz bridges. Smaller bundles of faggots were used as standings for the very considerable number of horses employed in that era.

Churchill VII AVRE with fascine on tilt-forward cradle

The military application of these 'fascines' goes back to classical times. They were used by the Romans to build up defences or to fill in ditches for impeding attack (the word 'fascine' derives from the Latin 'fasces' - a bundle). During the 1939-45 War, there was available a ready-made 'fascine', namely a convenient roll of chestnut pale fencing, also to be carried and dropped where required as fill-in or as a 'bridge'. Also, chestnut fencing, unrolled over muddy or soft ground, made an effective trackway for wheeled traffic. In its manufacture, palings are wired together, most often 75mm (3") apart, but spacing can be varied from 'close' (i.e. touching) to 125mm (5"). The number of lines of twisted wire was increased for greater strength, in order to be load-bearing. To meet the demand, fencing manufacturers were encouraged to convert any suitable timber into palings, even as sawn battens. This was a notable departure from normal, as the British Standards Institute had strict rules governing the use of sweet chestnut only for those manufacturers who sold fencing to BSI configuration.

Wadhurst and the surrounding district has many ancient sweet chestnut coppices, originally planted to provide charcoal for fuelling the Wealden iron industry. When coal replaced charcoal, the industry moved away to the Midlands. Fortunately, the introduction of hops to 'fuel' the brewing industry gave impetus to the coppice owners to maintain their still valuable source of this adaptable timber. Hop poles were needed in large numbers, especially in the early years when each hop 'hill' (plant) had its own pole to climb. Now, sadly, the requirement for chestnut products has dwindled.

Alternatives to chestnut fencing abound: fewer coppices are being harvested regularly on the optimum 12-14 year rotation; sweet chestnut, when allowed to grow on indefinitely, becomes useless for any other purpose than as charcoal so is another declining home product.

As a postscript to the use of 'fascines', the Gulf War of 1991 provided pictures of allied tanks going into battle carrying very large bundles of plastic piping, to be dropped into the 'berms' or defensive ditches - history repeating itself.

SOURCES

Hopping Down in Kent: Bignell, A [1977], Robert Hale
Technology in the Ancient World: Hodges, H [1996], Michael O'Mara
The Encircling Hop: Lawrence, M [1990], SAWD Publications
World War 1: Shermer, D [1975], Octopus Books

Interview with Jim Overy, Little Pell Farm.

CHAPTER 8: THE WOMEN'S WAR AT HOME
FEEDING THE FAMILY
HEATHER WOODWARD
One should eat to live, not live to eat.

The Background to Wartime food planning

Thanks to foresight and Government expertise, food rationing, introduced in January 1940, was so planned that the British should not suffer physically as a result of the limitation of goods. The disappearance of well-loved delicacies did, however, leave a sense of deprivation but people realised it was a 'necessary evil'.

Every home received a War Emergency leaflet whose 12th item was headed

Food Supplies.

Stocks of foodstuffs in the country are sufficient. In order to ensure that stocks are distributed fairly and to the best advantage, the Government are bringing into operation the plans for the organisation of food supplies which have already been prepared in collaboration with the food trades. Steps have been taken to prevent any sudden rise in the price, or the holding up of supplies. For the time being, you should continue to obtain supplies from your usual shops. You should limit your purchases to the quantities which you normally require.

Those in rural areas like Wadhurst were relatively well off as regards food supply, but even those in inner city areas were able to enjoy a balanced diet of adequate nourishment, making as economical a use as possible of the foodstuffs available.

But there's wisdom in women, of more than they have known

Rupert Brooke

The Wadhurst Approach

Josephine Bailey (née Maynard) lived with her family in a house with a large garden in Gloucester Road and her father *"certainly dug for victory"* because she remembers potatoes, vegetables and salad crops, plus soft fruits and an apple tree. Their garden produce was supplemented with eggs and rabbits - Josephine remembers having some home-made gloves made from their skins. There was also the bounty of blackberries and wild strawberries. Because there were no fridges, the Maynards' large cool larder held large crocks of salted runner beans and the spring glut of eggs put in isinglass.

Doreen Drury who lived in a *"two up two down"* in Gloucester Place, never remembered being hungry, despite rationing, possibly because she and her brothers had never known anything different and her Mum must have coped very well. Because their Father was a prisoner of war – at first reported missing - Mrs Hope had to manage the garden and the allotment helped by the three children. That provided vegetables and fruit and Doreen remembers helping to prepare gooseberries and blackcurrants which were bottled for use in the winter. When she went hop-picking in the summer to get extra money, Doreen recalls travelling there *"on an open lorry – no one worried about safety! I remember eating beetroot sandwiches – lovely!"*

As a result of the conscription of local men, women began to drive the delivery vans in the area – some even taking apples from the orchard next to the Old Vine in Cousley Wood up to the London markets.

> *Never before have the British people been so wisely fed*
> *or British women so sensibly interested in cooking.*
> Irene Veal [food writer]
> 'Recipes of the 1940s' [pubd. 1943] dedicated to Lord Woolton)

Feeding the Family and Useful Tips

Cooks had to be inventive, adapting old recipes and creating new ones if the family was not to go hungry. Nothing could be wasted: bacon rinds were put on joints to help make dripping or they were fried to flavour a soup; apple peelings were simmered in water till soft then strained so the liquid could be substituted for lemon juice to create pectin for jam-making. Tips and suggestions came from everywhere but particularly useful were the Ministry of Food official leaflets which appeared regularly, radio broadcasts such as the morning, 'The Kitchen Front', and women's magazines published on a weekly or monthly basis. Some gave practical tips and suggestions, others gave helpful recipes to get the best out of the rations.

"Of all the fish that swim the sea" runs the old saying, "the herring is the King." Certainly whether it is a question of flavour, food value or cheapness, we have to agree that the herring is worthy of his crown.

Consider the herring's food value. It is a very cheap source of the best body-building protein. It is an oily fish and its oil is distributed throughout its flesh, not all contained in its liver as is the case with the cod and halibut. Herring oil not only supplies an extraordinary high number of calories or energy-giving units, but it also contains two vitamins, A & D. Vitamin A strengthens our resistance to disease and Vitamin D is essential for sound bones and teeth.

That is why the herring is such a valuable food for young and old. It is a tasty food, too. This leaflet gives you a number of ways of serving it, whether for breakfast, dinner, tea or supper.

Food rationing ensured that everyone received their fair share of the limited food available. The irony of the situation was that, as a result, the population of Britain was much healthier during the War years than previously and, in some cases, since. The plan was for British agriculture to supply about ⅓ of the nation's food energy requirements, ⅔ of the calcium, ⅓ of the vitamin A, ⅖ of the vitamin B, and, as a result of hugely increased potato production, <u>all</u> the necessary vitamin C. A lot of explanation was needed to get the maximum vitamin C from vegetables by cooking them conservatively or by eating raw salads.

Handy Hint

How to Stop the Smell Filling the House when Cooking Cabbage

Simply pop a dry pastry crust in the pan on top of the veg. and then put the lid back on

---

[Bocking Collection]

Nora Tweedley remembers the excitement of the Cattle Market every Monday, [where the car park behind the Wadhurst Ironmongers and the Pharmacy is now]: "*cattle, pigs, sheep, cows, chickens and ducks and up some steps on the same staging were eggs, fruit and vegetables and everything was sold by auction. All the farmers were there, and the little smallholders*". In 1939, eggs at the market were 2/- a dozen and potatoes 6/- a stone. Rabbits were 9d and honey 1/3d a jar.

By Spring 1940, eggs were 2/7d and rabbits 1/6d, showing a considerable wartime inflation - especially as regards the rabbits.

The first market held under Government control was on 15ᵗʰ January 1940. Several visits and inspections were then made by the Military in September 1940 because they were proposing to requisition the Market. This came to nothing because the Ministry of Food took over the marketing of livestock

Rationing

Ration books, which had been ready since 1938, were eventually issued in January 1940. Every adult and every child had a ration book and prices were pegged so that all foodstuffs were accessible even to the poorest. A 'points' system was introduced for non-perishable goods that were too scarce to ration – which meant people could decide how they wanted to use these points.

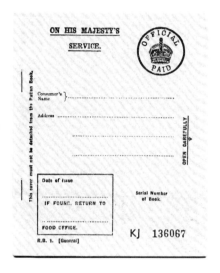

In Wadhurst, ration books had to be collected from the Commemoration Hall and long queues were guaranteed.

- **Wadhurst Grocers** advertised in the Parish magazine and in Kelly's directories, though the latter were not published during the War in order to save paper and possibly for security reasons. Housewives had to register at their favourite grocers where they would have to do their regular shopping. The shops were then allocated enough goods for their registered customers. In Wadhurst, the women had plenty of choice and what the grocers said about themselves is printed in italics in the entries below:-

- The International Stores [*now One Stop*] on the corner of Sheepwash [now Washwell] Lane. Each Wednesday a cycling salesman would call to collect the previous week's payment and write out the order for the current week which was delivered on Fridays.

- Gardners [*where Wine Rack and the Hospice shop are now*]: *The leading family grocer in Wadhurst district .... the store where the quality is better, the service better and prices right. A special feature is prompt attention to urgent telephone orders. If you want anything quickly, phone Wadhurst 5.* Gardner's departments included general drapery and millinery, gents' outfitting, ladies' and gents' boots and shoes, ironmongery and hardware, china and glass. It was also an agent for Achille Serre, dyers and cleaners.

[Bocking Collection]

- Durgates Dairy: *Licensed to sell Tuberculin Tested milk. Modern refrigeration installed.*

- Bayham Prospect [*now Nutshell*] near the Station run by A L Post

- Newington's in Sparrows Green [*now Costcutters*] was a general store and sold clothes, hardware and general furnishing, flower pots and garden implements as well as groceries.

- Tunbridge's in Sparrows Green [*now the Vets*]

- Wellington Stores, Sparrows Green: *The best of everything at the right price. Ready to give the best service at all times. It pays to shop here. (May 1936) Spring and Summer create a desire for appetising lunches, teas and suppers. Sole agents for Hill's noted pies etc delivered daily. (August 1938) Entirely re-organised. All clean new stock.*

- Rumary in Gloucester Place, Sparrows Green describes itself as an English and foreign fruiterer and potato merchant, and an agent for Lyons' and Crawley's cakes. Paraffin and oil could also be purchased there. Previously this had been Nugent's and later it was Voules: *Families waited upon daily.*

Rumary in Gloucester Place: 'fruiterer and potato merchant'

- Thunder in Pell Green
- Chapman in Cousley Wood: *Your kind patronage favourably solicited.*
- Oak Stores, Woods Green: *Ales, stout and cyder. Free delivery.*
- Martin in Woods Green.

Wadhurst Butchers were plentiful and the families of Wadhurst again registered with one of them. The Market was a dispersal centre during the wartime period and rationing control, which applied to most foods, meant that meat was allocated to the butchers and so housewives could no longer buy their meat direct as they had used to do.

By 1941, each person was given 16 points to buy the meat for 4 weeks from one of the following:-.

- Hoadley's opposite the Old Vine in Cousley Wood.
- Bert Norman's in Sparrows Green [*now John Cook*] at Gloucester Place. Bert lived in Old Station Road [*probably Greenhurst*] and kept his pigs at the bottom of the back garden. *High-class butcher.*

- Fred Chapman was in what is now the Durgates antique shop and he had his slaughterhouse in Jonas Lane. *The most up-to-date slaughter-house in the district, which ensures cleanliness. RSPCA Humane Killer used.* He was also a poulterer and game dealer.
- Ratcliff's was opposite the Clock House [*now Hairstyle*] before they moved along to where James Rogers is now: *Purveyor of choice English and Colonial meat. We meet your needs, you need our meat. Prompt delivery is feature of our service, ensuring a WELL COOKED JOINT on YOUR TABLE.* [his capital letters not ours.]
- Malpass [*now W J Crouch*] in the High Street and their slaughter-house was behind Forge Cottage in St James's Square: *A trial solicited. Humane pistol used for animals.*

Wadhurst Fishmongers

- Fred Chapman in Durgates provided fish as well as meat: *ice supplied.*
- Jones and Sons of Tunbridge Wells opposite the Clock House, also supplied poultry and game: *Families waited on daily.*
- E Keens was a fried fish shop in Sparrows Green.

Wadhurst Bakers

- Brooks, later Goldsmith, in the High Street.
- Boorman in Sparrows Green.

Wadhurst Fruiterers and Greengrocers

- Keens in the High Street – their shop would be completely destroyed in the Meteor crash in January 1956.
- Fruit Shop, High Street: *High-class English Fruit and Vegetables. Also Colonial and Empire Produce of every Description.*

Despite the fact that all these shops were available, quite predictably, in anticipation of any rationing that might be introduced, housewives spent the months before the outbreak of War, stocking-up their store cupboards. Dry goods at that time were sold in brown or blue paper bags. The author remembers well her Mother telling her, after the War, how devastated she had been in 1939 when she picked up a paper bag without checking properly – and poured salt into pounds of carefully-stored sugar. She checked everything very carefully from then on.

Food Supplies

Rationing was introduced gradually:

January 1940   4 oz a week of butter and bacon, and 8 oz of sugar a week. The latter was in short supply because of the pressure on shipping space.

March 1940   preserves, and 1/10d worth of meat. This was reduced to 1/2d worth in August 1942 and included all meat except rabbits or poultry. Offal was never rationed so that led to intense competition between housewives.

July 1940   2 oz per person per day of tea. Tea rationing ended in 1952. ½ lb a month of margarine and cooking fat, which meant 2 oz butter, 2 oz cooking fat and 4 oz margarine.

March 1941   1 lb a month of jam, marmalade or treacle.

By April 1941, unobtainable generally were onions, oranges, lemons, grapefruit and marmalade. Rare were bird-seed, cheese, chocolates, sweets, biscuits, tomato soup, eggs, meat, dried fruit. Wadhurst people could fill some of those gaps but by no means all.

May 1941   cheese. Miners and farm workers were given additional cheese. And in Wadhurst, those helping with the hop-picking "*got a bit of extra cheese*".

June 1941   30 eggs a year. One packet of powdered eggs to last eight weeks was equivalent to 12 eggs but, from all accounts, was not all that appetising.

November 1941   butter was reduced to 2 oz per week, margarine 4 oz and 3 eggs a month. Dog meat was now hard to find but there would be joy for the animals if they paid a visit to the kitchens of the houses where the soldiers were billeted.

January 1942   rice and dried fruit.

February 1942   tinned tomatoes and peas.

July 1942   syrup and treacle. 8 oz sweets and chocolates per month. 2 pints of milk a week in winter, 3 or 4 in summer.

August 1942   biscuits. These became very restricted as regards quality and variety. 350 different types were produced pre-war; now only twenty.

By 1942, austerity really was biting and food imports were running at less than half the pre-war level and the Japanese conquests in the Far East cut off Britain's normal sources of rice, sugar and tea in particular.

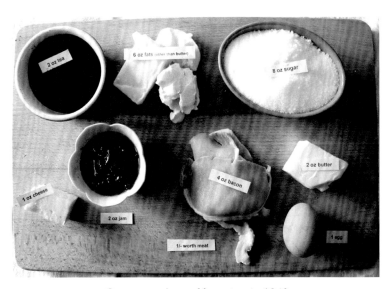

One person's <u>weekly</u> ration in 1942.
To this can be added meat to the value of 1/-; depending on the cut, this could buy about a pound of lower quality. Milk was rationed to 2 pints in winter and 3 or 4 in summer.

In The Times of Saturday 29ᵗʰ August 1942, its food correspondent reported:

> *From the beginning the Ministry of Food has worked on the basis that, while it cannot win this war, it could lose it. It has neglected no means of ensuring adequate rations, and, thus, has contributed to the maintenance of fighting vigour, productive capacity and good spirits.*
>
> *All the same it was important – and has grown more so – that food imports should use as little shipping space as possible. The first obvious step was to increase enormously food production here, but that done and extravagant fruit cut out, it was still necessary to reduce the bulk of our imports if ships were to be released for more direct war-making purposes.*

This requirement has been met through new achievements in Science.

Milk now comes as powder. During the next year, we shall import 100,000 tons of dried egg - the equivalent importation of egg in shell would be more than 500,000 tons, which would occupy more than six times the shipping space. Already samples of dried meat have reached this country. Products have also been achieved which, when reconstituted by adding water and cooked, are indistinguishable in appearance, colour and flavour from fresh foods.

1943   sausages came on ration.

In April 1943, one person reported that they had just had two visitors to supper and had opened a tin of salmon – *"24 points gone west!"*

Later in 1943   breakfast cereals, biscuits, canned fruit, condensed milk rationed.

As the War continued, more research was being done. Scientists discovered that, although the population was receiving an adequate diet and, in some cases, a better diet than before the War, the monotony of that diet led to a decline in the people's weight. Apparently in 1940/41, people (especially women) were not actually eating enough for their physiological needs. The introduction of more interesting Lend-Lease foods, such as tinned luncheon meat, ham loaves, dried eggs and more cheese in 1943, provided greater variety and improved people's health.

July 1944   bacon ration increased to 6 oz a week.
October 1944   cheese increased to 3 oz a week but milk still very short.
                ½ a pint of milk twice a week.

Even as the War was drawing to its close, in April 1945 food was still difficult and local residents remember that a lot of swopping went on – lard for washing soap, dripping for sugar, custard powder for seed potatoes.

The **"National Loaf"** was made with 82% wheatmeal, 10% white flour, 5% barley flour, 3% oat flour plus a little chalk and milk powder. With more grain being used than for the old white loaf, brown bread became the norm. No purely white bread was allowed after the spring of 1943. Bread was not rationed, and nor were potatoes, *"that puckish vegetable"*, according to Sir William Beveridge – vital because of their vitamin C content.

The National Loaf did not appeal to the tastes of many, it has to be said, despite the efforts of the Ministry of Food to popularise it:

> *Pat-a-loaf, pat-a-loaf*
> *Baker's Man,*
> *Bake me some Wheatmeal*
> *As fast as you can:*
> *It builds up my health*
> *And its taste is so good.*
> *I find that I <u>like</u>*
> *Eating just what I should.*

The public still remained somewhat sceptical.

Peter Wicker recalls that no one here was ever really hungry or short of food during the War:

> *Those dieticians knew what we could live on and we were pretty healthy*
> *.... and we got a bit of extra cheese when we were hop-picking.*

Incidentally, in The Times of 29th August 1942, amongst News in Brief items was the following:

> *Hop-pickers are specially asked to take with them to the hop-fields their*
> *own cups, plates, knives, forks, spoons, cooking utensils &c.*

'Mum and the gang'
Boys in caps [l] Jack Skilton [r] Peter Wicker   [Nora Tweedley]

168

There was no 'black market' in Wadhurst but one resident did once buy a leg of lamb and a big lump of lard for 12/6d from one of the soldiers. He just hoped he wouldn't be caught by the policeman because it had probably been stolen from some army base. The lamb was cut in half and shared with friends.

Everyone spent a lot of time and energy thinking and talking about food. It was not that they were hungry but meals could become repetitive, boring and very difficult to come by. Without the supplementary vegetables and fruit available around Wadhurst, not to mention game and poultry, the diet would have been very dreary as it was in other less fortunate parts of the country.

Acquiring food also entailed a great deal of that quintessentially British phenomenon, orderly queueing – which is, even today, much admired on the Continent.

One joke of the day recorded the tale of the old lady out shopping who saw a queue and, from force of habit, attached herself to it. After a quarter of an hour, having made little progress, she asked her neighbour what they were queueing for. *"Blood transfusion"* was the reply.

Another story, this time from Worthing, was that a lady saw a queue at Woolworths and went up to the shop assistant to enquire what the queue was for. *"It's for biscuits – but they've not arrived here yet."*

Any unwise request would inevitably receive the retort: *"Don't you know there's a war on?"*

One man had had the opportunity to go away for a few days and was waiting for his wife outside the greengrocer's. The greengrocer came out of the shop and asked him if he would mind not waiting outside because *"they'll form a queue. They always do."*

Residents of Wadhurst were still travelling up to Tunbridge Wells or London for work or even pleasure. A typical café meal in 1941 might cost

Soup	*1d.*
Choice of meat and two veg	*5d.*
Choice of pudding: rice or sultana batter	*2d.*
Cup of tea	*1d.*

British Restaurants were initially born as a result of the Blitz and were established on a non-profit-making basis. Meals were exceptionally cheap at 10d or 1/- a head and were self-service. One was in a hut in Grosvenor Gardens in Tunbridge Wells. Going there from school in 1945, Rosemary Potter describes *"horrible wet boiled cabbage, tapioca, squashed fly pie and lumpy custard"*.

Coping with the Restrictions

Rationing was hard but Wadhurst and its rural environs could provide additions to the larder and so many families had their menus enlivened, as Ruth Skilton remembers: *"with rabbit, pots of good stews and meat puddings, bacon puddings and roly-poly"*.

Rosemary Potter (niece of Mrs Doris Rabson) found that living in a village meant that people helped each other out with surplus from gardens and allotments. Her two grandmothers kept chickens which supplemented the egg ration, and her aunt Doris kept goats at Woods Green and the family, therefore, sometimes had cheese made from their milk. Most families kept chickens so there was little shortage of eggs (and spares could be kept in isinglass), fortunately, and an occasional chicken for the pot was a bonus.

Because her father needed sandwiches each day for his packed lunch and fillings were hard to come by, her mother used all their cheese ration on him, so Mrs Potter persuaded Rosemary that actually she disliked cheese. It was not until Rosemary left home as a teenager that she discovered the delicious tastes of cheese and was then told about her mother's subterfuge.

Joyce Anscombe (née Harmer) had the run of the fields around Sparrows Green as a child and remembers how resourceful and clever her mother was with food. Their mother was always cooking, it seemed to the family. They fed wonderfully – locally-caught rabbit, fish, sprats, herring, eels and especially a bacon suet pudding on Saturdays. Because her father was a full-time fireman, he was allowed extra rations of cheese, butter and such like.

Both Joyce and her sister, Jean, feel that, despite the severe rationing restrictions on food, they had a very healthy diet – plenty of home-made soups, eggs from their chickens and all their vegetables grown in their large garden. Joyce was delighted when fifteen bantam chicks hatched out and grief-stricken when one or two died.

The Harmer children used to raise pocket money and help the War effort by collecting acorns to sell to the farmers for their pigs, and jam-jars which had a special Ministry of Food logo on the bottom.

Jenn Hemsley normally went home for lunch because she lived close to the Primary School where the Youth Centre is now. When school meals and school milk were introduced, poor children had their milk free but parents who could afford it paid ½d for ⅓ of a pint of milk. In winter the milk was put next to the boiler to stop it freezing.

Evening canteens were run by the WVS ladies including Miss Scutter at the Drill Hall [*now Kingsley Court*] and St George's Hall.

Jo Bailey (née Maynard) remembers what she calls now "*strange food*":

dried locust beans	- chewed instead of sweets
dried powdered egg	- for baking or for omelettes
zanna	- a powder which, mixed with water, made a banana-tasting sandwich filling.

Children are always resourceful and Peggy Bartholomew recalls that, before the War, her brother Stuart and his two friends Cedric Gamlin and Jack Skilton were naughty with their pocket money. They used to put a halfpenny piece on the railway line so that the train could flatten it to the size of a penny, and then they would take it to one of the six shops which sold sweets in Wadhurst and buy a penny bar of chocolate! (No doubt, Stuart used similar initiative when he was in the Royal Marines during the War.) Rosemary Potter's family hoarded most of their sweet ration, saving it up for Christmas.

Peggy herself received 3d a week pocket money which she used to spend at the Three Oaks Stores. She used to buy a farthing's worth of sweets in a paper cone. To supplement their pocket money, Peggy and her sister Myrtle sold bags of plums as they fortunately had a big garden with plum, apple and pear trees.

Celebrating during the year

Everyone tried to make Christmas as special as possible despite the rationing and shortages. Turkey had all the trimmings but the treat for the Sinden family was a big tin of biscuits and that day was probably the only time they used the parlour or front room. The Christmas stockings for the four Sinden children were always full but not elaborate: always a pink mouse and an orange, but then useful items such as new pencils, brushes and combs.

Christmas cards were more or less abandoned because of the scarcity of paper and presents were, if given at all, practical rather than frivolous. Christmas tree decorations were made out of old sweet wrappers in Jennifer Hawkins' house and they had rabbit for dinner.

For a birthday party, there were no crackers, balloons or party hats, and an iced cake was very unlikely.

The 'iced' cake for weddings could be made with rice-paper replacing the icing as the crafty outside decoration. Almond icing for the cake itself was still allowed if it could be found, though it usually turned out to be peanuts.

The postmaster was Mr William Goble and Leonard Manktelow worked there. He would follow the wedding party to the house with the wedding telegrams. One was:

> *May the roof of your house never fall in and the folks inside never fall out.*

Advice, Recipes and Cooking Tips Galore

Housewives were given loads of advice on how to supplement and to make best use of whatever food they could lay their hands on.

As the Ministry of Food introduced in its first leaflet:

> *No country in the world grows vegetables better than we do, and probably no country in the world cooks them worse. For generations we have wasted our root vegetables by excessive peeling and over-cooking, and boiled most of the goodness out of our green vegetables – only to pour it down the sink.*

It went on to explain the importance of green vegetables as a valuable source of vitamin C, and also vitamins A and B, iron and calcium. They did warn that green peas and beans made a welcome change but could not take the place of leafy green vegetables as they contained little vitamin C.

An endless stream of advice kept coming from the Ministry of Food especially on the BBC Home Service at 8.15 each morning with its *Kitchen Front* including advice on Christmas pudding-making without eggs, preserving fruit without sugar, creating Pilchard Layer Loaf or corned beef rissoles – not to mention *"a new sweetmeat, a treat for kiddies – carrot stickjaw, deliciously brittle"*. One wonders how many were persuaded by that.

They extolled the virtues of the green vegetables we use regularly today but they also included the advice that *"broccoli tops, turnip tops and beetroot tops have good food value and are excellent if cooked like cabbage. So are the broad bean tops which gardeners always pick off."* The quantity should be 1½ lbs for 4 portions. Young nettles demanded 2 lbs for 4 portions and had to be picked young and tender, using gloves.

The following recipe suggests an innovative approach:

Brussels Sprouts à l'Italienne

1 lb Brussels sprouts	salt and pepper
1 oz margarine	pinch of grated nutmeg
1 oz flour	lemon substitute
1 pint milk and vegetable water	2 – 3 oz grated cheese

Cook the cleaned and washed sprouts in a little salted water until tender. Drain, keeping the vegetable water. Melt the fat, add the flour and cook for about 2 minutes. Add the liquid, bring to the boil and cook for 5 minutes. Add seasoning to taste, nutmeg and a few drops of lemon substitute and grated cheese. Mix thoroughly. Add the sprouts to the sauce and heat through. Serve hot.

Recipes abounded in official leaflets, in newspapers, popular women's magazines and, of course the Parish magazines. One of the most famous, or infamous according to one's taste, was:

Woolton Pie

named after the Minister of Food, Lord (Frederick) Woolton.

1 lb potatoes	1 tspn Marmite	1 lb cauliflower
½ lb oatmeal	1 lb swede	4 spring onions
1 lb carrots	1½ lb potatoes	1 oz cheese

Dice and boil 1 lb of potatoes, cauliflower, swede and carrots in salted water. Strain the vegetables and save ⅓ pint of cooking water.
Arrange the cooked vegetables in a large ovenproof dish.
Add the Marmite and oatmeal to the vegetable water and boil till thickened.
Pour the thickened water over the vegetables.
Add the chopped spring onions.
Boil and mash the remaining potatoes.
Top the pie with mashed potato and a little grated cheese.

Heat the pie in a moderate oven until golden brown (about one hour). Serve with brown gravy.

It has to be said that Rosemary Pope remembers that recipe with a shudder!

Another recipe which might not appeal to the modern palate was:

Dripping Cake

½ lb self-raising flour   2 oz clarified dripping
 OR ½ lb plain flour   3 oz sugar
4 teaspoons baking powder   3 oz currants or sultanas
½ teaspoon salt   ¼ pint milk
½ teaspoon mixed spice

Sift the flour, baking powder (if used), salt and spice together. Rub in the dripping, and add the sugar and fruit. Mix to a soft consistency with the milk and turn into a greased 6" cake tin. Bake in a moderate oven for 50 minutes.

N.B. If hard mutton dripping is used, it may be slightly warmed to make it easier to rub.

Miss D Pryce sent this next recipe into the Wadhurst Parish magazine.

Old Fashioned Shropshire Pie

Line a cooking plate with shortcrust pastry, put a layer of cold mashed potatoes, a layer of small pieces of streaky bacon, then place 3 or 4 eggs on top without breaking the yolks, and season with salt and pepper. Cover over with shortcrust pastry and bake in a moderate oven. Can be eaten hot or cold.

One popular pudding (War Cookery Leaflet No 13) seems to have been:

Apple Charlotte

1 lb apples (or other fruit)	2 –3 oz sugar	6 oz breadcrumbs
2 oz melted margarine	½ tspn cinnamon, nutmeg or mixed spice	

Prepare the fruit and cut into thin slices. Mix together breadcrumbs, sugar, spice and marg. Arrange a layer of breadcrumbs mixture in a greased pint-size pie-dish, then a layer of fruit and continue filling the dish in alternate layers finishing with a breadcrumb layer. Bake in a moderate oven for ¾ - 1 hour. Serve hot.

And there was the recipe named to show support for our colonial troops:

Anzac Biscuits

3 oz margarine	1 tsp bicarbonate of soda	3 oz sugar
3 oz plain flour	2 tblsp hot water	½ lb rolled oats
1 tablespoon syrup	½ tsp vanilla essence	

Cream margarine and sugar. Add syrup and vanilla essence. Dissolve bicarbonate of soda in hot water and add. Add flour and then oats to give a stiff consistency. Place teaspoons of the mixture on a tray, 2" apart; cook in a moderate oven for 20 minutes. Makes 36 biscuits.

Waste not, want not shows in this next recipe (Ministry of Food Leaflet "What's left in the LARDER" No 11) which used up stale bread:

Fairy Toast

Cut wafer-thin slices of bread and bake in a moderate oven until crisp and golden brown. Store in an air-tight tin. This is a good stand-by to have in place of bread or plain biscuits and it will keep for months.

How Can I Cook without Fat?

The Ministry of Food leaflet suggested that 'Mrs Carr' should cook:

Oven-Fried Fish – coated in flour, salt, pepper, nutmeg and milk then rolled in browned breadcrumbs. ½ hour in a hot oven.

Roast Potatoes – put in a roasting tin with salted water, comfortably without touching and cooked for 1½ hours. The water evaporates and leaves shiny golden balls with floury insides.

Sponge Cake – 4 reconstituted dried eggs, 3 oz sugar, 2 oz flour, 4 teaspoon baking powder, pinch of salt, a few drops of vanilla essence. Bake in two greased 6" sandwich tins in a hot oven for 10 minutes.

In hindsight, it is clear that the wartime population was healthier because of a diet rich in vegetables and low in sugar and dairy products. Lord Woolton was much criticised but he had done a good job.

Wadhurst Women's Institute

The Wadhurst WI was much to the fore during the War. The annual subscription was 2/- from 71 members before the War, dropping to 49 by 1940. In February 1940, they announced that *"the War Time Cookery Classes will shortly start"*, with the WI meeting part of the cost of hire of the Commemoration Hall, where ovens were available.

In August 1940, the WI arranged a centre for making jam with any surplus fruit grown in the village. It was open to everyone living in Wadhurst and the jam would be made by *"capable voluntary workers"*. The following year, under the ægis of the Ministry of Food, the WI Fruit Preservation Scheme worked for the five months of the fruit-growing season. The organisers needed to know in advance who would be likely to be donating what quantity

 of fruit so that they would have some idea of the amount of sugar for which they would have to obtain a permit. Fruit was bought at current market prices and the jam then made was to be sold at controlled prices. They emphasised that there seemed little chance of any sugar being released for private jam-making in 1941.

A month later, they were asking for 1-lb or 2-lb jam-jars which the Girl Guides would collect.

The Centre was at the Institute or at Old Monks in Cousley Wood, by kind invitation of Mrs G M Turner, and it was hoped that "*everyone will willingly co-operate by bringing their fruit to be made into jam*". Helpers were also needed to weigh, grade, prepare the fruit and make the jam. No doubt was left in the minds of the Wadhurst residents as to what was the right thing to do:

> *Though everyone would like to have their own sugar and make their own jam, it is not possible this year, and it is up to all to help the Ministry to make this war-time scheme a success.*

Quantities however small would be quite acceptable – for the Wadhurst Centre to be left with Miss Watson at The Lodge or Mrs W Gadd in the High Street; for the Cousley Wood Centre with Mrs Turner at Old Monks or Mrs Bocking at Spring Cottage.

The scheme leapt into action again the following year, for three days each week beginning on Monday 29th June. There was the usual plea for helpers and jam-jars and then "*THERE MUST BE NO WASTE!*" [their capitals not ours]. In the October, supplies of jams were available at most of the retailers and they planned to arrange a Fruit Canning Demonstration in the Institute during the first or second week of the month. By the end of the season, they reported that "*2,000 lbs of jam and jellies*" had been made.

By April 1943, the WI was outlining the enormous amount of work involved with the Wadhurst Fruit Preservation Scheme:

> *preparation of the room, fruit weighing, grading and cleaning, book-keeping, there are also the stocks of sugar and jars to be kept, errands to go, and lots of washing up to be done. When the day's jam-making is done, there is the job of finishing, labelling and tying down, also carrying across to the stores. This is just a rough idea of the many jobs involved and there are more which come along when the stock has to be sold, orders to be made up, transport to be arranged, and above all patience to be kept to an amicable degree.*

Mrs Bocking was very aware that the women of Wadhurst were already very busy but concluded:

> *So we put the scheme once again before you in the full knowledge you will give it your best consideration; it is a vital war job which we women have been pledged to do if possible in the interests of our own community.*

In June 1943, Mrs Tripp, Instructress in Rural Domestic Economy, gave a Fruit Preserving Demonstration at 2.30 pm. in the Old Billiard Room [*a room behind the Commemoration Hall containing one billiard table, and around which the Social Club was later built*]. That same month, however, a lack of sufficient support for the 1943 Scheme led to the announcement that it would not take place at all (perhaps they were all overwhelmed by the volume of work involved which had been outlined by Mrs Bocking) but the following month it was on again "*in spite of the adverse decision last month*". Mrs Tripp had paid a warm tribute to the Wadhurst Centre's work in 1942 as "*one of the best in East Sussex*" so it came back on stream for another season.

This time, they also hoped to undertake bottling and canning of fruit, under the supervision of Mrs Tripp, and now 7-lb jars were being sought. The irony was that there was very little surplus fruit eventually available to be dealt with in 1943, though a good plum and apple crop was anticipated. The children were then urged to bring in wild fruit like blackberries. By the end of the season, 838 lbs of jams and jellies had been made in addition to some bottling and canning – about a ⅓ of the previous year's quantity chiefly owing to the scarcity of soft fruits at the beginning of the season, though there had been a 'flood' of blackberries at the end.

A notable success of 1943 was Mrs Bocking herself. At the Produce Show in Hove, Mrs Bocking was awarded first awards for stone and soft fruit jams, fruit jelly and dried herbs and 2nd awards for bottled stone fruit and piccalilli. Out of a possible 150 marks, she obtained 142.

In March 1943, the Wadhurst WI organised a cookery demonstration by Miss Knapp, chiefly on 'New and Appetising Ways with Potatoes'.

As you all know, Lord Woolton appeals to our organisation to help to get the nation to eat more potatoes, and we have pledged ourselves to do so.

The competition for that month's meeting at St George's Hall was a War-Time Savoury, main item potatoes, along with recipe. There would also be a distribution of seed potatoes.

And so efforts were carefully honed and targeted so that the maximum benefit would be achieved with the minimum of wastage.

The restrictions continued for the duration and, in many cases, long after the War. Sweets and sugar cane came off ration only in 1953 just in time for the Coronation. Bread, never rationed during the War, was rationed afterwards, and tea continued to be rationed until 1952. We may have won the War politically, but economically and socially the country suffered long after.

SOURCES

The People's War: Calder, Angus [1969], Jonathan Cape
Despatches from the Home Front: McCooey, Chris [ed] [1994], JAK Books
Eating for Victory – reproductions of official 2nd World War leaflets, sourced from The National Archives, Kew.
Wadhurst Parish magazine and **Kelly's Directory for 1940**

The personal memories of local residents including
Joyce Anscombe, Peggy Bartholomew, Jennet Hemsley, Rosemary Pope, Rosemary Potter, Ruth Skilton, Nora Tweedley, and Peter Wicker.

DIG FOR VICTORY LEAFLET No.1. New Series

Vegetables for you and your family
every week of the year. Never a
week without food from your
garden or allotment. Not only
fresh peas and lettuce in June—
new potatoes in July, but all the
health-giving vegetables in WINTER
— when supplies are scarce - - - —
SAVOYS, SPROUTS, KALE,
SPROUTING BROCCOLI, ONIONS,
LEEKS, CARROTS, PARSNIPS and
BEET
Vegetables all the year round
if you
DIG WELL
AND CROP WISELY

Follow this Plan ➤

ISSUED BY THE MINISTRY OF AGRICULTURE

CHAPTER 9: BASSETT'S FORGE IN DURGATES THE WAR YEARS

JOHN MILLETT

Bassett's Forge housing complex in Durgates now marks the site of the Bassett family's thriving blacksmith's business which had been running in the village in some form since 1881. The forge finally closed in 1988 with the retirement of Rodney, who had worked there since 1923.

Background

The business was started in 1881 by James Bassett, a wheelwright, and his premises were where the Shell garage now stands. As the business grew, James moved to where the industrial estate now is. He had five sons, Fred, Ted, William, Charles and Jack. In 1902, Jack borrowed money from his uncle and bought land from Wadhurst Castle on the opposite side of the road. He cleared the site, built a forge, and started shoeing horses along with other blacksmith's work. In due course, a wheelwright's shop was built next to the forge, and his father James, and brothers Charlie and William moved across the road. A pair of cottages, Parkside, was built on the other side of the forge, and Charlie moved into the left side and Jack next to the forge on the right side. The wheelwright's business expanded into carriage building, and a fine two storey carriage house was built alongside the forge. Carriages of all sorts were built to order downstairs, then raised on a rope lift to the upper storey to be painted. This carriage house, converted into dwellings, together with the converted forge building, still stands today, with Parkside Cottage next door.

Jack had only one son, Rodney, born in 1908; he came into the business as an apprentice to his father at the age of 15. James Bassett, the founder of the business, died in 1940, having been predeceased by two of his sons, Ted and William. Fred, one of his other sons, had nothing to do with the business, and joined the railway, ending up as Station Master at a London Station!

181

Bassett's Forge during the Second World War

By the end of the 1930s, Bassett's Forge was a thriving business as farriers, general blacksmiths and carriage repairers. The carriage building side had all but ceased with the growth of the motor industry, although some farm carts were still made, and there was still a thriving repair, painting, and sign writing business.

Bassett's Forge [Bocking Collection]

Jack continued to be very much the boss in the forge, assisted by his son Rodney. Charlie Bassett was the wheelwright, helped by Mr Wilmshurst, and Wally Watts painted the wagons. Labour was, of course, scarce in the War, but there would undoubtedly have been other employees from time to time. Jack had a bungalow, named The Wilderness, built in the Marlpit, and he moved in there in the early 1940s. When he died in 1974, Rodney's daughter, Sheila, moved in with her family. When Jack moved out of Parkside, Rodney and his family, who had been living previously in Western Road, moved in. He lived there until his death in 1992. Sadly his wife Violet died in 1977, and his daughter Sheila looked after him from then on, and also helped with the shoeing in the forge. Although he became increasingly infirm after his retirement, he was a familiar figure standing in his garden, or waving from his window to one of his many friends.

During the War years, Violet Bassett kept the books, and sent out the accounts. All these customer account books, together with other papers, are now kept at the East Sussex Record Office in Lewes, and the writer spent a fascinating morning going through the books for the years 1940 – 1943 to see what was done in the business at that time. The account books revealed an amazing variety of activities in what was undoubtedly an important point in the village. The activities fell into four main categories but many other miscellaneous jobs were also undertaken.

Jack and Violet Bassett
[Bocking Collection]

Farriery

It must be remembered that these were still the days of the heavy working farm horse. Even though tractors were fast increasing in numbers, most farms had one or more horses. Most of these horses would need shoeing, or, if not, their feet would need trimming. The horse would be walked to one of the Wadhurst forges. This would sometimes mean quite a long walk by road or across country. The horses would be out in the fields in fine weather, but it is recorded that the farrier would expect a busy day if it was raining when he got up. There would then be a queue of working horses at the door!

There were also numerous hunting horses and ponies to be shod. In those days the price of a set of shoes seemed to vary from five to ten shillings, [*25 - 50 pence*]. Nowadays a set of shoes costs from £40 upwards! Most horses were brought to the forge, but as this entry from the account book shows, visits were sometimes made:

7th January 1941	Journey and paring 4 Hunters feet at Whiligh	8/6

It seems that a journey was made to Whiligh every month to trim feet or fit shoes.

Carriage repairs

There were several repairs to trailers and traps as these examples from the account book illustrate:

7th January 1940	Repairs to pony-trap making, fitting plate to broken shaft. Work 3½ hours. & collecting	18/6
October 1942	J Ratcliff, Butcher. Repairs to van: taking down rear wings, fitting new piping, replacing number plate cleaning down, painting and varnishing throughout. 50 hours	£6-10-0
April 1942	To building and supplying 1 new 4-wheeled trailer with ladder fitted to same as required, painting throughout	£35-0-0
April 1943	Repairs to trap. Alterations to springs etc. Cleaning down and varnishing etc.	£10-10-0

Work was also done directly to help the War effort:

4th January 1940	Uckfield RDC. To converting Ford utility van as fire tender reinforcing rear spring. Fit and fix in hose lockers, touch up work and varnish	£ 7 -10 -0
January 1943	National Fire Service: Work on vehicles and towing hitches. New starting handle, new lockers and ladder gantries	No price given

Machinery repairs

Farm machinery was worked hard and there were always repairs to make. Some examples:

April 1940	Making new iron plates as required for tractor Making new part for plough Repair plough Forging 8 new harrow tines	3/- 2/6 3/6 12/-
1942	Repair machinery for Ministry of Agriculture (this was probably from the WAC depot at Dewhurst, where machinery could be hired)	
June 1943	Repair to hay sweep, 2 new teeth to same; repairs to manure cart repairs to van (used for milk round)	

Wheelwrights

The shop was constantly repairing wheels for carts and carriages. Charlie was the expert at this and he was kept busy. Spokes had to be renewed and replacement tyres fitted. A wheel was made from three types of wood: the rim was of ash, the spokes of oak, and the hub of elm. If the spokes became loose the wheel would be immersed in water for some time to swell the spokes. An iron tyre was made by the blacksmith, the wheel was laid on a tyring platform and the almost red-hot tyre was picked off the forge by two men with tongs and fitted to the wheel. The hot tyre would expand to be fitted over the wooden rim and it would then be  immediately doused in water to shrink the tyre on to the wood and prevent the wood from burning. The tyre was then nailed on with tyre nails. The Kent Hop Company was a good customer as it needed a lot of repairs to cart wheels.

Miscellaneous jobs

The list in the ledgers included the following jobs:

Lawn Mower repairs
Sharpening tools
Supplying nuts, bolts, and rivets
Repair to milking stool
Gate ironwork
Repairs to locks
Repairs to stoves

Bassett's Forge   [Bocking Collection]

It also seems that the firm was into a bit of building and decorating and fencing as the following entries show:

March 1943	Wadhurst Church Wardens. To fixing gateposts upright to iron gate, nuts to gate hook, journey (?) and altering. 3 hours	7/6
March 1943	Whiligh. Repairing store at mansion, new shield bar, rebedding bricks and tiles. Repairs to plates	£1-2-6

Charlie also kept his eye on the furnace at the convent in Mayfield Lane [*now Weald Hall*]. This was a daily job. He also did some other jobs there, as this entry shows:

12th March 1943	The Sister Superior. To distempering room on veranda: ½ gal distemper 5 hours To cleaning windows all round 31 days' attention to furnace at 3/-	12/- £2-0-0 £4-13-0

It was also possible to purchase new tools such as shovels, axe handles, stirrup pumps and even pieces of wood at the forge. For example, two new shovels cost 11/3d and a stirrup pump cost £1. If you wanted something, there was every chance that Bassett's would have it, and despite the apparent chaos in every corner, as the writer can vouch, Rodney would be able to lay his hand on it at once!

No account of Bassett's Forge in wartime would be complete without referring to Rodney's service as a part-time fireman. He joined the fire brigade in 1925, and became a uniformed member in 1933. During the War he was promoted to part-time Section Leader, and subsequently, when East Sussex Fire Brigade took over in 1948, he was appointed Sub-Officer. After the War, Rodney claimed, and was awarded, the Defence Medal. This fire service commitment meant that Rodney was likely to be called away from the forge at any time, and no doubt he was kept busy in this respect during the War years.

Other forges in Wadhurst

Although Bassett's was the biggest and most prominent forge, there were also two others in the area.

Best Beech Forge and Wheelwrights
This was owned by the Gallups, and had been in the family since around 1845. The site of the forge was where Eaton's Garage stood, until it was developed for housing a few years ago. During the War years, trade was good, and many working horses went there to be shod. Apparently when the forge at Frant closed at the beginning of the War, horses from there made a cross-country trip to Best Beech. After the War, trade fell off with the demise of the working horse, and as the last Gallup had reached 70 years of age, the business closed around 1950.

Cousley Wood Forge
This forge was also owned by a member of the Gallup family - George, who was the eldest son of Frank at Best Beech. He took over from a Mr Ballard who died in 1914, so, at the outbreak of the Second World War, he was already in his mid-60s. He was a farrier and a blacksmith and was kept busy. He was known as 'old Gallup' by the locals, and could be seen working at the anvil until the forge finally closed shortly after the War.

The forge building still stands today, almost opposite the Old Vine, in the garden of the very attractive Ketley Cottage, which was moved from Rosemary Lane, Flimwell, when the reservoir was built. George Gallup's house was Elder Cottage next door.

There was also a wheelwright's shop in the triangle of Newbury Lane, also opposite the Old Vine.

The Cousley Wood forge [Bocking Collection]

It is not known whether George had a business connection with this shop, but they must certainly have worked together.

SOURCES

Rodney Bassett papers: East Sussex Record Office, Lewes
Sheila Waghorn. Personal photos.
The High Weald in Old Photographs: Harwood, B [1990],
      Alan Sutton Publishing

The Best Beech forge in earlier times   [early postcard]

*To mark the 40th Anniversary of the Dieppe Raid, this commemorative plaque was
unveiled at Newhaven Fort*
[Gote House Publishing]

Chapter 10: Canadian Forces in the Wadhurst Area

Martin Turner

This chapter tells something of the story of the troops and particularly the Canadian troops stationed in the Wadhurst and Tidebrook area from 1941 until the D-Day landings in Normandy in June 1944. In addition to information from official and published sources, it draws upon a number of eyewitness accounts from those living in the area at the time.

Background

With the dawning of the Second World War, Dominion troops once again fully supported the mother country, as they had in the First World War. The first convoy of Canadian troops docked in Liverpool on 19th December 1939 and they were followed by the initial squadron of the Royal Canadian Air Force on 25th February 1940. The USA did not enter the war until after the attack on Pearl Harbour on 7th December 1941. Thus, until Germany attacked the Soviet Union in June 1941, Canada was Britain's principal remaining ally. Records indicate that 500,000 Canadian Armed Services people served part of the War years in Britain.

COME ON CANADA !

The vast majority of Canadian soldiers who passed through Britain were volunteers, but why did they do it? In the early days few would have felt that Canada was directly threatened. The horrors of the First World War were well-documented and would have been vividly described by fathers and uncles. Some men would have volunteered because of family ties with Britain; others for idealistic reasons. There would have been those who joined because their friends had done so. No doubt some wanted to test themselves. Many could have been seeking adventure overseas and others might have sought escape from boring jobs or unemployment. In any event, the Canadian Army played a key rôle in the War and Britain was extremely fortunate to have had them on its side.

The arrival of the Canadians in Wadhurst

In mid-1941, the First and Second Canadian Divisions exchanged rôles with a British Division protecting part of the Sussex coast against German invasion. The first Canadian Troops arrived in the Wadhurst area at the end of 1941. During the period from then until the Canadian troops finally departed in 1944, elements from both Canadian Divisions came to the Wadhurst area at some time.

Prior to the arrival of the Canadians, a number of British units were billeted in the parish but there was a rapid turnover: as one unit moved out another moved in, sometimes for periods as short as three months. The South Wales Borderers were stationed in the area for a brief period when they came to provide defensive lines along the River Rother in preparation for a German invasion after the evacuation of Dunkirk on 27th May 1940. This deployment had taken place between 26th May and 4th June 1940. 13 Motor Coach Coy RASC stayed at Wadhurst Hall in 1940 long enough to have a formal unit photograph taken [see p. 204]. The 5th Loyal North Lancashire Regiment was stationed in the area from 11th July to 27th October 1940. They were succeeded by the Royal Scots Fusiliers who were initially billeted in Sharnden Manor. In February 1941 they were moved to Wadhurst Castle where they stayed until they embarked for Durban in South Africa in February 1942. Their stay therefore overlapped briefly with that of the Canadians.

The first Canadian regiment to arrive in Wadhurst was the 8th Canadian Reconnaissance Regiment. Contemporary records indicate they were in the area before Christmas 1941. Local resident, Roma Ogilvy Watson, has recounted that some of the officers had been invited to Christmas lunch by her mother.

The Canadian unit that stayed for the longest time in Wadhurst was the Saskatoon Light Infantry, which arrived in August 1942 and left on 14th January 1943. The Battalion Headquarters was established at Wadhurst Castle and the rest of the battalion was billeted in requisitioned houses within a five-mile radius. Other Canadian units stationed in Wadhurst at some time included:

> The Royal Regiment of Canada
> The South Saskatchewan Regiment
> The Toronto Scottish
> The Irish Regiment of Canada
> A French Canadian unit, probably The Fusiliers du Mont Royal or possibly The Royal 22nd Regiment
> The Algonquin Regiment
> The 85th Canadian Bridge Company Army Service Corps.

In addition to the Canadians there was also a small American Specialist Air Force unit based at Buss's Green Farm, Cousley Wood, for a short period.

Germans examine a Canadian Churchill Tank after the Battle of Dieppe
[Canada: Dept. of National Defence]

Two of these Canadian units had suffered major losses during the ill-fated Dieppe Raid [*Operation Jubilee*] on 19ᵗʰ August 1942 in which Canadian forces played the major part. 174 men (about one third of the total strength) of the Royal Regiment of Canada were killed. Many others were either wounded or captured. The South Saskatchewan Regiment lost 71 men in the raid.

Altogether nearly 5,000 soldiers of the Second Canadian Division and 1,000 British commandos had been landed on the coast of occupied France as part of Operation Jubilee - the only major Combined Forces' assault on France prior to the Normandy invasion of June 1944. Despite air support from Allied fighters and bombers and a naval fleet of 237 ships and landing barges, the raid was a disaster. Of the 6,000 troops landed, over a thousand were killed, of whom 907 were Canadians. A further 1,874 were captured. Only 336 of the 2,210 who returned to England came back unharmed.

Two Canadians were recognised with the Victoria Cross for actions at Dieppe: Lieutenant Colonel Merritt of the South Saskatchewan Regiment and Honorary Captain John Foote of the Royal Hamilton Light Infantry.

The value of the Dieppe Raid is a matter of some controversy. Some historians feel that it was largely because of Dieppe that the Allies decided not to attempt an assault on a seaport in their first invasion of occupied western Europe; others would point to the large number of amphibious operations before and after Dieppe as evidence that nothing new was learned there. In any event, the Dieppe Raid illustrated the absolute necessity of close communications in combined operations.

Location of the Canadian Units in the Wadhurst area

Troops were billeted in at least 23 different houses in the Wadhurst and Tidebrook area. There is no evidence to suggest that any troops were accommodated in tents. Units were constantly on the move as different deployments and manoeuvres took place and often they were moved after three months or so, sometimes even less. It is quite probable that units were moved around as often as they were, to prevent boredom, to test map reading (all the signposts were taken down during the War) and to test ration supply problems. There was even an instruction that rations should be picked up at night to get the Quartermaster and drivers used to night work. Moving so often and relocating to new billets was seen as good practice for the forthcoming mobile War that would follow the D-Day invasion.

Knowledge of which units were located in each location is incomplete. The War Diaries of units usually show where the Headquarters were billeted but rarely give the requisitioned houses used by sub-units. The information available on the houses used and their possible occupancy is summarised in Table 1.

Table 1: Houses in the Wadhurst and Tidebrook area occupied by Canadian troops 1941-1943

Location	House (s)	Occupancy
Tidebrook	Tidebrook Place, Sharnden Manor	Tidebrook Place was occupied by the Royal Regiment of Canada in 1942
Station Hill	Marling House, Puck Hill, Highfields House (later Wadhurst Conference Centre), Burwood	Burwood for some of its occupation was used as the soldiers' canteen
Partridges Lane	Riverhall	Mention is made in the Saskatoon Light Infantry War Diaries for October 1942 of Riverhall being used as the men's mess but this may not have been for very long
Faircrouch Lane	Faircrouch House	Probably only occupied as an Officers' Mess
Mayfield Lane	Kirkstone, Westwind	No details known
Best Beech / Tidebrook Road	Broadfields, Gill Wood	No details known

Location	House (s)	Occupancy
Mark Cross Road	Beechlands, Saddlers	No details known
Wadhurst Castle and Lodge	The Battalion Headquarters of the Saskatoon Light Infantry were at Wadhurst Castle from August 1942 until January 1943. The Irish Regiment of Canada was at the Castle from 17th March to mid-May 1943 [and see below]	
Wadhurst High Street	'The Olde Tuck Shop' (now the Post Office)	'The Olde Tuck Shop', run by Mrs Keen and Miss Hawkins, was requisitioned as an issue point for the daily supply of food for outlying requisitioned houses
Lower High Street	Moseham, Highfields, Uplands (a large residential house later demolished)	According to Peter Wicker, the Algonquin Regiment were billeted 'all over'. In addition to Wadhurst Castle they occupied Highfields and Uplands
Churchsettle Lane	Olives Manor	No information available
Cousley Wood	Buckland House	Buckland House was occupied for a period by a French Canadian unit. Used as a vehicle repair centre for some time and later accidentally burnt down by the Canadians

Table 1 [cont]

* Notes: *Wadhurst Hall also functioned as a prisoner of war camp at various periods during the war for both Italian and (later) German POWs.*

Captain H C Payne of the Regiment was billeted at Round Oak with Mr Llewelyn Jones who then owned Round Oak. Other known occupants of the Castle at some time were the Toronto Scottish and the Algonquin Regiment.

An interesting question is what happened to the owners of the requisitioned houses in Wadhurst. It would appear that most moved away. At least no record has been found of them continuing to live in their houses, although, in other areas of the country, it was not unknown for owners to continue living in a small part of their house.

The life of the Canadians in Wadhurst

The life of the Canadians in Wadhurst was typical of the Canadian troops in Sussex. There were periods of toil and arduous training exercises and also periods of frustration and inactivity. The tragic experience of the Dieppe raid cast a dark shadow.

Some insights on the life of these troops and their relationship with the community in which they found themselves can be gained from a study of Canadian official records such as Unit War diaries, and contemporary diaries - notably the 1942 diary of the Tidebrook resident and author, Miss Editha Blaikley. The recollections of those who lived in Wadhurst during the War years have also been valuable. Some of what follows is based on interviews with Nora Manktelow who was a teenage girl during the War years and who worked as a land girl at Buckhurst Place [*now demolished*] from 1943 onwards. Norman Gingell, Nora Tweedley, Walter Hodder and Ken Jones also contributed some of their memories.

Table 2: Excerpts from the Saskatoon Light Infantry Battalion Standing Orders

Reveille	0615		Supper	1715
Breakfast	0700		Retreat	1800
First Parade	0800		Roll Call	2245
All offices open	0800		Lights out	2300
Dinner	1215	(On Sunday both Reveille and Breakfast were an hour later)		
* Gardens of all Requisitioned Properties are out of bounds				
* No general sleeping-out passes will be granted				
* A maximum of one 48-hour pass every three months together with one week-end pass from after duty (1200 hrs) Saturday until 2359 hrs Sunday per month may be given				

Military matters and manoeuvres

An indication of the routine life of the soldiers can be gained from the Battalion Standing Orders shown in Table 2. As would be expected, there were regular parades and inspections. For example, the Unit War Diary of the Saskatoon Light Infantry records that on 13th November 1942 Mr J W Estey, Attorney General of Saskatchewan, inspected the Battalion on parade on Wadhurst cricket ground accompanied by Major General Salmon of 1 Canadian Corps. Ten days later, the diary records that a Battalion march past took place in front of the Rock Robin with the 1 Canadian Division Band.

The troops were regularly engaged in training exercises and military manoeuvres and these inevitably impinged on the local community, as Editha Blaikely's lively diary entry for 26th May 1942 illustrates:

The night was rather disturbed by manoeuvre noises - explosions like trench mortars between midnight and 1.0 am. And after that much traffic on the road. The activities increased during Whit Monday. Two soldiers came and asked for bread saying they were cut off from supplies and hadn't any food for several hours, so Annie gave them a small loaf which was rather hard to spare as we were a little short. Later two more soldiers came, wanting a wash so Annie gave them a tub of cold water outside and expressed the hope that they didn't want to strip too far!

Four or five enormous tanks rattled down the road scattering lumps of mud as they went. In the morning we found that the army had been all over Tidebrook and had damaged some of Gilbert's fencing (not maliciously). The explosions we had heard were the signal of the blowing up of Tidebrook bridge at the foot of the hill. All today there has been a half barrier there with a notice "this bridge has been destroyed". Soldiers walked all around my cottage and in and out of the front gate, and leaned against the railings or stood along the hedge across the road awaiting fresh orders. One, leaning against the railing, said he had been hit and that his helmet being off was a sign that he had been killed. " If you were a casualty we might help you," I said, "but if you have been killed there is nothing to be done". He laughed and agreed to that. One of them told Annie that she had been helping the enemy yesterday. We didn't know the difference as all were in khaki of course, but he said the enemy had nets over their helmets. The Canadians it appeared were being defeated and pressed back to the coast.

> *The Westons were also rather annoyed because yesterday the soldiers had gone across their ground and done some damage. On being asked whether they couldn't keep to the path they said they went where the officer led. After all it is war, and going straight for their objective is no doubt good practise [sic].*

Her entries for June show that members of the local community were sometimes involved in a supporting role (e.g in manning canteens) and that exercises sometimes involved the local Home Guard:

> *June 7th. Yesterday we started the canteen at Sharnden House for 350 men, Canadian troops and Home Guard who are doing some biggish practise together this coming fortnight.*

> *June 14th. Yesterday was a tremendous day for the Canadians at Sharnden who were going to put the Home Guard through their paces with live ammunition. There was a great rally of Home Guard from Tidebrook, Mayfield, Wadhurst, Frant and I suppose Mark Cross. These included local cadets, some of them charming and eager boys of about 14.*

> *June 17th. This afternoon I went up to the canteen at Sharnden, we had a pleasant busy afternoon. The Canadians are very grateful and we like them. They say they haven't been so well looked after since they left Canada.*

Nora Manktelow remembers manoeuvres taking place at Wadhurst Hall:

> *I do recall manoeuvres up at Wadhurst Hall. I used to go up there by bicycle and have a swim in the lake - it was my only way of having a swim. The troops used to come and have pretend invasions (not while I was there!) with landing craft. They used to throw explosives into the water and when I went down swimming all these fish would be dead on top of the water. Why I never had any trouble, I don't know, but I never did.*

After Norman Gingell came to Earlye Farm in 1942, he could not remember the Canadians exercising or doing manoeuvres over the farm, although it seemed probable that they might have done prior to his arrival, since there were gaps in hedges large enough for a tank to have gone through. He said that there had been a small 100-yard range at neighbouring Lightlands (Grid Reference 596334) and you could still see the bank into which they fired.

The extent to which the local population had knowledge of the involvement of the Canadians in military actions against the Germans is open to question. For example Nora Manktelow does not recall being aware of the Dieppe Raid taking place but Editha Blaikley was clearly aware as her diary entry for 19th August 1942 [*the day of Operation Jubilee*] illustrates:

> *While I was having breakfast this morning Mrs Haffenden came across to let us know (our wireless being worn out) that if we heard great noises there was to be a raid on . I gather the Commando raid involved all services.*

Relationship with the local community

The Canadian troops appeared to have made every effort to forge good relations with the host community. For example, they were sensitive to the issue of food rationing. An instruction in the Battalion diary of the Saskatoon Light Infantry stated:

> O.C.s [*Officers Commanding*] will ensure that when on the march or in convoy, troops are forbidden to fall out for the purpose of entry to shops of any town or village in which they are stopped. (This can mean) that no supplies are then available to the inhabitants. Conduct of this nature is not only a breach of march discipline, but is also calculated to damage the good feeling which should exist between the army and the civil population.

Contacts with the local inhabitants were fostered through such events as church parades and, less formally, by entertainments and dances. According to the Battalion diary of the Saskatoon Light Infantry, church parades for the 1000 hrs Sunday Service in Wadhurst Parish Church were fairly regular. An example entry on 17th September 1942 reads 'Church Parade at 1000 hours for Battalion HQ, B and D Companies'. Church parades to Tidebrook Church were also arranged, but far less frequently. Editha Blaikley noted in her diary on 10th May 1942 that as she entered church she was confronted by "*rows and rows of Canadian soldiers*". On 16th August she noted that "*there was to have been a church parade of several hundred Scottish Canadians at Tidebrook at*

10 am. But the weather was so bad that their Colonel wouldn't let them come so far."

There are many references to dances and other entertainments arranged either by or for the Canadians and the locals. The following quotations give some impression of their nature:

> *Concert party featuring local talent given by Mrs Llewelyn Jones for the troops, in the village hall. Supper for officers after at local pub. All officers detailed to attend – show fair, food fair, artistes fair (Battalion diary entry, 8th October 1942)*

> *A group of officers attended a dance at Wadhurst Hall organised by 1 Canadian Division Ammunition Company (Battalion diary entry, 21st November 1942)*

> *I remember dances at Wadhurst Hall and other places too. The Canadians used to send a lorry down to pick us up (Nora Manktelow)*

> *I remember a time when the Saskatoon Light Infantry were in Wadhurst Castle, I went to a Christmas party there once (Nora Manktelow)*

> *The dances were great, someone made tea and we had buns. They were mainly Canadians but I do remember some fisticuffs with the Canadians and the French Canadians (Nora Manktelow)*

> *We used to have wonderful dances with Mr. Gobles (sic) and his Band. Mrs Gobles was one of the members and someone on the violin. I suppose there were five of them altogether. It was one shilling a night entrance fee, they played from 7 to 10 and we never stopped dancing (Nora Manktelow)*

Some Wadhurst and Tidebrook residents were involved in running canteens for the troops. There were canteens at several sites. The canteen at Sharnden has been mentioned in the previous section. Nora Tweedley remembers the Salvation Army Hall [*which was next to the present Primary School before being demolished*] being used as a canteen, run for troops only, by the WVS and serving tea, coffee and cakes made by the ladies. St George's Hall, the Drill Hall and the Best Beech Hut were also used for this purpose. Local women also helped with laundry. Nora recalls helping her mother do the laundry at the Castle Inn on Station Hill for Canadian officers billeted at

Faircrouch. She remembers that soap was not rationed and that they were paid weekly. Not all their laundry was done at the Castle Inn: Lou Skilton - as a married lady - washed the officers' underwear, brought to her at Rock Robin Cottages in a pillowcase by a batman; her unmarried daughter Nora was, however, allowed to do the ironing!

There are many reports of the favourable impression created by individual Canadian soldiers. One of Editha Blaikley's first encounters with a Canadian soldier is described in her diary entry for 10th March 1942:

> *I went out to leave knitting wool at Sharnden Lodge for Mrs Pomfret and her friend and was challenged at the entrance to Sharnden House by a Canadian soldier. He was gentle and apologetic about it and, when I passed him again on my way back, explained that the adjutant had just ticked him off for letting a gentleman pass in a car without question. I told him I was glad that he had not asked for my identity card as I had left it at home and he assured me that was all right. This is a fresh detachment and every unit has its own orders and practices about sentry work etc.*

In later entries, Editha Blaikley regrets that the presence of the Canadians had ruined the drive of Tidebrook Place due to the heavy regimental traffic but was at pains to stress that no reflection was intended on the soldiers. She went on to state that "*individually I have found Canadians very well-mannered and discreet*".

When Norman Gingell was working at Earlye Farm in 1942, soldiers from the Saskatoon Light Infantry were staying at nearby Riverhall. He recalls that some of them had been good friends and that some had come in for cups of tea on occasions and to play cards. Nora Manktelow remembers that the Saskatoons were real country people who loved helping with farming and used to help with the hop-picking.

The generosity of some soldiers was also commented on. Nora Tweedley remembers the large numbers of scarves, balaclavas, gloves and socks sent to Canadian troops by their relatives. Because there were far more than they required, the surplus was sometimes donated to local people.

Some strong attachments developed between Canadian soldiers and local girls. As early as 17th June 1942, Editha Blaikley was noting in her diary that:

> *.... many of them are marrying English girls. I trust these are all well authenticated as bachelors! Miss Sands is marrying one on Saturday.*

Nora Manktelow recalls that " *it was quite the done thing to get married to a Canadian and quite a few did*". At least half a dozen of her friends married Canadians and went to Canada after the War. However, although some of these marriages proved happy, some did not. In some cases budding relationships had a tragic end. For example, a land girl living with Walter Hodder's family in Tidebrook had a Canadian boy friend who was killed in the Dieppe raid.

Records indicate that overall some 40,000 British/Canadian marriages resulted and that between 7,000 and 8,000 former Canadian armed services personnel settled in Sussex after the War. In addition, not surprisingly, there were many transitory relationships and flirtations. The following light-hearted reminiscences of Nora Manktelow illustrate this:

> *I remember an amusing incident when I went to a dance in Tonbridge with one lad. When we got to the station to come back the ticket man said the train for Wadhurst was the second train in. We got on the platform and there was a train there, so we counted that as one and got on the next train: we finished up at Ashford! My mother and father were, of course, doing their nut, they did not have a telephone. He wrote a nice letter to my parents apologising and he received a week confined to barracks. I did not keep up with any of the soldiers - they could have been married or anything. We did not have any trouble, nobody was being burgled nor girls being raped or anything. Occasionally a person got pregnant but maybe that was their own fault.*
>
> *Then we had the Toronto Irish, they were here a long time and were in Wadhurst Castle with the Lodge as the guard room. They wore a green gingery-coloured kilt. I knew the man working in the Quartermaster's Stores and I brought him home to my Mum and Dad, as you do. One day he said "if I get you a nice joint of meat could you cook it for us for a Sunday lunch?" My mother said "yes", of course, and he used to*

bring along tins of sardines and milk and things that you couldn't get. Mother was over the moon. Sitting round having this Sunday lunch they called for milk. We did not have anything like that, only had water at the table. The Toronto Irish wore a beret with a feather in it and these lovely kilts. I was offered one of them and turned it down. I then saw another girl wearing one and thought why the heck did I do that!

I used to have a Canadian boy friend called Smokey; he was a despatch rider. He was lovely he was: he looked like Clark Gable with a little moustache. I can't remember what regiment he was in.

One of the boy's mothers wrote to me from Canada; they hoped we were going to get married and they were getting a 'hope chest' together. I thought what was a hope chest? Anyway once they went away that was it. In the war years it was 'Hello' and 'Goodbye'.

Nora eventually married in 1949. Her husband was in the RAF and had returned to Britain having served in the Far East. They met at a dance in Lamberhurst.

Problems and accidents

Although the Canadians were generally liked and established good relations with the inhabitants of the Wadhurst area, their sojourn was not without a few problems. Occasional reports of misdemeanours by Canadian troops appeared in the Battalion diary of the Saskatoon Light Infantry, for example:

Two soldiers were charged with burglary and were sentenced to 12 months' imprisonment with hard labour.

One soldier was charged with indecency and sentenced to three years' penal servitude.

A soldier absent without leave for 21 days 2 hours and 40 minutes was awarded one year's detention.

Two soldiers were tried for disclosing the location of certain military units - *"an act calculated to imperil the success of part of His Majesties* [sic] *Forces."* Both were sentenced to two years' imprisonment.

There were clearly tensions between the Canadians and the French Canadian forces. Nora Manktelow, as we read before, remembers *"some fisticuffs"* between the Canadians and the French Canadians at local dances. Ken Jones, who was living in Wadhurst until being called up in 1943, has vivid memories of this animosity:

> *We soon began to see the differences between the French Canadians and the others. There were fights between units in the High Street when windows were broken in the Queen's Head and blood was spilled. This was after I was called up to the RAF in November 1943. I understand that the French Canadians were banned from Wadhurst thereafter. My father was the signalman at Wadhurst Station throughout the War. The last train on Saturday nights was always a problem with most of the soldiers well-inebriated and the collection of tickets a hopeless task. The French Canadians were the worst to deal with and in the end lorries with Service police met the train. My father said he had never seen such treatment meted out by those police. Admittedly many of the soldiers were fighting drunk. The use of the revolver butt was commonplace and the men bundled into the lorries to go to Wadhurst Hall.*

During their stay in Wadhurst some of the Canadian troops suffered serious illness due to food poisoning as Editha Blaikely recorded in her diary entry for 28ᵗʰ May 1942:

> *This morning we were sorry to hear at the post office that a large number of soldiers had been taken ill from ptomaine poisoning (from fishcakes made from tinned salmon) over a hundred being taken to hospital and I think more than 20 were dying. Poor Miss Weston's kind heart was wrung by the sight of one of them in pain, and asked an officer who came whether she couldn't give him a cup of tea, the officer himself looked ill but said that she musn't give them anything as they were on iron rations! I do think that is carrying it too far. A man dying of ptomaine poisoning is no case for iron rations. I believe these are Canadians who we have been told are the enemy. (The soldiers were taking the part of "the enemy" in an exercise at the time).*

Sadly, there were also accidents involving the troops that had tragic consequences for members of the local community.

The author's grandmother, who lived in Lower Cousley Wood, was killed in 1942 by a Canadian soldier on a motorcycle. She had been visiting and found she was a bit early for the bus home, so decided to walk one stop closer to save a penny on the fare. She was waiting at the Balaclava Inn [*now Dobbin's Inn*] when two Canadian soldiers on motorcycles approached from the Cousley Wood direction. The first turned right to go down Balaclava Lane, not realising that the second motorcyclist was overtaking him at the time. They collided with each other and skidded into my grandmother waiting for her bus.

Troops in Wadhurst after the departure of the Canadians

All the Canadian troops had left the Wadhurst area well before D-Day. Some, such as the Saskatoon Light Infantry, had moved to Crowborough. Although the Canadians had left, Wadhurst was far from deserted. As Nora Manktelow remembers:

> *During the build-up to D-Day we never ever had a dull moment because not only were the regiments coming and going .... thousands of troops not just a few hundred - thousands. Tanks and lorries going right through the village all night long being parked up George Street and us going out with tea for them, they didn't drive over the fields just going from A to B.*

The last troops to be stationed in the Wadhurst area were Royal Artillery Light Air Defence Units armed with the Bofors Light Anti-Aircraft Gun and with searchlight support. The guns were sited during the time of the V1 attack on England which commenced in June 1944. Two were positioned in a field west north west of Downgate in the Parish of Tidebrook at GR610299. There were two other light anti-aircraft sites in the Wadhurst area: one about 200 metres south of Pennybridge (Grid Square 6130) and one at about 300 metres east of Earls Farm (Grid Square 5930). However the Bofors was found not to be very effective against the V1 which flew at between 2,000 and 3,000 feet, at the very top height of effectiveness for the Bofors. The guns were withdrawn after a short time. There was also a Searchlight Unit in Snape, close to Foxes Bank Farm during this period.

So we can see, from the eye witness accounts recorded in this chapter, that the Canadian troops living amongst the Wadhurst community were well-received.

It is surprising considering the pressures that the troops were under, so far from home and very often with not enough to occupy them fully, that there was apparently little conflict, but on the contrary much appreciation, affection and respect. Troubles, when they did arise, seem to have been principally between the English- and the French-speaking men of that great country which came so quickly to the aid of Britain at such a critical period in its history.

SOURCES

No Soldier : The 1942 Diary of Editha Blaikley
The Maple Leaf Army in Britain: Longstaff-Tyrrell, Peter [2002],
Gote House Publishing Co
Canucks by the Sea: Ockenden, Michael [2006],
Eastbourne Local History Society
The War Diaries (WO179) held at The National Archives, Kew
under the name of each unit

Interviews with and/or letters from residents or past residents of Wadhurst including:
Norman Gingell, Walter Hodder, Kenneth Jones, Nora Manktelow, Roma Ogilvy Watson, Nora Tweedley and Peter Wicker.

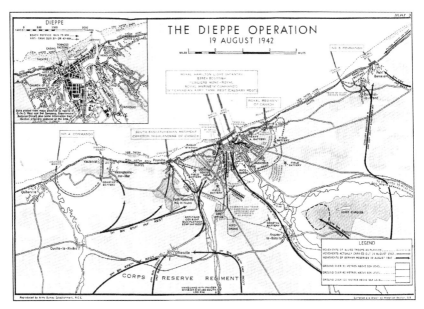

The Dieppe Operation 19th August 1942 [Canadian National Archives]

13 Motor Coach Coy RASC - Wadhurst Hall - 1940 [WHS]

CHAPTER 11: WARTIME MEMORIES OF A VILLAGE GIRL
ROSEMARY POPE

Early life

I am an only child born in Wadhurst in 1930. My father was the local carrier based at Wadhurst Station. He had taken the business in 1916 when my parents married and moved into the cottage near the station where I still live. My mother did not work outside the home after their marriage; she did my father's accounts and correspondence, helped in the garden and was very busy in the house.

I wish to set the scene of my childhood before considering the effect the 1939-45 War had on me and others living in Wadhurst. Like many cottagers we had a large garden mostly given over to growing fruit and vegetables. We were completely self-sufficient in vegetables but bought eating apples locally as a treat for Christmas. Mum, Dad and I worked hard in the garden and I was taught the correct way to use tools and harvest crops.

Looking back, I feel I had an idyllic childhood. Both of my parents encouraged me to do things with them (that was how I learnt to do practical things outside and in the house) and taught me about the countryside, wild life and farming.

However, compared with the way we live now, life and work were hard. Our rented cottage had no electricity or gas and one cold water tap in the scullery. All cooking and baking was done on the kitchen range which was fuelled by coal and some wood. The wood was obtained by cutting and clearing a patch of woodland on the nearby farm – with permission, of course.

Washday was usually Monday when the copper in the outside copper house was filled with water by hand, the fire lit and the clothes boiled. The clothes were then rinsed again by hand and finally put through the mangle [*a machine with two heavy rubber rollers through which clothes were passed*].

Ironing was managed with flat irons heated on the kitchen range. As we had no electricity, our lighting was by oil lamps downstairs, but I went to bed by candlelight.

Our bath water was heated in the copper and our baths taken in a large zinc bath. Our one toilet was 'up the garden' and I will only say it was <u>not</u> a flush.

Rosemary Pope's father's lorry outside Tappington Cottages 1938

I have mentioned that my father was the local carrier. There was very little motorised traffic in the 1930s and all goods for the local shops came by rail. My father was responsible for the delivery from the station to the individual shops – large sacks of flour, rice, dried fruit, sugar and cases of tinned fruit, golden syrup etc. This was heavy work and he also delivered the girls' trunks to Wadhurst College, in Mayfield Lane, and brought them back to the station at the end of term. Some of the builders and farmers had materials brought by rail but a few collected from the station themselves.

For entertainment, I saw a few films at the cinema in Tunbridge Wells before 1939, one still clearly remembered was 'Snow White'. Of course, we did not have television but one radio in our living room which was tuned in every evening at 5 pm. for Children's Hour with Uncle Mac followed by the News and Weather forecast at 6 pm.

This radio ran with an accumulator, we had two – one on charge at Mr C Baldwin's, the other in use. They were changed weekly; Mr Baldwin's shop was where Magpie and the Sandwich Shop are at present.

There were no other children living near by so I had few playmates although I do not remember being concerned about this. Occasionally my parents took me to Hastings for a day – travelling by train. My school holidays were spent playing in our large garden or going with Dad in his lorry delivering around the village. I really enjoyed this and I learnt about the isolated farms and many lanes in Wadhurst which otherwise I should never have visited.

I do not wish to give the impression that I had a 'deprived' childhood. This was the normal life style for a working family before 1939. In fact, my parents were fairly well-off compared with many local families. I have the accounts for my father's business in early 1930 and his profit was far more than a working man earned in a week. There was no National Health and no unemployment benefit and I can still remember local children during this period who suffered poverty, and mothers who wondered how to keep their families fed.

Conditions in the War years

Looking back this was the end of my carefree childhood. I was nine and a half at the outbreak of War and fifteen when peace was declared so a large chunk of my 'growing up' years was during the War. I clearly remember standing in our garden on 3rd September at 11 am. when the air raid siren sounded. It meant little to me but how did my parents feel? They had married during the First World War and many of their friends had lost their lives then.

At first in 1939 nothing much changed. A man visited us and issued identity cards (I still have mine) and also gas masks – horrid smelly things. The gas masks were in cardboard boxes and Mum made a case for mine from spare material. To start with everyone carried their masks everywhere – I carried mine to school – but I believe the general public soon got tired of this and finally only officials carried them e.g. ARP wardens and the police.

An official gas mask

I do not remember ration books being issued but it was certainly after the identity cards as your identity number was on your ration book. The ration books caused a slight problem to my parents as you then had to register with one retailer for your groceries. As my father was in business he had always used most of the retailers in the village for different goods supporting the businesses that supported him. We eventually registered with the International Stores. Milk was rationed and, as I was a child, I had extra. This was delivered daily. We registered with Ratcliff for meat and, if you were lucky, you could occasionally buy offal which was unrationed. Bread was not rationed until after the war; in 1947 I think.

The black-out was very strict and the local police and/or ARP would visit you

 if your house had a chink of light showing after black-out time. I think you were warned at first but if you repeated the offence, there was a punishment, a fine I believe. My mother lined the front room curtains with old curtain material and together my parents made shutters for our back rooms. A result of the black-out was that there were no street lights, all vehicles on the roads had tiny slit lights and torches were also limited to slit lights. However, small advantages of the black-out were that I learnt to walk around in the dark and I was able to enjoy the night sky and moonlight.

There were very few vehicles on the road, just a few commercial lorries and vans which were issued with limited petrol, coloured red. This was meant to prevent you using it for your private car. Most people walked or cycled and some farmers/smallholders had their own pony and trap to travel to the village. My father was allowed petrol for his business but it must have been very limited as I remember that on the hills round the local lanes he often 'coasted' the lorry. He was not the only one to do this. At some time during the War I remember females taking over the driving of delivery vans. The men had, I presume, been conscripted and goods were delivered by all grocers/bakers etc. The shop at Best Beech had a woman delivering at one time – there was no testing done during the War!

My mother was a very good cook and so all our meals, even after rationing, were satisfying and I never remember feeling hungry. We were self-sufficient in fruit and vegetables and adding veg. made the meat go further. The Sussex '10 to 1' pie was often used (10 pieces of veg. to 1 piece of meat) and covered with a pie-crust. We also harvested blackberries from the hedgerows, mushrooms from the fields and even chestnuts from the woods. Nothing was wasted. Oranges and bananas disappeared from the shops but very young children were issued with orange juice and/or rose hip syrup. Local people collected rose hips but I cannot remember who made them into syrup – was it the WI? My parents and I gave up sugar in our drinks for the War effort - this enabled my Mum to make about fifty pounds of jam each year from the fruit grown in our garden. (Strangely, I have not taken sugar in tea or coffee since.)

Preserving the fruit and vegetables we grew was a major part of life in late summer and autumn. Some fruit, like plums and wild blackberries, was bottled - that is put into Kilner jars, half sealed, then placed in large saucepans and boiled and finally tightly sealed. This certainly kept the fruit well but think of the pounds of blackberries picked by Mum and myself. Runner beans were salted down in a large crock, a layer of beans and then a layer of salt until the crock was full, and the final layer was salt.

I suspect it was illegal but my parents were asked by the retailer who supplied our groceries if we would take our entire ration in butter, instead of some butter and some margarine, as a certain local mother could not afford butter so wanted to take all of her family ration in margarine. This, I think, proves that there was poverty in Wadhurst during the War.

Clothing was obtained on coupons and my mother was constantly mending garments that today would be thrown away. Sheets were turned sides to middle, towels cut down to face cloths or dish cloths and adults clothes cut down to fit me. Utility was the label on all garments and furniture for no trimming or decoration was allowed. I can remember during the period just after the War when parachute nylon was suddenly available and the 'New Look' appeared, the teenagers (I was one) went mad with long very full skirts. During the War I believe hats were not on coupons and certainly photos of young women then often show them wearing hats. I was still wearing my school hats.

Coal was also rationed and our only cooking and heating fuel was for the kitchen range. However, during the winter when there was little gardening to be done, my father would clear a piece of woodland for the local farmer. Mum and I helped. This was hard work, especially when I had to get one end of a cross-cut saw and Dad was the other end. I feel country people must have managed in the War better than town dwellers with their gardens etc. Dad even caught an occasional wild rabbit, a delicious meal.

One amusing thing I remember: when there was a country-wide glut of a certain vegetable, extra good qualities in this food were discovered and widely advertised by the Ministry of Food. For example, it was widely advertised that carrots contained vitamin A and helped you see in the dark - which was very useful in the black-out.

I remember clearly that during the early part of the War all signposts were removed from roads and the names on railway stations, post offices etc were also taken down. This was to confuse the Germans if they invaded. It certainly confused the locals in unfamiliar areas or when someone was trying to discover which station they had arrived at – remember there was very limited lighting. Perhaps they then thought of the poster at most stations *"Is your journey really necessary?"* All local maps were to be handed in to the police. My father did not obey this order but our maps were well hidden. Consequently, I have some road/rail maps of 1920/30.

Certainly after Dunkirk there was a fear and expectation of an invasion and if any stranger asked directions he was suspected – was he a spy?

Specific conditions in Wadhurst and how they affected my life

Soon after the outbreak of War, evacuees from London arrived in the village and were billeted on local families. At last I had a playmate, Eileen, who lived with a family nearby and played with me on Saturday. There were several cases of diphtheria in the village around this period and a baby who lived in Dewhurst Cottages died. Rightly or wrongly, the evacuees were blamed for the outbreak. Later during the war immunisation was introduced. Many of the evacuees settled into the village well, like the Brockley Boys, but others returned to London finding life away from family too distressing. Also London was not attacked until Autumn 1940 so it felt as safe as Wadhurst.

Did we feel safe? After Dunkirk we had to cope with the 'Battle of Britain'. I overheard the porters at Wadhurst station discussing the trainloads of wounded and exhausted soldiers returning from France through Tonbridge but I never felt frightened. I believe my parents did a great job keeping my life as calm as possible and during the dogfights overhead in the summer of 1940 I watched with others, standing in the road or garden, cheering as a German plane came down in flames. That summer there were endless blue skies and the farmers were rushing to get in their crops, the hops and fruit being gathered all to the sound of the gunfire and screeching planes. We continued to work in our garden; Dad went round in his lorry often hindered by the display above. Sometimes machine guns were fired at the ground and I remember some chickens at the station being killed this way.

After the first summer came the winter and that to me was more frightening - maybe I realised more about the War. The drone of heavy bombers passing over most nights, especially in moonlight, kept you awake or even if you were asleep the explosion of a bomb dropped nearby would shake you awake. I remember the shock of waking when a bomb fell on Edge Hill and the lady, Mrs Carr I believe, lost her arm. I also remember standing outside our back door one night and seeing a vivid red glow in the sky. I was told that was the direction of London – I expect I remember the night as so much of London was destroyed by fire.

Life in the village went on – many of the young men were 'called up' so women took on some of their jobs. My father helped the local farmer gather in his hay and corn as there was no young labour. This work was done in the evening after my father's day work as a carrier. His carrier's work became disrupted – trains from London were often delayed or could not get through and a large warehouse at New Cross, owned by Sutton Carriers, was completely destroyed and never rebuilt. My father worked on commission for Sutton and, with the cut in railway traffic due to rationing, his income was much depleted. He did not get paid for helping the farmer but a load of manure would be put over our hedge in the winter.

I continued attending a small private school at Durgates, travelling by bus in both directions. My parents had planned for me to attend a larger school in Tunbridge Wells as I became older but the War made them decide that I would stay near them. This was also the reason that they declined my aunt's offer to send me to Canada – where she lived. These decisions obviously made a difference to my life. I could have been brought up with cousins in Canada or drowned, as one boatload of children crossing the Atlantic was sunk by U-boats [*the s.s. City of Benares – 17th September 1940*].

However, I had a special friend, Bernice, at school. She lived at Flimwell and we stayed with each other for weekends. Bernice's father was in the army stationed in Ireland. He died there from polio in 1941 and her mother went to Ireland leaving Bernice with us. Bernice did not know about her Dad's death and my parents told me - I suppose to prepare me for any difficult questions. One of my aunts had died a few months before so I was learning at a young age to face death. Just as well, because, in 1944, when Bernice and I were fourteen, she went to stay with an aunt and uncle in Snodland, Kent, for August Bank holiday and a doodlebug fell on the house and they were all killed.

Although Wadhurst was only twenty miles from the coast, travelling there was very restricted. I had three uncles and many cousins who lived in the Hawkhurst/Sandhurst area. Before 1939 we had visited them regularly but at the outbreak of War, unless you lived in Hawkhurst or farther on, you could not go over the Flimwell crossroads. There was not always a policeman there but you could not risk paying a fare through and then being turned back. It became easier as the risk of invasion decreased and my Dad was always allowed through because of his special police card. So for a long period I did not see my cousins and during that time many of them joined the Forces. I did not see the sea until 1946 when the coastline and the cliffs were still mined in places and festooned with barbed wire with many concrete barriers.

George Pope - with Police Special helmet, armband and whistle

I mentioned my Dad's special police card. He joined the 'Specials' in the 1920s and during the War went out one evening a week on patrol with Bert Norman who was the butcher in Gloucester Place. He was also expected to attend any incident if possible, e.g. any bombing, and always went to bed with his clothes neatly laid

216

out for a quick exit. Most men in the village who were above the age for 'call-up' were in the Home Guard, ARP or police and all had uniform.

Possibly the biggest effect on village life after the arrival of the evacuees was made by the soldiers who were billeted in many of the large houses. These included: Faircrouch, Marling Place, Burwood, Redgates, Highfields [*later Fryerning and then FTA*], Uplands, Riverhall, Wadhurst Castle, Wadhurst Hall, Olives Manor, Gill Wood and Buckland House. The latter was burnt down by Canadian or American soldiers by accident and never rebuilt. We had various English regiments who stayed for a brief period then moved on but the ones I remember most were the Canadians, both French and Scottish. The Scottish had a pipe and drum band and sometimes went on church parade from Wadhurst Castle. It made a welcome splash of colour.

Most of the soldiers seemed well-behaved although my parents caught some scrumping apples in our garden! Dances in the Commemoration Hall meant they could meet up with the village girls and some marriages followed. The Canadians were here from the end of 1941 and left in 1944 before D-Day. I went with my Dad to deliver something to a cottage in Wadhurst Park grounds and the whole length of the drive had piles of ammunition, bren gun carriers, tanks etc. hidden under the trees. My Dad had to show his police pass and I was only a child but my Dad said "*You are not to tell anyone what you have seen*" and until very recently I have not mentioned it.

While the soldiers were here they did manoeuvres, driving heavy tanks along our roads, which destroyed the surface, and setting up machine guns to practise firing. I had measles in the summer of 1943 and lay in bed with a feverish headache while guns were firing two fields away from the house.

1943 was a sad year for my mother; from before her marriage, she had a close friend who was a war widow from the 1914-18 war. She lived in Tunbridge Wells. Her husband was killed before their son Bert was born. Tragically, Bert went down in a submarine in the Med in 1943. My mother had knitted oiled socks and pullovers for him. After Bert's death, his mother hid herself away on Remembrance Sundays for the remainder of her life.

I have not mentioned if we, as a family, took any measures for safety. We did not have an air raid shelter, but Mum and I went under the stairs, sat on a large trunk and my Mum sang very loudly old choruses from her childhood. In the tin trunk were blankets and clothes – and my Dad buried in our garden a tin trunk containing birth certificates, savings certificates and lists of stocks and shares that my parents owned – to protect them from fire, I suppose.

In 1943 I left the private school in Durgates and transferred to a larger school in Tunbridge Wells travelling to and fro by train as we lived near the station. From there I won a scholarship to the Girls' Technical Institute at Tonbridge, starting there in April 1944 and again travelling by train. Shortly after joining the school we all had a really frightening day. The building was close to Tonbridge station, a tall ugly structure with cellars; it is now, I believe, the town library. On this day we were confined to these cellars for all the hours of school; normally we were allowed into the town during lunch hours. Nobody told us why we were confined and we read, sang and got more frustrated as the day wore on. The next day classes were as normal in the building and gradually we learnt that an unknown weapon had exploded in Kent early the previous day – this was the first 'doodlebug'. After that day we became accustomed to the sound of the doodlebug's engine above and the silence when the engine stopped, waiting for the explosion.

Dressed for 'Wings for Victory' 1943

During August of that year one fell and exploded on the railway line almost opposite our house. Some of our ceilings came down, three of our windows were smashed and a 'chair' from the rail landed on the gable end of our cottage and damaged the roof. No one was hurt. We often watched our airmen put the wing of their plane under the doodlebug when it was about to crash and turn it away from buildings into fields and woods or even attempt to shoot them down before they reached London.

Throughout the War Wadhurst held fund-raising days for the War effort. Adults and children dressed in costume, and there were games and fun activities. I remember one time called 'Wings for Victory' but cannot recall any other titles.

I have no memories of VE celebrations since, unfortunately, I was in bed with a sickness bug, feeling most annoyed. At some time around this time the church bells rang out, was it on 8th May or on Sunday? The bells were silent for the duration of the War as they were to be rung as the warning of an invasion.

My father retired in December 1945 and the following summer took me by train to Canterbury for my first visit. He had worked and lived near the city before moving to Wadhurst. It was the first time I had seen the damage bombs had inflicted on some of our local towns and it made a lasting impression. The cathedral still stood up over the city and I had the thrill of watching the Roman pavement being uncovered from the ruins of a cellar.

Although the War had ended, I remember the winter of 1947 being very difficult. We had heavy frost and snow for weeks, bread was rationed, coal was almost unobtainable as it was frozen at the pits and depression was nationwide. Not what had been expected after the troubles of wartime?

I apologise if any of my memories are inaccurate but it all happened a long time ago. Maybe this will stir up your own memories.

George Pope in his Police Special overcoat

8th June, 1946

To-day, as we celebrate victory, I send this personal message to you and all other boys and girls at school. For you have shared in the hardships and dangers of a total war and you have shared no less in the triumph of the Allied Nations.

I know you will always feel proud to belong to a country which was capable of such supreme effort; proud, too, of parents and elder brothers and sisters who by their courage, endurance and enterprise brought victory. May these qualities be yours as you grow up and join in the common effort to establish among the nations of the world unity and peace.

George R.I.

The message sent by King George VI to school children across the country at the end of the War

CHAPTER 12: THE IMPACT OF THE WAR ON WADHURST SCHOOL

DAVID JAMES

Background

Wadhurst School was one of three in the parish covering the ages five to fourteen. Its headteacher was Mr C B Mould. His colleague at Tidebrook was Miss Wadeson.

Wadhurst School House c 1934   [Margaret Muir]

Tidebrook School had opened in 1859 but was soon to face closure after the destruction caused by a flying bomb in August 1944. The Cousley Wood School, built in 1864, was under the headship of Miss Larcombe, and the small number of pupils would lead to its closure in 1949. It claimed to have the longest serving teacher, since a former pupil, Miss Funge, had joined the staff in 1898 and continued there until her retirement in 1947.

There were two other schools that were becoming established as European tensions increased following Hitler's election as German Chancellor in 1933. Miss Mulliner had founded Wadhurst College for senior girls in 1930 and their number rose to 162 during the War. Although the College was uncomfortably on the flight path of the Luftwaffe, she staunchly resisted thoughts of evacuation. The Sacred Heart School, also in Mayfield Lane, had its first intake of 11 children in 1935.

Cousley Wood—Sunday School group 1935/36
Photographic postcard by Cousins, of Camden Road, Tunbridge Wells
[Bocking Collection]

Wadhurst School itself was located in the Lower High Street at what is now the Youth and Community Centre extension of Uplands Community College. Almost all the children spent their whole school life at the school, but they had the option of taking examinations at the age of 11 for entry to selective schools in Kent. In June 1939, for example, John Ratcliff, Sidney Rumary and Derek Vidler were offered places at the Skinners' School, and Audrey Farley and Dorothy Styles qualified for the Tunbridge Wells Girls' Grammar School. Others transferred later to continue their education beyond the age of 14, like Jenn Hemsley who obtained a place at Tonbridge Technical School for Girls in 1947.

With two classes for the infants, taught by Miss Mould and Mrs Manktelow, and five junior classes, the school was very pressurised with 280 children. There were some 40 children in each class in very small rooms. The cramped conditions were not helped by poor heating. Molly Codd (*née Davies*), a pupil in the 1930s, remembers "*the large coal-fired stoves which didn't give out much heat. If you sat at the back of the class you froze.*" The problems continued. The School Log Book entry for 27th January 1943 declared: "*The stove smoked so badly in Standard IV that I had to send two classes out for a nature ramble*". At the end of January 1945 the school closed for a week as the lavatories were frozen and the coke supply was almost exhausted. The lavatories were often a source of complaint from the boys as they were in the open at the back of the playground, and consisted of slabs of slate with a gully that fed into a drain.

A move to Sparrows Green?

In the immediate pre-war years, there was much enthusiasm over the possibility of a move to a new school. The opportunity arose after the Hadlow Report of 1926 had recommended two stages of education, primary schools for children between the ages of 5 and 11, and secondary schools to cover ages 11-15. The Education Act of 1936 duly planned to raise the school leaving age to 15 in 1939 and authorised grants of 75% towards the cost of building church schools for senior pupils. By May 1937 the managers of Wadhurst School had determined to build such a school on the five and a half acre site at Sparrows Green corner. It would provide places for 240 pupils from the parishes of Ticehurst and Wadhurst, and it was estimated that it would cost £1,000 to purchase the land and a further £17,000 for the building. The Church of England was expected to contribute £5,000 and the local community agreed to help. A 'Two Day Sale' in the Commemoration Hall in November 1937 was opened by the Marchioness of Abergavenny and raised £300.

The Parish magazine for November 1938 gave the grim warning: "*After our experience last month* [the Munich Crisis] *we dare not leave to haphazard and last minute arrangements such matters as ARP and other precautionary measures*". It was balanced, however, by the exciting news that the Church was within £750 of its target figure and plans for the new building had been agreed and submitted to the Board of Education.

It was not to be. The shortage of timber during the War meant that the builders had gone as far as they could by April 1940. Furthermore the structure had suffered damage during the preceding month when four bombs struck Sparrows Green. June brought both the tragic news of casualties at Dunkirk and the sombre decision not to continue with the building beyond the recommendation to roof it over and to make it weatherproof. It became a store for materials that had been acquired already and was used for other purposes. Jenn Hemsley remembers it being a billet for firemen who needed a break from their experiences in the London blitz.

NOBODY WAS HURT when a bomb fell in a town in the South East.

The local press photo of the bombing, which damaged the new school during construction

Inevitably, wistful thoughts and frustrations continued to be expressed. In the October 1941 Parish magazine the Revd. E Mannering declared: "*All we can do at present is to use our imagination and see it, we hope, filled with nearly 300 children over 11, meeting at their Assembly in the fine hall and then moving off to the spacious and well-lighted classrooms and learning science and arts and crafts as well as the 3Rs .... organised games in the playground and in the playing fields. May the dream come true of a better school for the boys and girls of Wadhurst and the neighbouring villages."* In July the Diocesan Inspector, the Revd. Arthur Miles, prodding where he could, reported for the benefit of the authorities that *"with the hold up of the new Senior School the work of this school has to be carried on still in conditions which are not ideal for such large numbers".*

The December 1944 Parish magazine bemoaned that *"our present buildings have had to serve for all ages at a time when it seems impossible to get even repainting done and damage from blast has been incurred".* The wheels of progress, however, were beginning to turn again. Earlier that year, the Butler Act had determined three phases for education, primary, secondary and further, and confirmed the raising of the school leaving age to 15. This was implemented in April 1947 and the completion of the new school had become urgent. It opened as the new secondary school in 1949, with the recognition that it would become the centre for primary education as soon as a site for a new secondary school had been secured and developed.

Life at Wadhurst School

The structure of the school year was different from that in the 21st century, tending to close for the summer holidays in the third week in August and reopening a month later, to suit the needs of agriculture. However, this did not quite fit the season for picking hops, and the school Log Book for 20th September 1943 recorded that *"200 children are absent owing to hop-picking".* The LEA had had to grant a week's extension to the holidays in both 1940 and 1941 when so few children materialised at the start of term, *"thirty children only being present on account of hop-picking".*

There was no school transport and children walked to school. The long lunch break between the summer sessions (9 am. - noon, 1.30 - 4 pm.) enabled many children to return home for lunch. Frank Bishop remembers his mid-day walk to his home at the Old Vine, Cousley Wood, during the lunch break. Others took sandwiches, which had to be eaten outside unless it was raining, however cold it was.

1942

Wadhurst School Canteen Fund

AN

AUCTION SALE

IN AID OF THE ABOVE

will be conducted by

___

Mr. E. B. WATSON

in the

Hall of Commemoration, Wadhurst

at 2.30 p.m.

On SATURDAY, JUNE 6th

___

GIFTS INVITED, to be brought to the Hall
before 11 a.m. on Saturday morning.

COME AND BUY, and so help to provide hot
dinners for our Children next winter.

A change occurred in 1942. School milk had already been introduced, although families who could afford it were asked to pay a halfpenny for the third of a pint bottle. A meeting of the managers in January agreed to plan for the introduction of school meals. They had hoped that facilities could have been included in the Sparrows Green project, but instead agreed to fund a hut on the school field to serve as a kitchen. The meals would be eaten in the classrooms. The LEA would provide the equipment, the cost of overheads and the wages of the cook. The managers determined to raise £100 for the facility through private donation and an auction sale on 6th June.

Consequently the School Log for 2nd November 1942 recorded: "*Today the school canteen commenced. 215 children sat down at one sitting to a two-course dinner. It was successful. Eight to ten helpers come to the school each day at 12 - 12.30 pm. and serve out the meal. Mrs Cogger is the cook.*" However, Jenn Hemsley recalls that the attraction of this novelty on the first day meant that "*insufficient food had been cooked for everyone so they had to send out for bread to give to those without anything*". As the May edition of the Parish magazine had observed: "*At the present time the need for school dinners is all the greater because an extra ration of 1d a day of meat per child is allowed for this purpose*". The meals cost 4d a day.

Frank Bishop, whose school career straddled the schools at Cousley Wood and Wadhurst, remembers that "*children were taught basic reading, writing and arithmetic, using chalk and slates to write on*". Des Mansfield recalled Mr Mould coming into his class at least once a week to test the children's skills of mental arithmetic. It was not the era of rewards or gold stars.

> *He would tap you on the shoulder with his cane and ask "What are 7x7s?" or something similar, and if you gave him the wrong*

answer he would tap a bit harder until you gave him the right answer. We certainly learnt our times tables quickly, and have never regretted it since.

There were wooden desks with sloping tops and a hole in the right hand corner for the inkwell. As well as subjects like history, geography and physical education, there were different subjects for boys and girls. Mrs Newington took needlework lessons for the senior girls, who also joined others from Tidebrook and Cousley Wood for cookery, mainly baking, with Miss Knapp, all crowding round a single cooker. Meanwhile the boys learnt basic carpentry and joined the Headmaster for gardening at the school allotment.

1938 Wadhurst School Cricket team
l to r: back row : Mr MacQueen - Arthur Percy - Noel Carley - Vic Blake -
Gordon Miller - Fred Galloway
middle : Arthur Freeman - Charlie Thompsett? - Eric Barden - Ron Thompsett -
Donald Beeney
front : Freddy Hodges - Ron Thorpe   [Cosham Collection]

They played football on the field behind the church and cricket on the Institute field, while the girls' games comprised mainly stoolball and shinty.

The Muirs [caretaker's daughters] at play

Less formal games took place on the playground where girls enjoyed hopscotch and skipping. The boys were separated, often kicking an old pig's bladder which they had obtained from the local butcher, who still had an abattoir at the back of his premises. During the summer Mr Mould encouraged their cricket skills by placing a penny as a target on the dustbin that they used as a wicket.

The curriculum was enriched by Mrs Newington's music. A special concert had been arranged just before the War to raise funds for the new school building. The choir often travelled to festivals in the Pump Room at Tunbridge Wells, securing several prizes. There were also school trips, to the Aldershot Tattoo and to Hampton Court, and the children particularly enjoyed 'Maggie's Specials', the Sunday School treat which Mrs Manktelow arranged each year before the War, taking them by train to the beach at Hastings and including tea at Leacock's café.

Christianity lay at the core of the School. The vicar took Assembly each week, often choosing 'Hills of the North, Rejoice' as the hymn. The Diocesan Inspector in July 1943 noted that *"a delightful spirit and a very real sense of worship is developed"*. He was impressed by the Scripture lessons in each class. With the Infants he considered that *"excellent methods are used by the teacher with these little folk"*. With the Junior class III he found the teacher's *"lesson on the Wicked Husbandman aroused the interest and sustained the attention of her class"*. He cajoled the managers to provide more hymn books and prayer books to assist the spiritual development of the children.

Precautions during the War years

As early as 19th April 1939 Colonel W E Hume-Spry, the Honorary Organiser of the Air Raid Precautions Department in Battle, had written to the Director of Education at Lewes warning:

> *The chief danger we have to face in this district area, apart from spray, is the indiscriminate dropping of bombs by enemy bombers who cannot get through to their military objectives or who wish to lighten their machines in order to get away from our fighters. For all we know there may be at least 20 heavy bombers at any one period, each carrying 40 - 50 50lb bombs with some 800 - 1,000 of such bombs which they want to get rid of as quickly as possible and which they will drop wherever they happen to be passing.*

The ARP organiser in Wadhurst had already visited the school to give his initial thoughts to shape the managers' recommendations to the LEA. On 28th May 1940, immediately after the German blitzkrieg into the Low Countries and France, the School Log Book recorded that *"workmen have started putting wire-netting under the ceiling in all the porches in order to prevent plaster falling on the children in the event of a bombing attack – the children will be put in the porches which I consider much safer than the classrooms"*.

WADHURST SCHOOL children prepare to dig for victory. My picture from the past shows scholars of Wadhurst Voluntary Primary School with their headmaster, Mr C. B. Mould, all set for a gardening session at nearby allotments, during the early days of the last war

Wadhurst School 'Dig for Victory'
l to r back: G Pearce - A Hemsley - ?? - Arthur Lavender - Bernard Hemsley - John Cook - ?? - Mr C B Mould - Albert Turner - ??
seated: ?? - ?? - Ted Anscombe - Norman Elkins - Eric Avis - Don Buchanan
front: Len Hazelden - David Price - Edward Newick - Brian Hogden

[Courier]

The action was prudent as the 'Battle of Britain' soon followed. On 1st October *"the children went into the air raid shelters [porches] for three periods"*. Three days later they were in them again. For additional security on 16th July *"the gardening class have commenced digging trenches in the playing field. This is an extra precaution in case the school was hit."*

There were several other safety measures. In May 1940 the Government curtailed the week's holiday *"owing to expected air raids"*. Black-out curtains were fixed to all the windows in November 1941. The previous month a policeman had addressed the school *"on the dangers of picking up things dropped from aeroplanes"*. The Log Book for July 1943 reported that *"an ARP man from Lewes visited the school to show and give instructions on the German anti-personnel bomb. All gas masks have been inspected by class teachers."*

Schools were given guidance in the event of invasion. A letter from the Director of Education in July 1941 referred to the Board of Education's Memorandum No. 282 and informed headteachers *"in confidence that in the event of invasion schools should remain open unless and until authoritative instructions are received by them to the contrary"*. Despite Hitler's diversion to Russia in 'Operation Barbarossa', the threat of invasion remained sufficiently real in 1942 for the Director to issue a further circular in May (EE627), stating:

> *It is expected that there will be some period of warning before a threatened invasion, though this may not be possible, on which the order 'Stand to' will be given to the Army and the Home Guard. It is unlikely that schools will be closed during this period but transport facilities will be greatly restricted.*

Under such circumstances children and teachers were expected to report to the nearest school, and headteachers, in consultation with the chairmen of managers and *"other prominent local officers"*, could *"act very largely on their own responsibility"*.

Hitler's decision to launch V1 rockets in 1944 brought renewed danger. Just over a fortnight before the devastation at Tidebrook School, the Wadhurst Log

Book recorded that *"owing to Wadhurst School being in the 'Flying Bomb' area"* the authorities decided to offer voluntary evacuation to the children.

> *Twenty-three left this morning at 9 am. for an unknown destination in the West. Miss Larcombe accompanied the party; she should return in the course of a day or two. During the past fortnight the school has received damage from blast; windows, a ceiling and tiles have been broken.*

> *At a meeting of parents, under the chairmanship of the Vicar, it was agreed that the Headmaster's suggestion of installing electric bells in each room and having a rota of children acting as spotters to give the alarm so that children could shelter in the porches, was satisfactory. It was also decided that the school should adopt the times of school sessions as used during the winter, and this suggestion was forwarded to the LEA for approval.*

By the end of the month, five Morrison tables had been delivered and erected. The Director of Education's Circular No. EE687 of 12th July 1944 had given guidance on the protection of children from flying bombs. While Morrison tables would be provided for infants, *"for the remainder of the school the best protection that can be provided at present is for children to take up their 'shelter positions' immediately on the sounding of the spotter's warning"*.

Suggestions were also given for the digging of slit trenches.

Cousley Wood School - 'Salute the Soldier' Week May 1944
[Bocking Collection]

Other effects of the War

The school responded to the sense of community spirit that the War generated. £426 6s 2d was gathered during 'Salute the Soldier Week' in May 1944. Children were encouraged by the East Sussex Bulletin No. 55 to collect and dry medicinal plants with the warning that "*damage to growing crops should be carefully avoided and permission should be obtained beforehand from any farmers or other owners on whose land collecting expeditions are arranged*".

The arrival of evacuees in September 1939 added to the pressures of a congested school. There were 30 Infants, 37 Juniors, the Headmistress and eight assistants from Elfrida School, Lewisham. In addition 50 children came from elsewhere to stay with friends. By October they had been assimilated into the school's age groups instead of working as separate units, and the County had provided additional furniture. Each year a nurse and doctor from London would come to inspect the evacuees, and an official visited from time to time to check on numbers. East Sussex Bulletin No. 55 of 1942 provided guidance on how householders who were accommodating unaccompanied children could obtain a clothing entitlement for them. The evacuation provided other opportunities as well and, in July 1941, the senior boys challenged a team from Brockley County Grammar School to a cricket match.

The War disturbed the normal life of the school through the departure of staff on military service and the arrival of temporary replacements for its duration. Mr McQueen was called up to join the Army in April 1940. Mr Wood joined the Navy in November 1941, and Mr Keast became a member of the RAF base at Cardington in August 1942. They all returned safely to the school in the summer of 1946. However, military service continued to have an effect when Mr Brabben was called up in October 1946.

There were moments of great sadness. Several former pupils died on military service. The Parish magazine of September 1944, for example, recorded:

> The latest additions to our Roll of Honour are the names of James Willett and Leonard Manktelow. Both belonged to old Wadhurst families and were boys in our Day Schools, both sang in the choir, Leonard at the Parish Church, and Jim at Cousley Wood School. And

now both are fallen in Normandy and their untimely deaths are part of Victory.

There was also inspiration for the pupils. The July 1941 edition of the magazine had delighted in the news that the George Medal had been awarded to Rose Ede, recalling proudly "*that not so long ago she attended our Day School*".

The closing months of the War brought further changes. If the evacuation of 23 children to the West Country in the summer of 1944 had created some space in the school, it was filled very soon afterwards. Whereas he responded very willingly to the emergency, there was a certain wryness in the Headmaster's comment at the start of the winter term in 1945: "*Owing to Tidebrook School being hit by a Flying Bomb the children were transferred to Mark Cross School. As they were somewhat crowded there the LEA have decided to send them to this school.*"

The end of the War

The dangerous years were soon to be over. The School was closed on 8th and 9th May for the VE Day celebrations and again on 15th and 16th August for VJ Day. Mr Mould wrote feelingly in the School Log Book:

> *The war is over and danger to us at School is at an end. I thank Almighty God that not one of us was ever hurt, especially at that time when Flying Bombs were passing over the school and crashing round about during school hours. I thank Him for the courage He gave to the staff and myself that enabled us to carry on our school duties. I thank Him for the lives of the staff who enlisted and will now return safely to their duty in this school again.*

The children themselves could delight again in the pleasures of peacetime. On 18th July there was the first 'Maggie's Special' since 1939, and 450 children and parents played excitedly on the sand at Hastings. Their traditional café may have declared apologetically "*no staff, no food*", but things really were beginning to return to normal.

SOURCES

The Education of Wadhurst: Ascott, K F [1998], The Book Guild
Wadhurst, Town of the High Weald: Savidge, A and Mason, O
[1988], Meresborough Books
The Log Book of Wadhurst Church School
Wadhurst Parish magazines
ESRO documents of the Director of Education and of Battle RDC

The personal memories of local residents including:
Frank Bishop, Molly Codd, Jenn Hemsley and Des Mansfield.

CHAPTER 13: UNEXPECTED VISITORS
REFUGEES, EVACUEES AND PRISONERS OF WAR
MICHAEL HARTE

War, the threat of War, and its aftermath, brought unexpected visitors to our community. The Parish magazine for December 1937 records:

THE BURTT MEMORIAL HOME, WADHURST

The Children's Holiday Home has had a large number of little visitors since it was opened on September 25th of this year. It is very remarkable to watch the improvement in the children's health from week to week. A jolly, happy party of boys and girls enjoy themselves immensely both outside in the lovely grounds, indoors in their cheery playroom, and elsewhere in the house. At the moment of writing [November 16th], there are fewer children than usual, but probably Christmas will see their numbers increased once more, and the home full.

The love and care shown by Matron and staff is very evident, and a delightful welcome awaits any visitor who goes to see the home. Matron will be glad of warm clothing to fit children of the ages between 4 years and 12 years, also toys and provisions.

In 1933, Mary Hamlyn Whitty, of Dewhurst Lodge, died and the property was sold; in 1937 the big house became the Burtt Memorial Home. Mary was an active Christian and there is still a room in the old stables known as the Mission Room. As to the Burtt connection, the following is an extract from David Mander's book 'More Light, More Power - An Illustrated History of Shoreditch'.

Most notable among the nonconformists was the Hoxton Market Christian Mission. The founders, saddlers, John and Lewis Burtt, had themselves been rescued from the streets and educated in a Ragged School. They took children into their basement workshop and offered them shelter, warmth, food and second-hand clothes. With the help of members of Rectory Road Congregational Church in Hackney, the brothers started home visits, and five years after their work had begun, funds allowed them to acquire premises in Hoxton Market in 1886. Religious activity included meetings, a local Band of Hope and Bible classes. The Hoxton Market premises were rebuilt in 1904 and further enlarged in 1914. During the First World War the Mission played a strong social role in supporting families whose principal wage earners were in the armed services, and in the hard times of the post-war decades helped with assisted emigration; as well as feeding and clothing children. Replacement boots were a speciality, while the slogan 'Daddy Burtt's for dinner' became part of Hoxton folklore. After the death of the last of the Burtt brothers in 1937, a memorial home was opened at Wadhurst in Sussex, moving to Bognor Regis in 1948, giving convalescence space to sick children. In the Second World War the Mission helped to evacuate local disabled people, first to Hastings in East Sussex, then Malvern in Worcestershire, and finally to Heanor in Derbyshire. The Mission premises, gutted in an oil bomb fire on 10 May 1941, were rebuilt and re-opened in 1952. The Mission survived the creation of the welfare state and did not close until the early 1980s.

In the East Sussex Record Office [AMS5813/5 20 Mar 1623], there is a record of transactions dealing with Wadhurst almshouses, whereby Thomas Whitfeild [TW] of the Inner Temple, London gent conveys in trust

> to John Hatley clerk, vicar of Wadhurst, William Fowle, Thomas Saunder and Robert Wemborne gents, Alexander Butcher and William Weston junior yeomen, all of Wadhurst 3 dwelling houses with land in Wadhurst, 2 of which abutt E on Sparrowes Green, the third in or near Weeke quarter [*Shoesmiths and Woods Green*], inhabited by 2 poor couples In trust to place such poor persons of Wadhurst therein as they shall see fit, relatives of TW aged over 40 without dwellings to be preferred; inhabitants may be ejected (whether men or women) on becoming takers of woods and under-woods, common hedge breakers or trespassers in woods or otherwise notoriously wicked or scandalous in life or conversations. Trustees may appoint up to 3 of the principal inhabitants to maintain their number at 6.

One of the witnesses was a John Burtt. Was this link with the past why the home was set up in Wadhurst?

The home continued to operate through the War and in January 1943 the Parish magazine recorded:

> WADHURST YOUTH GROUP. The Group celebrated its first birthday in November after a successful year. During the past year they have given an Entertainment in the Commemoration Hall, also at Ticehurst and Best

Beech Hut. At the Burtt Memorial Home Fete in July they gave a display of Dutch and Maypole Dancing. .... A Pantomime is being held on January 16th in the Commemoration Hall, in aid of the Merchant Navy Comforts Fund. Please give this your generous support.

In May 1943:

BURTT MEMORIAL HOME. It is hoped to hold a 'Bring and Buy' Sale, probably on Wednesday, July 7th, during the afternoon. The Matron will be pleased to have contributions to the sale or gifts in kind for the Home.

That is the last mention of the Burtt Memorial Home in the Parish magazine.

Refugees

The next unexpected visitors also feature in the Parish magazine. In January 1939:

REFUGEES

As many already know a meeting was held in the Commemoration Hall on December 16th, at which it was unanimously decided to go forward with a scheme for housing a "Non-Aryan" Christian family in Wadhurst as a communal effort to deal with a tiny fraction of the wide-spread distress caused by this terrible problem. It should be clearly understood that the Home Office regulations, which must be fulfilled before refugees are allowed to land, are designed to ensure the interests of British workers. No refugee will be allowed in to take a job, for which a British worker is available, and an unlimited guarantee of maintenance has to be given by those who ask for a permit for a refugee to enter England. No doubt a certain number of refugees can be profitably absorbed in British industry, but for the great majority the time which they spend in England must be a time of preparation and waiting until they can be found new homes overseas.

In May 1939:
OUR GUESTS

Dear Mr Mannering,
We are anxious to express our deeply felt gratitude for all the kind and helpful assistance we have met with since we have come here. We came from a foreign country but we found friends here who had prepared a home for us at "Burwood" [*opposite Great Durgates in Station Road*]. And by making this home so comfortable and providing everything for us you have eased the grief we felt on having to leave our native country and our relations. We thank you and Mrs Mannering with all our hearts for your kindness. We also thank the committee that has taken responsibility for this

work of real Christian charity and we thank all the men and women who had a share in making this work succeed. But above all we are grateful to God who by His Holy Ghost has made the minds and the hands of men willing to perform a work of real brotherly love. "Unto Him be glory in the Church by Christ Jesus throughout all ages, world without end."

The occupants of "Burwood"
Pastor Karle and family; Edith Ehrhardt and family; Otto Frey.

All did not continue so smoothly for these refugees from Nazi Germany. In July 1940, the vicar had to report that they had all been interned in the Isle of Man:

"BURWOOD"
As most people already know Mrs Karle and Mrs Ehrhardt and their families had to leave Wadhurst on June 14th. Thus a piece of practical Christian sympathy for the oppressed came to an end after 15 months, and may be numbered among the casualties of war. We print two letters from Mrs Ehrhardt and Mrs Karle, which should be of interest.

"Burwood" June 13th

Dear Mr Mannering,
Would you say to all people in the parish that we thank them so much for all they have done for us! We are most thankful for this peaceful year in the beautiful house and garden. We are thankful to those who have worked for us and to those who have been kind to us, the strangers, and to those who dislike us as Germans for having borne us patiently. We are very sorry to leave Wadhurst that we have come to love. We hope and wish that it may remain the peaceful village even in these times. We hope and pray that this terrible war may soon be ended by a good and lasting peace.

With special thanks to you and to Mrs Mannering,
Yours very sincerely, E Ehrhardt.

"Elim Woodlands", June 18th.

Dear Mr Mannering,
Having come to a kind of rest now, I am able to thank Mrs Mannering and you and all the friends in Wadhurst for all your kindness. Now we have left it we know that we had a real home there, not as strangers, but as friends in a Christian community. We are kindly treated here and the children are enjoying themselves in the large garden. What will happen to us in the next days we do not know, but that is time for everyone to learn how to be patient.

Yours sincerely, Anna Maria Karle.

August 1942: VISIT OF PASTOR KARLE. The friends of Pastor Karle will be interested to hear that he will shortly be visiting Wadhurst. On Monday, August 10th, he will speak in the Methodist Schoolroom, where there will be an opportunity for all to meet him.

Despite the similarity in names, there is no connection between this Karle family and the family of Professor Paul Kahle, who lived in Wadhurst Park after the war.

The refugee-related entries continue:

October 1942: WADHURST FUND FOR REFUGEES. At a meeting of the Committee held recently the Hon Treasurer, Mr R Newberry, reported that there was a balance of nearly £145. It was unanimously decided that this should be handed over to the Committee responsible for helping Pastors and their families who were brought over before the war, as this was the purpose for which the money was subscribed.

Evacuated schools

During the Second World War, Wadhurst saw an inflow of evacuees - escaping the threat of Hitler's bombs. One large group came from Brockley School, Hilly Fields, London SE4. There is no mention of this in the Parish magazine but the School magazine - The Raven, published in April 1940 - records the following:

THE EVACUATION

Masters were summoned back to School nearly three weeks before the end of the Summer Vacation. Then came a strenuous week at School rehearsing manoeuvres for a probable evacuation. On Saturday, September 2nd, in accordance with instructions from the Council, some 300 boys, together with some 30 sisters and younger brothers, and some 30 masters and escorts, entrained at Ladywell Station for an unknown destination. Ordered to detrain at Crowborough, supplied there with two days' iron rations, thence conveyed by a fleet of motor-coaches to Wadhurst, Sussex, where we were received by the local billeting committee with cocoa and biscuits. Remainder of day occupied in distributing boys, sisters, staff and escorts to billets over a wide area. War declared next day (September 3rd). Next ten days busily occupied in attending to billeting difficulties and in organising improvised schooling. School opened on the advertised day for beginning of new term (September 13th) in three widely separated village halls - Hall of Commemoration, Best Beech Institute, St George's Hall - where limited time-table and curriculum have been pursued since.

After this start in Wadhurst, split between three sites, in 1940 those boys from Brockley School, who had not by then drifted back to Lewisham, moved to Oakover House in Ticehurst for the rest of their stay. Much more detail about their life in Wadhurst, and later in Ticehurst, has been provided by three boys from Brockley School - Bill Christmas, Don Henderson and Eric Clarkson. They each had a different view of local life and their recollections can be found in the Annex to this chapter.

In September 1939, Elfrida School in Lewisham, however, took a different approach. Their children were placed within our local schools. There were 30 Infants, 37 Juniors, the Headmistress and eight assistants placed in the Wadhurst School; to these were added a further 50 children, who came to stay with friends. The 30 Tidebrook children, then in the school, were joined by 45 evacuees and three teachers from Elfrida School. The consequent crowding only eased in November when the junior girls from Elfrida School transferred to Frant, and others drifted back to Lewisham. By the end of term just 14 evacuees were still at the Tidebrook school.

LEAVE HITLER TO ME SONNY— <u>YOU</u> OUGHT TO BE OUT OF LONDON

ISSUED BY THE MINISTRY OF HEALTH

Other groups

The next arrivals were rather different. The Parish magazine records:

> July 1941: MONK'S PARK has now been opened as a hostel for old people, who have been bombed out of their homes in London, and at present there are 34 living there. Mrs Phillips, the Matron, would be glad to welcome visitors who would drop in and chat with the old people. She would also be grateful for help in any of the following ways. Clothing is needed, as in most cases they have lost all their possessions. Gifts of vegetables and fruit would be welcome, also a few more walking sticks. A short Service is being conducted on Sunday mornings by Mr Bryant. For this hymn-books, preferably A. and M. are needed, so if anybody has a spare hymn-book or two, it would be a kindly act to send them along to Monk's Park, or to leave them at the Vicarage.

Nothing more is known of this venture: presumably all went back to Lambeth after the War – or even earlier if their homes had been made habitable.

In November 1940, another group arrived in Wadhurst, for whom there is only one mention in the Parish magazine:

> Wadhurst has many visitors in these days from more vulnerable areas, and it is difficult in any way to keep pace with the movement of population. May I offer a special word of welcome to the staff and students of St John's Hall, Highbury, who have had to leave their good buildings in London and are now in somewhat cramped quarters in Wadhurst. They will use the Parish Church as their chapel on Sunday, and also during the week. I am sure that their help will be extremely useful in various ways and will readily be forthcoming.

St John's Hall has, however, an interesting history. Founded by the Dissenter movement, Highbury College, designed by John Davies in Ionic style and reminiscent of the British Museum, was built in 1825-6. The grounds of about 5 acres extended north-west behind the college; 1½ acres on the east side was added in 1835 and a smaller plot on the west side in 1854 when the college had become a training school for schoolmasters. In the 1850s Highbury Congregational College amalgamated with the ministerial training wing of Homerton College in the East End to form New College, London. Homerton went on to specialise in training teachers, moved to Cambridge in 1894, and is now a full College of the University. The Highbury site was sold in 1866 to the Church of England who formed the London School of Divinity –

sometimes regarded as 'the back door into the Ministry'. In 1913 Woolwich Arsenal Football Club moved north to Highbury, dropping Woolwich from its name. Their chairman, Henry Norris, took a 20-year lease on part of the grounds of St John's Hall for £20,000. The new Arsenal Stadium [also called Highbury] was built there. St John's Hall burnt down in 1946 and was replaced by a block of flats; the college moved to Nottingham and became St John's College – one of its staff, between 1970 and 1975, was George Carey [Archbishop of Canterbury 1991- 2003].

Another group came to Wadhurst – as recorded in the Parish magazine for September 1943 – obviously to work! But nothing more is known of this.

> Sep 43: WANTED. For the Land Girls' Hostel, the gift or loan of a ping-pong table and darts board. Would anyone who could help with either of these please get in touch with the Warden, Mrs Thorpe, Braeside.

After the end of the War in Europe, in August 1945 the Parish magazine reported an appeal for help:

> YOUNG PEOPLE FROM OCCUPIED COUNTRIES: An opportunity occurs to show our gratitude for having been spared the horrors of invasion in a very practical way. The children from Holland are being brought to England for a two-months' holiday in as large a number as there are homes offered for them. A party of children, aged 8 to 14, is expected in Tunbridge Wells in October, and I have been appointed Wadhurst representative of their Reception Committee. Invitations are asked for one or two children in homes [preferably where there are children], of all types, as the Central Committee tries to send the children to homes more or less like their own.
>
> There is no billeting payment, the children are not ill, and come provided with ration cards, and clothing for the two months, and the Committee is responsible for medical attention if required, pocket money etc.
>
> Will anyone in Wadhurst who has already sent an invitation to the Central Office, or who would like to help by taking a little guest for one month or two months, write to me or come to see me for further particulars? Dutch children learn English at school!   Ann M Boyd [Hill House, Wadhurst].

There is no information in later issues about Wadhurst's response to this appeal. However, some Wadhurst families took up Ann Boyd's request and had Dutch children to stay. In all seven children, from around Amsterdam, came here, after a short stay in a camp in Crowborough. Most of them ended up in Hill House with Ann Boyd; one stayed with Martin Turner's aunt and a 15-year old Dutch girl stayed for two months over Christmas with Kathy Mitchell: sShe is still in regular contact with a few of those, who are still alive, and their children and grandchildren; she is also still in contact with one of the German prisoners of war, who came to Wadhurst Hall - and stayed.

Prisoners of War

The final set of unexpected visitors to Wadhurst were POWs. There was a camp set up in Wadhurst Hall which has not been formally recorded and little is known about its early days. Certainly it was used to house Italian POWs, as at least one group left their mark in the conservatory of Olives Manor; POWs are believed to have constructed Bankside, leaving an inscription on the kerb stones.

Several local residents remember German POWs working on the farm: Darby's Farm, Buttons Farm, Dewhurst Farm and Cousley Wood Farm all had labourers at some period during and after the War; they were remembered particularly for their skills at woodwork. Heather Russell (née Topp - one of the children rescued from Buttons Farm) remembers the toys they made for children, especially for Christmas. One has left a mural of his home town, Hildesheim, lovingly painted in the apex of the barn roof of 'The Loft', Dewhurst Lane.

A prisoner of war's recollection of Hildesheim - in 'The Loft', Dewhurst Lane

Some have made their home in Wadhurst and their recollections lend a human dimension to what was a depressing and frightening time for many.

Hans Degenkolb explains that he had been called up into the German Pioneer Corps in May 1941 [aged 18] and was serving on the Russian Front. In May 1944 he was sent home on leave. He continues – having heard on the wireless:

Every soldier had got to report back to his troop. What I had to do, I had to pack up all my belongings, walk to the railway station, towards the east and I came as far as the border of Germany and Poland; then the military police stopped the train and told us to get out of it and next to it stood an empty train facing Germany and we had to board that train, go back to Germany again and all the way to France [HD explained earlier that they did not understand what was happening until part way through the return journey when they learnt that the second front had started in the west]. *And they took us all the way to the bottom of the Pyrenees. Cor - we didn't know what to make of it seeing it was a strange country to us – the first time I had been in France. When the others went, we had to do other repair jobs – I was in the Pioneer Corps, like your Royal Engineers – we had to do all the heavy work, sometimes we had to repair some bridges and everything – been a lot of broken bridges during the war before. So it went on and on.*

Later on, I was issued with a motor bike and I took over as a despatch rider. They gave me a leather case, maps and a rifle and everything. I went round and round the country – it was all strange to me. I went round for hours and hours – I was told I had to look for number so and so – another Pioneer group: no sign of it. I went round and round – the landscape was all flat, couldn't see nobody. I heard a lot of shooting and bombarding – I was used to all that and I took no notice. I lost a lot of time and kept looking at my watch; I was afraid as it gets dark – you couldn't switch the lights on – and I went round and round and looked and looked – no signs of anybody. And I went around a bit further – cor – there they were - some American soldiers came each side out of the ditch with their rifles pointing at me. Dear, oh dear, that was the end of my war. Cor, dear oh dear. And one tall soldier – taller than I was – he got hold of my tu,nic and he pulled me off the motorbike like a rabbit. And another he wanted to start the motorbike up and he couldn't –

I don't know what happened to the motorbike later on. One soldier took me away and that was the end of my war.

And after a few weeks we were all collected behind a big barbed wire fence – no shelter or nothing - raining like mad – we were all huddled in behind barbed wire. Another few days later they took us out of the camp and we had to board a big lorry and then they took us to the port of Marseille. We had to board an American ship there and they took us all the way to America – what a lovely trip. We was afraid you see – the war was still on – and we went across the Atlantic and we were afraid our U boats were still about in the Atlantic.

After some time in America, he was told that he was to be shipped back to East Germany:

We went on this big ship across the Atlantic again, back to Germany. And one day we were all happy amongst our colleagues and a news flash came through the ship's loudspeaker "You are heading for Liverpool". Huh! Ha! You ought to hear all the noise. What the hell do we want to go to Liverpool for if we have signed all our papers to go back to Germany. We couldn't believe it – that's how it is – as a soldier you had to be quiet and take orders and that's how it went. Cor, dear, oh dear. After that little excitement when we looked out of the ship – another new country – again sorting us out like in a cattle market and we was only a little group - oh, a hundred – and they took us to the railway station and that's when we came to Wadhurst all the way from Liverpool – Wadhurst Station and when we looked out of the window we could see Wadhurst station. Huh - and in the railway yard when we got out of the train we could see a load of army lorries all lined up and they told us : "Get in there". And we said to each other: "I wonder how the hell it turns out now". Dear, dear. That's when we went to Wadhurst Hall – what they call Wadhurst Park now.

There is still one building left at Wadhurst Park from those days, which – it has been suggested – was once part of the camp. It is now used as a garage; but its construction of square concrete panels bolted together does not tie in with Hans' recollections of living in Nissen huts; maybe the garage was an ancillary building in the camp or was built later on the footings of an earlier hut.

Outside and inside of the remaining building of the POW camp in Wadhurst Park

In any event, Hans and his colleagues had to build additional Nissen huts on their arrival in Wadhurst.

Life in the camp was pretty informal; there were no British military guards and the POWs largely ran their daily life themselves. The senior German there was Willi Pesch:

Herr Willi Pesch - senior German in the Wadhurst Hall POW camp

[Photo lent by Heather Russell]

After a while, Hans continued:

> *They told us we'd got to work on the farm. And each one was given a bicycle and we went, sixteen of us, on bicycles – we went from the camp to Cousley Wood Farm – between Wadhurst and Lamberhurst. Sixteen of us and the problem was – you see – we drive on the right and we had to learn to drive on the left. God, God, dear, dear. But we got used to it. When we came on that farm, it was a hop and fruit farm - sixteen*

acres of hops and fourteen acres of fruit. And we said: "What have we got to do down here then?" "Oh", they said "you've got to go down the hop garden and do hop training - twiddle the hops up the string". You see the hops went as high as that. And when we came there – to the hop garden – I said to my colleague, I said "what are they – grapes?" He said: "you fool", he said, "they're hops not grapes". Because of course when I was in France they grew the grapes just the same as hops. He said "you fool – hops"; he said "you've got to twiddle all the hops up the strings". Good God – you see - because it's the first time I see hops.

He was then told that he was to be moved to live at Cousley Wood Farm.

It was the best life I ever had. You see the farmer found out I was a carpenter by trade and when we came there, the farmer had nothing – no implement shed, no tractor shed – nothing. And he asked me if I could build all them sheds. And I stayed there for seventeen years.

Before I had a chance to move out to the farm, the camp commander told us you'd got to make your mind up if you want to stop here or go home. So I wrote a letter to my mother – of course she was still alive – what shall I do? And so many times before when I wrote letters they was all blacked out by the Russians. You see like you do when you are a long time away, you ask a lot of questions, and my mother wanted to answer back – it was all blacked out. So many letters all blacked out.

He later married a neighbouring farmer's daughter and now lives in Frant.

Another POW has a local connection through marriage. In 1943 Hans Kaupert, born in Breslau in Silesia [now in Poland] was called up and served as a wireless operator; once trained, he was sent to La Rochelle – fortunately for him, as the rest of his colleagues went to the Russian front. By 1944 it was clear the War was lost and, as the Americans advanced and Hans' unit moved east along the Loire, one day his commanding officer gave his men a choice: either try and get back to Germany, facing the increasing number of French partisans - or surrender. Hardly surprising that the second choice was preferred; later that day a couple of American officers and several soldiers arrived to discuss the necessary details. After a period of captivity in France, on a very poor diet of 900 calories a day, Hans was shipped to America and then, in 1946, to England, where he was interned in the POW camp at Robertsbridge.

Here he met a Land Army girl from Wadhurst – Freda Kennard, one of seven sisters. They married and after a while arranged to live in one of the cottages at Earlye Farm; while here Hans worked at Wessons Farm in Buckhurst Lane and also did work for Capt. Dennis [of Dennis trucks] at Riverhall. Hans now lives in Lamberhurst Quarter.

Local residents also have memories of POWs in Wadhurst. Nora Manktelow recalls seeing gangs of Italian prisoners of war digging ditches across the fields near Buckhurst Place. She particularly remembers their "*lovely singing*" of opera as they worked. She also has memories of two German POWs who came to work daily on the farm at Buckhurst Place:

> *One was Adolf and one was Werner. They had a big O on their backs to identify them as POWs. Their conduct was so good that they were allowed to live in the dairy on the farm and stay there. I remember these Germans having great hunks of black bread for their dinner. One wet day they were sitting in the boiler room and Mr Bradshaw, who owned Buckhurst Place, gave them a pound of pickled onions and they ate them all in one go.*

After the war several German ex-POWs continued to live and work in the Wadhurst area. John [Dobbin] Willett, now of the Dobbin's Inn, at the bottom of Balaclava Hill, had a sister who married an ex-POW by the name of Adolph Cosh. There were also other local marriages to ex-POWs.

Other personal stories

Finally, the BBC Second World War archive records a couple of individual evacuees who came to Wadhurst. Ann's father was in the League of Nations in Geneva.

> *In 1936/38 it packed up and he went to work for the International Court in the Hague, where I lived and went to school. We had a German maid in the Hague and, when there were rumours of war, my father asked her if she wanted to go back to Germany and she said "No, I'll be waiting for Hitler to come here." I remember when war broke out. My father's face fell at the dining room table. It wasn't until November that my*

father decided to send us to boarding school in the UK. We took the Rotterdam, a ferry, to Gravesend. We had to put on lifebelts. On arrival at Gravesend I remember hearing the man on the land wanting to know a password. "Red white white red" - I remember this being said and repeated. I remember it was all blacked out at the station, except for an eerie blue light.

My father went back to the Hague with a Christmas pudding made by his sister-in-law. He went back by plane and had to pay extra for the weight of the pudding. My mother went to Brussels to see her mother. Then the Germans came to Holland and the whole International Court went to sleep at the Spanish Embassy under the Spanish flag because Spain was neutral. The diplomats were respected and the Germans sent them by special train to Geneva. I was in boarding school in the UK, age 7, and knew practically no English. I spoke French.

Eventually, maybe in 1940, my mother came over on a ferry and met up with us. She came in full mourning dress including a black veil, because of her mother's death. We lived on a farm in digs. The rumour in the village, Wadhurst, was that my mother was a German spy. By summer of 1940 the music teacher shared our digs and entertained soldiers in the village. She gave me a German bullet that had been cleaned out. It was later confiscated at boarding school and I never got it back. When there were dogfights, the gym mistress blew a whistle - two short whistles followed by a long one - and we had to go to the cellars. Once there was a dogfight immediately overhead. I remember streams of German bombers, even in daylight. I got to know the sound of German planes. There were mattresses on the floor in corridors to accommodate all the children in boarding school.

We moved to Malvern, but only for two weeks because there was a terrific raid. We went to Ambleside in Lake District. We changed digs five times because people were suspicious of my mother's foreign accent. We didn't know what was happening to my father. Eventually we heard he'd arrived in the UK. He had had time mountaineering with friends in Geneva. Then he went to Portugal and got a merchant navy ship to the UK. The sun kept rising in a different place, as the ship was zigzagging all the time for safety. It took a month to get from Portugal to the UK. The BBC wanted my father because he spoke several languages. He spent the rest of the war working in censorship. He allowed a mention of Croydon airport, and was told off! He had to sleep, eat etc. at the BBC in London. They slept in dormitories and Wilfred Pickles complained about my father's snoring!

My father got us back to Wadhurst and we stayed there for the rest of the war. I remember hearing the first doodlebug. I recognised it as a very frightening sound. There was a nasty flame at the back. We had a very good view from school. One came down in the middle of Wadhurst and killed one or two people. The RAF threw out tin foil [called 'window'] to cause interference to communications. It landed in the school grounds. My father retired from the BBC at 60 and he went to Germany after the War and visited the Reichstag and picked up some carpet underlay as a memento. Then the International Court started up again and he went back.

Heather Simpson was another evacuee, with a delightful descriptive style:

In September 1939 I was 19 years old. I had left school two years earlier and I worked for my living as secretary to the managing director of a firm of coffee merchants in the city of London. Quite grown-up you might think. No. I was still a minor, two years away from getting 'the key to the door' at the age of 21 when I would legally become an adult no longer within the care and control of my parents. Even in those pre-war days there were a few enterprising and adventurous souls who managed to fly from the nest but as a general rule a girl lived at home until she married and did as her parents told her. That is how it came about that after the momentous declaration of war on the 3rd September I allowed myself to be evacuated with my mother from our house in Lee to Wadhurst in Kent [sic]. Father wanted us out of the way for a while until he could find out how the war was going and how much extra time he would have to spend at the Blackheath Bank where he was manager. It had all been arranged and I had not been included in any of the discussions. I was just told. I felt most unhappy about it all. I felt bad about leaving Daddy even if it was what he wanted and I felt as if I were running away. What would people think? I left home reluctantly and grumpily, but when I got to Wadhurst I couldn't help being glad that I had come.

Our new temporary home was a little wooden house in the middle of a field. Aptly it was called "Field Cottage". The September sun shone on the lovely silvery wood of the cottage walls and made it as warm as a garden shed in high summer. Also in a field between the lane and the cottage was a pen of big fat geese who set up a tremendous honking when anyone approached. Did you know that geese are wonderful watchdogs? They are not nice creatures though. However kindly one speaks to them they just hiss angrily in reply.

England in the autumn of 1939 seems in my memory to have had a distinctive atmosphere about it. That September the sun shone brilliantly, enveloping everything in a golden embrace. The skies were blue and clear and quiet. No planes disturbed the song of the birds. Along the lane leading to our cottage the hedges were full of blackberries, huge, glowing and oozing juice, already half-stewed by the sun. In all the Kentish orchards and gardens, trees were laden with ripe fruit and on the grass beneath the heavy branches wasps tottered about amongst the fallen fruit in a droning drunken stupor. None of the fruit went to waste and, in Wadhurst kitchens, housewives busily stirred jam and bottled the best fruit (no home freezers, remember) ready for the hard times ahead. As autumn wore on and the nights became crisply cold the country took on an old fashioned air of cosiness. People collected fallen branches to burn and to eke out the coal ration, so a lovely smell of wood smoke filled the air. Traffic was at a minimum as petrol was rationed, so a great quiet hung over little towns and villages.

However we knew that we must expect air attacks from Germany, so it was important that no light should be allowed to show and act as a guide to the enemy bombers. A complete black-out had been imposed and at dusk black-out curtains were put up and Air Raid Wardens did their rounds, making sure that no chink of light shone in the velvety darkness. All street lights were switched off for the duration of the war, but in a remarkably short time we got accustomed to finding our way about in the blackness of night with only a small pocket torch to cast a glow-worm's light on our path. The hunt for No. 8 batteries to use in our trusty torches became one of the great pursuits of the war.

We called this period of time the Phoney War, because nothing seemed to be happening. Out in the darkness across the sea the enemy was

251

prowling and plotting, but we had battened down the hatches ready for the storm and we slept soundly in our warm beds. I had already got a job to go to in Wadhurst. I suppose growing up in London had made me somewhat arrogant in my attitude towards "country folk".

On my first Saturday there I marched into the Post Office cum village store and asked what I could do to help, just as if it were a Battle Zone. Surprisingly there was a job for me. The local Corn and Coal Merchant had a vacancy for a Secretary/Book-keeper and I soon settled down to work in the little dark office behind the shop. I adored the shop, with its open sacks of chicken feed, corn and bran and dog biscuits sold by the scoop, with its bags of coal and Coalite, its firelighters, bean poles, balls of twine, flower seeds and garden gnomes. I loved it if the shop manager was out humping things about in the store and then, when I heard the shop bell, I would hurry into the shop to weigh out dog biscuits or bone-meal or bird seed for the canary. The Coal Merchant, Mr Jones, was a sick man. He always sat in the office in his trilby hat and mittens, from which protruded his poor red arthritic fingers. As winter came on he sat in his overcoat and muffler too. He had a chronic cough and swigged cough mixture straight from the bottle - about half a bottle at a time. Mr Jones was very nice to me, as were the shop manager, Mr Clark, and the 14-year-old lad who swept up.

Mother and I joined the Home Nursing class in the village hall. We had done First Aid in London the year before. Home Nursing seemed to consist mainly of bandaging, which I loved. I could bandage heads, noses, jaws, arms, legs, fingers and toes. I had missed my vocation. I should have been apprenticed to an Egyptian mummifier. Also we knitted for the troops. After tea we carefully checked the black-out curtains, banked up the fire, turned on the wireless and got out the khaki wool. I was hopeless, but in the course of time I turned out a balaclava helmet for a giant and mittens that might possibly have fitted a midget. Father joined us on Friday nights to spend the week-end in Wadhurst.

In the New Year the weather became bitterly cold and the Kentish [sic] fields were covered in soft white snow, pretty as a Christmas card. In January Mr Clark was called up, leaving me with a lot of extra work, so a gentleman (I mean a Gentleman) came in to help with the accounts.

He was middle-aged and fierce looking and he wore hairy, ginger-coloured plus fours and jacket that rather clashed with his ruddy complexion. But he was kind. He spent his sweet ration on bars of Fry's Chocolate Cream for me. He was shocked to discover that Mr Jones didn't provide afternoon tea and so he arranged for the pub opposite to supply a pot of tea for us all, which he paid for each day. The Lad was sent over to collect the tray stacked with cups and saucers, teapot, hot water jug, bowl of sugar lumps, etc. His face was a picture when he brought it back - a mixture of embarrassment, tolerance and plain amazement at the strange ways of the gentry. The Gentleman was always threatening to take me out to dinner, but the weather was too bad and the roads too icy to arrange a date, much to my relief, ungrateful girl that I was.

The bad weather made it hard for Father to live alone and to pay his weekend visits to Wadhurst, so in March Mother and I returned to London.

SOURCES

Wadhurst Parish magazines

WW2 People's War: the online archive of wartime memories contributed by members of the public and gathered by the BBC. The archive can be found at www.bbc.co.uk/ww2peopleswar

The personal memories of local residents including:

Kathy Mitchell, Heather Russell, Hans Degenkolb, Jim Gray and Hans Kaupert.

St George's Hall

*Brockley School
started in these
buildings in
Wadhurst*

Best Beech Hall

Commemoration Hall

and then moved to

Oakover House in Ticehurst

Annex

BROCKLEY SCHOOL – INDIVIDUAL MEMORIES
Recollections of Don Henderson:

I was one of some three hundred boys and masters who left Lewisham South Station on the morning of Saturday 2nd September 1939 carrying a small suitcase, gas mask and a stamped addressed postcard to let my anxious parents know of my arrival at an unknown destination.

We were, later that day, to arrive in Wadhurst, via Crowborough, in a fleet of Southdown coaches and be deposited outside the Hall of Commemoration earlier than the reception committee seemed to anticipate. To its credit however, we were all assigned to foster homes by the evening having been fed, medically examined and documented. Thus, the invasion of this pleasant East Sussex market town by Brockley County Grammar School had started and, for myself, was to lead to some pleasant and never to be forgotten years even now in the year 2002.

In spite of much being written about unhappy evacuees and foster parents due to varying circumstances, the majority of boys had little to complain of and settled quickly to life in lovely surroundings.

Luckily I was not unused to the countryside and had often paid visits to Sevenoaks, Tonbridge and the Weald from my home in Bromley and I did not find myself 'fazed' in any way.

My first lodging was with Mr H C Corke at "Tanners", Turners Green and after the first night I reported to the Hall of Commemoration along with the staff and boys who had to find a way there somehow. Standing there we heard Mr Chamberlain's announcement at 11 am. on a relayed radio belonging, I think, to Mr Goble of the Post Office. Within a minute the sirens had wailed but there was no panic and we disposed ourselves to the playing field behind the hall and began what was, for many, the first of several days of freedom before arrangements for school were commenced.

This meant three venues for boys and masters viz: (1) The Comm. Hall (2) St. George's Hall in Sparrows Green (3) A Scout Hut in Mayfield Lane. Desks, books and other equipment arrived from S.E. London and 'The Brockley Cabbages' settled down to the quiet first few months of 'The Phoney War' in Wadhurst and surrounding districts. Teaching was done under some difficulty but there was never any lack of discipline, respect or drive under our superb headmaster, Dr Sinclair, and the excellent staff of older masters too old for active war service. In this period, too, many of us received more personal equipment from home and some were lucky enough to have bicycles which were necessary if you were housed some five miles away from Wadhurst.

After one week at "Tanners" I was moved to a rather primitive cottage in Buckhurst Lane and learned what it was like to walk to school. One compensation there, however, was the delicious blackberry pies made by Mrs. Harmer but, after my father had sent down a Hercules bicycle (£2.10s), I was removed again into Keens and Hawkins Bakery in the High Street. This shop is now the present post office and is of course very much changed. There I remained until March 1940 when the place went into liquidation and I made another move to be in Western Rd. with Mr & Mrs Walter Baldwin.

After the initial worry that London would be shattered by bombing had passed, almost half the school had returned there if parents consented. I had three days at home that Christmas but as most of my other friends had also evacuated it seemed that life with the school at Wadhurst was the better option even though it turned out to be a cold, bitter winter.

There was a memorable party in Commem. Hall in which we combined with Wadhurst School and friendships, some long lasting, were made. We were encouraged to join with such organisations as the church choir, youth group, Scouts etc. For myself at this time I took the opportunity to play Rugby for School 1st XV. Most games were played on Sparrows Green Playing Field. I also played soccer for Wadhurst Rangers on the same field and later for Wadhurst Town in the village. The Air Training Corps, formed later, also ran a team which played on the field by the church behind Hill House, now wired off by the path to "Step Stile".

By the lovely summer of 1940 those of us who remained were well-integrated into life in the High Weald. We were encouraged to learn as much of local history and geography as we possibly could and my love of the area, already instilled, caused me to roam all over the "hurst" and "den" villages and to this day I remember every lane and turning particularly in "the Wealden Iron" area which I later chose for my thesis before becoming a teacher.

But — guns had been heard in the distance at Dunkirk and I remember the order for bells to be silenced until threat of invasion had begun. It seemed to make little difference to the life of the village, though suddenly there were more soldiers about and Canadians arrived in the area and there were quite a number in the Snape Wood vicinity.

Then, overhead in the lovely blue skies of this momentous summer, began "The Battle of Britain". Dogfights raged high in the sky above, patterned with many vapour trails. In spite of many claims by both sides very few aircraft came down in Wadhurst Parish. Spent bullets and cartridge cases became prized possessions and stories were told of our escapades and narrow escapes but there was very little damage to the district, much more happening in the tragedy of 1956 [*the RAF Meteor jet crash on the High Street*].

Boys were released from school to assist on local farms at five old pence per hour and the school had its allotments on land adjoining Sheepwash [*Washwell*] Lane which was able to produce useful amounts of vegetables. Later in the year we were involved in both fruit and hop-picking, myself at Cousley Wood.

During this summer the LDV had been formed and boys over sixteen years of age could participate as messenger boys. I was assigned to a platoon which kept guard in a small hut in Brinkers Lane. The only requirement was a bicycle with a blacked-out headlamp on which to ride with a warning to the police station should parachutists land. I found myself in the same outfit as my headmaster who was an entirely different man under these circumstances but who reverted to type a few hours later when back at school.

My love for cricket was amply satisfied during this summer as we took over the field on which Wadhurst played for the duration of the stay there until re-evacuation in 1944. This was a lovely experience on a good wicket with expansive views over Snape Wood at the lower end and, at the upper, the shingled spire of the church. We enjoyed matches against local schools, London schools evacuated within the area, RAF and Army teams. We also played as guests for other villages who were 'short' and on the Neville Ground at Tunbridge Wells and Linden Park. No shortage of good cricket under our masters and the watchful eye of Mr Meech, the groundsman.

Later in 1940, the school obtained the use of Oakover House in Ticehurst and subsequently some eighty of us left to be domiciled in three large houses, twenty or thirty in each. These were (1) Steelands in Ticehurst Square [*now Apsley House*] (2) The Courthope House [*Whiligh*] at Shover's Green (3) Abbey Lea on the Stonegate Rd.

Obviously in many ways this was more convenient for schooling and fostering arrangements but those boys still in Wadhurst needed to cycle the necessary miles.

Those of us who wished not to sever ties made with Wadhurst of course remained in touch. There were visits to the Assembly Rooms for classical orchestral concerts in Tunbridge Wells, Cinema Shows in the Salvation Army Hut at Sparrows Green and Pantomime rehearsals with the Youth Club.

One of the school activities which had been able to continue was the school orchestra led by Mr Tom Pickles. We provided music for the pantomimes and visits to Old Peoples' Homes in the area, often being helped by Mrs Page and Joyce Law a local piano teacher.

So, by and by, although I now resided in Ticehurst, again with kindly people, I kept up my cricket activities until I joined the RAF in 1942 and returned as often as possible when on leave to play football and to see friends whom I would never have known had it not been for that "nasty little Adolf".

The second set of recollections comes from Bill Christmas:

'BROCKLEY' - AT WADHURST - AND AFTER

Yes, on September 2nd 1939, the whole school - together with masters, their wives and assistants left South East London (by a devious route) en route for Wadhurst. This was part of the Government's plan - Code name 'Operation Pied Piper'. My late mother (widowed when I was a small boy) was a Council employee and therefore allowed to join us, but neither she nor any of the masters, wives or assistants were paid. Any money allocated was paid directly to their billet.

As previously reported, we all arrived at Wadhurst Commemoration Hall. The Billeting Officer and his staff were very surprised to see 300 boys, aged 11-16+, accompanied by adults. Wadhurst had been expecting mothers and babies and, as a result, some homes had been prepared with cots, baby clothes and toys! A dozen other boys and myself (with my mother in charge) were allocated the top floor of the Vicarage, the home of the Reverend Ernest Mannering, his wife, their cook and a maid. Coincidentally, the Rev. Mannering's previous post had been at St. Peter's Church, Brockley, so he already knew our home area.

Life at the Vicarage was very pleasant. Lessons were taken in the Commemoration Hall across the road and during this period (known as the 'phoney war') there were opportunities for exploring the countryside, including visiting the site of the iron mines, near the Miners' Arms public house. Iron from these mines was used for the gravestones in Wadhurst Church.

It was at Wadhurst Church, on September 3rd 1939, that we heard the Declaration of War and later, at the same church, I was confirmed by the Bishop of Chichester, Dr Bell.

That period ended, however, with the increasing privations of war, in turn resulting in the "calling up" of the Vicar's staff and the subsequent necessity to close the top floor of his house. My mother therefore returned to London to take up paid employment at one of the Fire Brigade Stations, in Surrey Docks.

I was moved, temporarily, to the old Post Office, Wallcrouch. Then, with a dozen others, to a tea-hut - 'The Woodlands' at Flimwell crossroads - just in time for the very severe winter of 1940. The hut was poorly heated and, being so far from Wadhurst, we had to use the irregular 84 bus (it is still operating). Therefore most of us missed occasional lessons as well as some of the social events described by Don Henderson.

By then moves were afoot to acquire 'Oakover', a large beautiful house in Ticehurst. The Drewe family had moved out and agreed that the house and grounds could be used as a school building. It might otherwise have been commandeered by the Canadian Army, who were in the area. The house was made ready for us: protection on the floors, certain rooms containing valuable furniture locked and one glass case in the entrance hall (containing a collection of stuffed birds) boarded up.

The war was 'hotting up': the Battle of Britain was being fought above our heads and on the 7th September 1940, London was set ablaze. In Sussex we could see the vivid glow in the night sky very clearly. Ironically, it was my mother's birthday and, in response to my birthday card, declared she didn't want any more 'returns of the day' - not that day - having recently escaped from blazing Surrey Docks with her life. In fact whenever I went home during the ensuing 4 years for Christmas, Easter or summer holidays, there was always an air raid; this meant sleeping under the Morrison 'table' shelter [see p. 90] or in the Anderson 'garden' shelter [p.78].

Entertainment in and around school has not been mentioned but I must recall the travelling cinema in the hall at Sparrows Green. It broke down frequently, either en route or in the middle of the film - but at least it had pictures with sound! We also went to Tunbridge Wells for more modern shows and for shopping but were, of course, restricted by rationing. Other milder amusement in Wadhurst was watching the mental patients from Ticehurst House Mental Institution (still there but renamed) out walking with their carers. Which was which?! By now I was a member of the school ATC, resulting in being given the prefix number 928 when I joined the RAF. Anyone else remember that?....

Finally, I must acquaint my readers with the fate of the Brockley School building. It still stands, at the top of Hilly Fields, but is home to Lewisham Prendergast Girls' School (whose old building in Rushey Green was demolished). I was present at the time of the transfer, a few years ago, and was delighted to see that the Governors had graciously allowed the fine mural in the main hall to remain in situ. Ex-scholars will remember that it depicted the boys in rugby gear.

Eric Clarkson recalls his experiences from 2 September 1939 through to mid-July 1940.

It all began in the last days of peace in 1939. We had been away on holiday at Barmouth for three weeks, that is my Dad and Mum, my brother who could only have two weeks' holiday, a friend of ours Cyril Worsell, and my uncle Cyril and his son Trevor who was a little younger than me. We had had a good time learning to sail, going for long walks, and playing cricket on the sands. But the threat of war was always there.

All good things have to come to an end and so it was with this holiday. No sooner had we returned than I had to report back to school. School for me was what we now call year 12. I had not done very well in my General Schools' exams in May 1939 and I was due to repeat the course work in my 6th year at

Grammar School. School for me was Brockley County School in Lewisham.

"*We had to report at school today and prepare for evacuation.*" So reads my diary entry for 28th August 1939. Next day it reads "*Did the same as yesterday, lot of Gas Mask drill*" - I should add that we had had Gas Masks from the year before in 1938.

Friday 1st September the entry reads "*Told this afternoon to prepare to evacuate the next morning*".

So it was that some 250 – 300 boys assembled in the school hall and walked down to the local station at Ladywell. As I recall my mother was there to see us off. This would have been about 10 o'clock. At school we had been given a brown paper carrier bag, and we all had our Gas Masks and a medium-sized suitcase which contained a change of clothes. In the carrier bag were things which were to keep us going until we got some food. The contents were: a packet of Rich Tea biscuits, some sandwiches, an apple and an orange, a tin of Condensed Milk, but best of all a big bar of chocolate.

Because I was one of the older children we didn't need to have a label with our name on, it was assumed we knew who we were!

Once on the train you can imagine that we discussed among ourselves where we might be going. Well, the train puffed its way through many unfamiliar stations on the southern outskirts of London. All we could tell was that we were going in a southerly direction. Eventually after about two hours we drew into a small station called Jarvisbrook, it's now called Crowborough. Lined up outside were a large number of country buses and into these we piled for onward move to our destination. This turned out to be Wadhurst, a small village in E. Sussex.

On arrival, we then had a roll call to be sure that no-one had got lost on the way. We were told to wait outside the hall and await the billeting officer to come and allocate us to whoever were to be our hosts.

My friend Colin Boxall and I had agreed that if were possible we should stick together, but time went by and nobody came to pick us out. I expect that they took one look at us and thought we would take a lot of feeding.

Fortunately it was a lovely summer's day and not unpleasant to be outside. About three o'clock, a smart car drew up and a young man only a couple of years older than us came up to the billeting officer and asked if there were four boys together. Quick as a flash a couple standing near us, Charlie Rye and Geoff Roberts with whom we were fairly friendly, put up our hands.

Off we went, going back about two miles from the direction from which we had come. This young man was at University and training to be a Doctor. The car in which we were riding was a Triumph Vitesse which was quite a posh car for those days. Soon we were delivered to the front door of a big house called

'Bensfield'.

The lady who owned it was called Mrs Leete and it was her grandson who had picked us up from the village.

Once indoors we found that we had been allocated two bedrooms with twin beds in both, so Colin and I shared one room and left Charlie and Geoff to share the other.

At first we ate with the servants of whom there were five, three maids, a cook and a kitchen maid. Outside there were two gardeners who each lived in a semi-detached house in the grounds of this very large house. It must have had at least 20 rooms besides the usual 'offices'. There was also a chauffeur called Fillery who didn't seem to care for us much.

At first we had our meals with the servants but Mrs Leete soon realised that this was not the best use of the space she had available especially as we needed room to do our homework. So she kindly let us have the use of her dining room.

We were fortunate because not only did we have plenty of good food but were very well treated. We even had the use of a half-size billiard table and a table tennis table in the games room.

Some of our friends were not so lucky. In a few homes the food was neither good or plentiful. Some of our lads even found that they already had some occupants in their beds!

Mrs Leete like all other folk who had evacuees was paid 10/6 a week or 52½ pence in today's money. This was paid by the Government.

On Sunday 3rd September I went to the parish church in Wadhurst but we were only there for about fifteen minutes before a message was brought in to the Vicar saying that war had been declared and he said we should all go home. Shortly after leaving the church we heard the wailing sound of the Air Raid Siren and we all wondered what was going to happen. Actually the 'All Clear' sounded not long after. We had had the first of many false alarms.

It was some days before we went to school again. It seemed that no one had told us that we should turn up on the Monday. In the meantime one of the gardeners decided that with these four lads he could occupy their time profitably in what he called 'thistle dodging' which meant going into one of the fields surrounding the house and chopping down thistles.

What we eventually found had been arranged was that three village halls had been hired, and these were used until we got a more permanent building in May 1940. The building which we used as a school was in Ticehurst a few miles farther on from Wadhurst and was called 'Oakover'. It was in that building that I re-sat my exams and was pleased with my results when they were given as I had matriculated.

The winter of 1939/40 was very snowy and we found a toboggan in the garage and set about making good use of it. Unfortunately it was a bit old and one day as three of us were aboard we went over a hump and when we landed, one of the wooden bars broke.

As we tumbled off I tore my trousers on the screw head and had to get one of the parlour maids to mend it for me which she did quite cheerfully. The cook was excellent and we really enjoyed the meals she prepared.

In May 1940, following the Dunkirk evacuation, Mr. Anthony Eden made a broadcast asking for volunteers to form Local Defence Volunteer (LDV) groups. This name was later changed to the Home Guard. We were too young to join but we enrolled as runners. At first there were no weapons available but the day came when P.14 rifles arrived; these used .303 ammunition but had been in store since the end of the 1st World War and were covered in thick grease. Fortunately we boys were excused the job of removing all the grease - that was left to the volunteers!!

The following gives an indication of the generosity of Mrs Leete:

When we went to 'Oakover' in May 1940 Mrs Leete was very concerned about our midday meal because there were no cooking facilities which could cope with 200 or so boys. We had to make do with corned beef and potato chips with an apple for desert. So she arranged that we should go to the local public house and made the proviso that we had a master who was willing to be with us. She paid for our meal, which I think was 1/6d, but I think that Mr Walmsley had to pay for his meal himself. Incidentally we became a co-ed school because Mr Walmsley's daughter, Sonia, was the only girl in the school and she also had her meal with us.

After I had left school I went back to see Mrs Leete at least a couple of times but by then the school had been moved to S. Wales.

I eventually left school in July 1940 and went back to London before the blitz started in September 1940, and got a job with the Metropolitan Water Board, but that's another story.

Don Henderson and Bill Christmas gave their recollections to the Wadhurst History Society. Eric Clarkson's recollections come from the BBC's project 'WW2 People's War' - an online archive of wartime memories contributed by

CHAPTER 14: THE WOMEN'S WAR AT HOME
THE LIGHTER SIDE OF LIFE WITH SERIOUS UNDERTONES
HEATHER WOODWARD

"This is a war of the unknown heroes.
The whole of the warring nations are engaged, not only soldiers,
but the entire population, men, women and children."

Winston S Churchill

Left at home, often bewildered and frightened, many with their fathers, uncles and other older members of the family away in the Forces, the young people of Wadhurst were involved in many ways with the War effort, thanks in large part to the useful skills learnt in the years prior to the War, through the wide range of youth activities available in Wadhurst. The adults guided and encouraged the youngsters so that they would actively help in meaningful ways. The adults were also very aware of the need for the young to enjoy their youth and, as today, the youth organisations provided stability, comradeship and purposeful activity for the younger members of the community.

All age groups would gather regularly for entertainments in one of the Wadhurst halls and various distractions would bring colour and brightness to what was often a very grim period. They were also very good at entertaining themselves. The youngest members of the family, however, must have felt particularly hard done by, in the summer of 1942, when "*all toys which included rubber, cork, hemp, kapok, celluloid or plastic derived from celluloid, casein or synthetic resin*" were outlawed. There was a relaxing of that regulation in the short periods before the Christmases of 1942 and 1943 but that was all.

Youth Organisations in Wadhurst

These included the Brownies where they had lots of fun helped by Miss Elaine Avis, the much-liked Brown Owl. There were also the Guides, Cubs, Scouts and Rangers, the ATC, the Hill House Girls' Club (started on 19th February 1936) which was particularly good at producing knitted patchwork blankets much appreciated by the Finnish Relief Fund, and the boys enjoyed their own Boys' Club in St George's Hall run by Mr Clemmence, the local policeman, where they learnt, among other things, boxing. There were also the Junior Red Cross Detachment, the Methodist Wesley Guild, Wadhurst College and the Wadhurst Youth Group which was established in 1942.

The Wesley Guild invited a group of German POWs to a social evening one Christmas and after 'eats and carols', they asked the prisoners to sing a carol. They chose to sing *Silent Night* in German which brought tears to many who were present.

The Scouts enjoyed their yearly camp under canvas but were dismayed to find in 1938 that their Scoutmaster did not eat porridge or drink cocoa: *"That was an omission so strange and inexplicable that we felt considerable anxiety"*. The Scouts lost their Scoutmaster in July 1939 when Capt. Charters had to rejoin the Royal Engineers for an indefinite period.

In early 1941, Peter Wicker's big treat was as one of the *Cubs*, whose group was run by Miss Collyer and Miss Kelsey, when they

> *were picked up on the Friday afternoon and taken to Miss Kelsey's house at Riseden where each boy was provided with a kit bag. [We] camped, cooked and played games all week-end before being returned to school on Monday morning.*

Peter has no recollection of taking any spare clothes with him for this adventure so he assumes they must have arrived back at school a bit dirty and dishevelled. Certainly, a good time had been had by all the Cubs, and their parents had had a welcome break from all their responsibilities.

The 1ˢᵗ Wadhurst Guides, led by their Captain, Miss Daphne Courthope of Whiligh, were regularly appealing for any old clothes which they could mend and then distribute to people living in bombed areas. They also appealed for large numbers of cotton reels which were sent up to the War Office or Air Ministry.

The 2nd Wadhurst Guides, run by Miss Gwenda Clements, met at the Cricket Pavilion at the Sparrows Green playing fields and also used to go to her house in the evenings during the War to sew and make things – quite often using felt hats. Jean Hayward (née Sinden) remembers camping under canvas during the War in the grounds of Wadhurst College in Mayfield Lane, and they were allowed to use the school's swimming pool because it was the summer holidays and the girls had gone home. Needless to say, there was great rivalry between the two Guide companies.

Eileen Codd (née Davis) remembers that the Guides learned many useful skills including cooking, sewing and First Aid and they also went to the swimming baths in Tunbridge Wells.

Josephine Bailey was a Brownie and one year remembers a fête in the vicarage garden and they all dressed up to represent the nations of the world. Meanwhile, Miss Beryl Courthope ran the Rangers who were very active in supporting people and helping out those in need.

The Air Training Corps was created, in 1941, by the expansion of the former Air Defence Cadet Corps to recruit young boys of 16 and over, to prepare themselves for subsequent service in the Royal Air Force. The ATC Wadhurst Flight was initially lead by Mr Keast, a local schoolmaster who had originally formed a small group for aircraft model-making with balsa wood, thin paper, glue and a sharp razor blade. When Mr Keast was called up, William Goble, the local postmaster and shopkeeper, having been granted a commission in the RAF Volunteer Reserve, became the commanding officer until its disbandment at the end of the War. Don Hemsley was the first senior cadet and was followed by Ken Jones.

The Flight worked hard during the winter months to prepare for their proficiency examinations which included mathematics, Morse code, drill and physical training, navigation, gas, flying theory and practical engineering. Des Mansfield had worked hard along with all the others to master Morse and he was preparing to try to get into the RAF - until his General Manager forced him to resign from the ATC because he was working for Post Office Telephones, a reserved occupation, and, as a member of the ATC, would be liable to be called up. To Des's frustration he had to join the Cranbrook Home Guard because that was nearest to where he was employed. Eventually, he was transferred to the Ticehurst Home Guard, near where he lived, but he never managed to get into the RAF.

The ATC's first visit to an RAF Station was to Biggin Hill in the summer of 1941 where they inspected Spitfires of the two active squadrons stationed there, and a flight of Blenheim bombers. Six cadets had their first flight in a Tiger Moth flown by a Spitfire pilot whilst other cadets examined a captured German Messerschmitt 109 fighter. In the September of the same year, Cadets Jones and Vidler spent a week at Biggin Hill watching the Spitfires taking off and returning from operations over France and spending most of their time polishing the perspex windows of the Blenheims and assisting the ground staff. This provided a valuable insight into the workings and life of the RAF.

In March 1942, the cadets were looking forward to attending a rigging class at the Squadron Headquarters in Tunbridge Wells where a glider was in the course of construction. Gliding was to become a regular part of their training once spring had arrived. In the summer of 1942, cadets visited RAF Detling where they were given flights in an Avro Anson over Tunbridge Wells, where the green dome of the Opera House was particularly conspicuous. With the arrival of Canadian troops in Wadhurst, a friendly relationship was built up and cadets were allowed to use the assault course established in the woods near the Best Beech Inn. In return, senior cadets gave instruction in aircraft recognition in preparation for the coming assault on Europe.

F/O Goble met a lot of people through his work in his shop which sold sweets and gifts [*now Jackie Martel*] and he was able to arrange talks by local serving men and others on leave.

Particularly memorable to Don Hemsley, Ken Jones and Ken Midmer were those given by a Free French officer and by Lt. Donald Ogilvy Watson D.S.C.

a submarine commander, who was to die in the sinking of HM Submarine Unbeaten on 11th November 1942.

Two cadets died while in the Forces: George Sales of Turret House, Tappington was killed on his first operation as a navigator in September 1943 and is buried in Hanover Cemetery; Roy Cook died on a training flight as an air gunner in April 1945 and is buried in Wadhurst Churchyard.

The Tunbridge Wells Advertiser published a photograph in 1943 of the ATC when a standard was presented to the Flight. Ken Midmer is the standard bearer, the escort was John Walters and Don Hemsley is immediately behind the iron railing post. The drummer is John Ratcliff wearing the Skinners' School Officers' Training Corps uniform. William Goble is on the far right and the tall gentleman is Mr du Vallon, chairman of the Flight Welfare Committee. The Revd. E Mannering carried out the dedication and the other officer is from the mother squadron in Tunbridge Wells.

The Youth Group was run by Miss Gwenda Clements, and within the first year of its existence, the youngsters had given an entertainment in the Commemoration Hall, another in Ticehurst and in the Best Beech Hut. For their January pantomime in the Commemoration Hall in aid of the Merchant Navy Comforts Fund, the younger children took part as rabbits, imps and fairies. Because of clothes' rationing, finding costumes could be a problem and Jo Bailey remembers wearing 'fairy wrap' made up of a borrowed net curtain attached to each little finger by a curtain ring. In another year, the imps wore head-dresses made of cleaned rabbit bones including skull bones which the adults painted various colours and attached to strips of tape.

Sports in Wadhurst included *football* and *cricket* for which there was, and still is, a strong following but, of course, activity was much reduced because so many of the boys were in the Forces. The Sparrows Green Rovers played in blue and yellow.

The Tennis Club was pleased with its newly enlarged and re-turfed courts in January 1938. By April 1939, however, there was considerable concern in the Tennis Club because of the shortage of women: "*At present the proportion is about three men to one lady.*" [Ironic - bearing in mind the situation which would develop during the years to follow]. There was also the 'Rabbits' Tennis Club where members could remain only as long as they were still 'rabbits' at the game. "*Any undue proficiency will lead to removal to more exalted circles.*" Many youngsters played tennis in the evenings at Wesley House Tennis Club in the Lower High Street which was, at that time, the residence of the Methodist Minister.

There was also at least one *Quoits* pitch down at the Railway Tavern [*which became the Rock Robin*] opposite the station.

The Boys' Club was given a fine new billiard table by Mrs Hollis in 1937 and this was declared a welcome addition to their equipment "*especially as it will enable the final of the billiards tournament to be played under conditions calling rather more for good judgement than good luck*".

Cycling was popular and the youngsters used to run races along the roads. A good circuit was down Churchsettle Lane and around Snape. They also used to go fishing.

Helping the War Effort

All the children did a great deal of collecting of salvage over the War years and in April 1943 the Youth Group was appealing especially for rubber, locks and keys. They were delighted to be able to announce a couple of months later that this appeal had resulted in "*four tons of rubber and a considerable amount of iron being collected*". The national campaign for salvage enrolled hundreds of thousands of young people as 'Cogs' whose official Cog battle song was "There'll Always Be a Dustbin".

Jean Hayward used to make camouflage nets and was paid 2/6d a time. She was supplied with the string and started off with one stitch, increasing at each end of each second row and then, once she had reached the required breadth decreasing back to one. She made several of them.

'Maggie's Special'

Before the war, the highlight of the year for many families was the very formal-sounding Combined Sunday Schools' Outing which travelled down to Hastings on '**Maggie's Special**' [Mrs Margaret Manktelow, one of the Primary School teachers, organised this annual fondly-remembered day-trip], leaving Wadhurst Station for Hastings at 7.30 am. "*There were loads of Sunday schools in the village*", remembers Nora Tweedley, who was a member of the tin Mission Church over the railway bridge near where the tip is now.

Mrs Margaret Manktelow

> *If you went to Sunday School so many times a year, you were given a ticket and you went on Maggie's Special. Some people were lucky and could walk to the station; others came in horse and cart or whatever other conveyance was available. And we had a bucket and spade on the front of the train because it was Maggie's Special. You always saved up for your trip to the sea.*

Joan Griffin (née Reed) remembered being taken to the station in Heasman's charabanc or Lavender's coal lorry and holding paper streamers out of the train windows.

Frank Bishop also felt that Maggie's Special was the real highlight of the year and many children were accompanied by their parents.

> *Some had a fish and chip lunch which was especially delicious and then the whole group met up again to enjoy a free tea of sandwiches and cake. Everyone had to wear a coloured [yellow] ribbon pinned to their clothes so that they could be easily identified.*

During the war, the outing was impossible so the Sunday School Party became the highlight in the Commemoration Hall. Almost 200 children enjoyed the "*conjuring and ventriloquism, a wonderful tea and finally apples and a pencil or book to take the place of the oranges and toys of earlier years*".

In August 1945, a welcome return -

> *for the first time since 1939, the United Sunday School Outing was held again and about 450 children and parents went by special train to Hastings and thoroughly enjoyed a long summer day by the sea, which some of the younger children were seeing for the first time. Our usual tea-place had been bombed, and no caterers were ready to receive us. But Mrs Manktelow was quite undaunted, and secured an excellent place for tea in the Hall of the Central Methodist Church, and an abundant supply of food was taken by road from Wadhurst, so that in due course all were fed.*

Children did not, of course, always want to be roaming outside, and they looked forward to their magazines and comics coming out, usually each week: The Beano Comic, The Rainbow, The Hotspur, Tiny Tots, The Champion, Boy's Own, Girls' Crystal, The Magnet, Radio Fun, The Wizard, The Rover were all eagerly awaited.

Dances

Three dances were held in Wadhurst each week, two in Ticehurst. These included cricket club dances and football club dances. None of them could finish later than 10.30 pm. because of the black-out and there always had to be a live band. Dancing to records was 'not done', remembers Des Mansfield, whose first dancing lessons were at the 6d village 'hop' where teenagers like him gained the confidence to go to dances. He particularly liked Frank Chacksfield's four-piece band – Frank came from Battle and became very famous later.

From July 1940 onwards, weekly fund-raising dances in the Commemoration Hall were organised on Wednesday evenings by Mr and Mrs Edward Carr and had Mr Fred Still, who was also the caretaker of the Commemoration Hall, as the Master of Ceremonies. The money raised was given to numerous projects. In the first six months, £40 had been shared between the special needs at the Kent and Sussex Hospital and a local War Comforts Fund. A detailed inventory of later contributions was explained in July 1941:

Purchase of wool for comforts for the Royal Sussex Regt and Royal West Kent Regt Prisoners of War	£23 7s 0
Two pianos for billets in Wadhurst and tuning the pianos already in billets	£21 1s 0
War Weapons Week	£7 18s 6½d
Wool-gathering Fête	£2 16s 0

Mr Still had also organised a very successful series of Saturday evening dances and as a result over £80 had been given to local charities. Over 300 people had attended the 'Farewell Dance'.

The main highlight of the week for teenagers – though that name hadn't been invented then – was the Commemoration Hall dance – they paid 2/6d each to hear Bill Goble and his band: Mr (William) Goble, the postmaster, Mrs Anderson, the piano player, whose husband worked on the Courthope Estate, and Mr Vic Blackford.

Before Noel Carley joined the Forces, he recalls, like Roma Ogilvy Watson, that *"Wadhurst carried on as usual"*. When the Canadians arrived and were billeted at Wadhurst Hall, they had a very good dance band which performed in the Commemoration Hall nearly every Saturday night. In fact all the regiments had their own dance bands and would play either at the Commemoration Hall or Wadhurst Hall. Mind you, Des Mansfield does recall that some fights broke out between RAF members and the Canadian soldiers or the Canadians between themselves, *"but a good time was had by all"*. Nothing, of course, like the fight that was going on overhead and he remembers one night, during a Wadhurst dance, that they heard several explosions. It turned out these were the bombs dropped at the entrance to Darby's Lane; and at a dance in Ticehurst he heard the bombs dropped at the end of Churchsettle Lane.

The Theatre

The Osiris Repertory Company, invited by the Youth Group, presented, on one occasion, Sheridan's *She Stoops to Conquer* in the Commemoration Hall with tickets priced at 2/6d, 1/6d or 9d. A very special treat for some children was to be taken to see a pantomime at the Opera House [*now Wetherspoons*] in Tunbridge Wells. And, of course, one boast in London, after the first week of the War, was *We never closed!*

The Wireless

The spirit of the People's War

Angus Calder

The importance of the radio, especially during the War years, cannot be over-emphasised. Among other things, it established routines for every family when all age groups would sit round listening to the news broadcasts in the evenings at 6 and 9 pm., and the major, often unscheduled, speeches, made by the Prime Minister, initially Neville Chamberlain, and then Winston Churchill from May 1940 onwards.

Certainly Churchill's well-crafted speeches of encouragement, advice and persuasion kept the spirits of the nation raised and the War effort campaigns energised. He used the radio to great effect, cajoling and encouraging unity on the Home Front.

The radio became what has been described as a "*new weapon in modern warfare*" as it advised, admonished, warned:

Careless Talk Costs Lives
Be Like Dad, Keep Mum

These messages were backed up by a poster campaign:

The BBC - "The Voice Of Britain"

Do not believe the tale the milkman tells;
No troops have mutinied at Potters Bar.
Nor are there submarines at Tunbridge Wells
The BBC will warn us when there are.

A.P.Herbert

The BBC would become an essential cog of the fighting, world-wide War as it broadcast its vital messages to Europe and the Far East in 47 different languages. It had used only 8 languages before the War. The messages to Britain of the former lieutenant of Oswald Mosley, William Joyce, the American-Irish-Englishman, (soon nicknamed Lord Haw-Haw because of his manner of speaking): "*Germany* (Joyce pronounced it Jairmeny) *calling, Germany calling*" showed, however, that blatant propaganda does not always work. On one occasion, he accurately mentioned Snape Wood where they were charcoal burning. Eventually, however, some of his scripts were so ludicrously inept and false, that his broadcasts became a target of ridicule.

So important was the BBC that, where people were still not connected to mains electricity, they would listen through old crystal sets, as did Des Mansfield's father. Every now and again, he managed to find the radio station with the crystal and sit with the earphones listening to it. Conventional radios could be powered by an 'accumulator', a very large type of battery which could be charged at a central depot. Noel Carley remembers that they were always "*glued to the radio*" which consisted of an accumulator battery and a large dry battery. Rosemary Pope's family had a radio which ran with an accumulator and it had to be charged weekly by Mr Baldwin, who had the shop where Magpie and the Sandwich Shop now are. The Popes had two accumulators therefore – one on charge, one being used.

The 'wireless' was to provide many hours of genuine distraction for the people at home and especially the families – distraction which was increasingly needed.

On 3rd September 1939, after a long hot summer, everyone knew Mr Chamberlain was going to broadcast so families gathered round the wireless to listen to the clipped tones of the Prime Minister:

I am speaking to you from the Cabinet Room at 10 Downing Street. This morning the British Ambassador in Berlin handed the German Government an official note stating that unless we heard from them by eleven o'clock, that they were prepared at once to withdraw their troops from Poland, a state of war would exist between us. I have to tell you now that no such undertaking has been received, and consequently this country is at war with Germany.

Not everyone heard it, though, because the announcement, at 11 o'clock, was broadcast during morning church services.

On the wireless, *The Home Service* had a varied programme, some of it quite serious and this met the needs of a great deal of the population. It regularly included all types of music, literary talks as well as comedy and debates and quizzes.

5.20 pm: Children's Hour was broadcast every night (at 5.15 pm. on Sundays). *We are the Ovaltinies* was a favourite song. On his 9th Birthday, one little boy was told to listen to Children's Hour and a voice said: "*Would Desmond Mansfield like to look in his Father's gun cupboard? Happy Birthday.*" His parents had bought him an air-gun which he quickly learnt how to use. Des had fun with that gun but was never allowed to shoot birds.

Everyone who listened to Children's Hour was particularly fond of Uncle Mac [Donald McCullough] with his warm voice ending each broadcast with "*Goodnight, Children - everywhere*", and there was Toy Town with Larry the Lamb. Other favourite programmes included Just William, Norman and Henry Bones (the Boy Detectives) and Dick Barton who came on later in the evening at 6.45.

6 pm: The News Bulletin was followed by the *News in Norwegian* (this was the only place in the schedule where the latter could be fitted). Announcers and newsreaders like Frank Phillips, Alvar Liddell, Stuart Hibberd, Frederick Allen et al. were better known than most Cabinet Ministers. In Manchester, Wilfred Pickles was the first newsreader without the distinctive BBC 'received' accent. The main news broadcast, though, was at 9 pm. The *National Anthems of the Allies* were played on Sunday evenings at 8.45, just before the main news.

The Radio Doctor, Dr Charles Hill, continued his once-a-week broadcasting from 1941 until 1950 in his unmistakeable, intimate throaty tones, waxing lyrical about the virtues of *"my old friend the dandelion leaf"* and admonishing his listeners with

> *Don't come over all superior at the mention of fish and chips – it's first-class grub. That's true whether it's dished up with dignity to the duke in his dining-room, or scoffed by the nipper from a newspaper spread out on his knees.*

Dr Hill was delighted that the war was destroying the ritual of the Sunday joint: *"Hot on Sunday, cold on Monday, and if there's anything left, hashed or murdered on Tuesday".*

When recalling the wartime years, even now people in Wadhurst remember, with much affection, shows like

It's That Man Again (ITMA), first broadcast on 19th September 1939, starring Tommy Handley with his friendly northern accent. Handley managed to lift the nation's spirits as listeners giggled at ITMA's absurdities. The script-writer, Ted Kavanagh, aimed at a laugh every 11 seconds with the outrageous puns, crazy situations and grotesque sound effects. Mrs Mopp, (played by Dorothy Summers), besides her various catch-phrases, kept things going with her lavatorial *doubles entendres.* There was also the ineffectual German spy, Funf, with his feet of sauerkraut, and the Office of Twerps at the Ministry of Aggravation (a combination of Agriculture and Information). Tommy Handley was ably helped by the versatile mimic, Jack Train, in keeping the programmes absolutely up-to-date. Jack Train created characters like the Squire of the Manor of Much Fiddling, and the Mayor of the seaside resort, Foaming at the Mouth, whose motto was: *"Loosen the Green Belt, tuck in the blue prints and paint the town red".* Amongst others in the cast were many who became stars in their own right after the War: Molly Weir, Deryck Guyler, Hattie Jacques, Maurice Denham, Carleton Hobbs to name but five of a very talented set. Some of them even came to Wadhurst once, after the War.

Part of ITMA's success was that it never lost its homeliness, its topicality or its directness. In one episode, Mrs Mopp presented the mayor with *"a jar of carrot jelly strained through my own jumper".* In 1943, when the duty on drink was increased, Colonel Chinstrap (Jack Train) asked: *"Why must the Chancellor always tax necessities?"* - no doubt voicing the opinion of many, not only in Wadhurst.

The cast of ITMA - Tommy Handley [centre right]

This was the show that established many catch-phrases:

Mrs Mopp, the Corporation Cleaner: *"Can I do you now, sir?"*
Ali Oop, the pedlar: *"I go – I come back."*
"I don't mind if I do." when being offered a drink.

The BBC Engineering Division organised voluntary spare time munitions work in the evenings but, when it came to choosing <u>which</u> evening, everyone was adamant they could not do Thursday evening because that was the evening for ITMA and Tommy Handley.

Band Waggon featured the diminutive, 'big-hearted' Arthur Askey and Richard 'Stinker' Murdoch.

Hi Gang was a success with Vic Oliver, Ben Lyon, and Bebe Daniels.

The infatigable *Sandy Macpherson* played 'live' on his theatre organ to an otherwise empty London studio.

Regular radio band leaders included Geraldo, Mantovani, Billy Cotton with his signature tune *Somebody Stole My Gal*, Victor Sylvester and *You're Dancing on my Heart*, Henry Hall with *Here's to the Next Time*, Jack Hylton and *Soldiers in the Park*, Ambrose with *When Day Is Done* and Joe Loss *In the Mood*.

The Sunday Service on one occasion was relayed from an air raid shelter in London and

> *was almost too poignantly pathetic in its setting. The hymns sung for the most part by folks now sheltering every night in the crypt of the church had a significance they never had before.*

Henry Hall's Guest Night had everyone swaying to the live dance music.

The Forces' Programme provided light entertainment and a sentimental link between scattered friends and relatives, and regularly attracted 60% of all listeners; *Forces' Favourites* was one of the new request programmes linking scattered families and friends.

In 1941, *The Robinsons*, the first-ever soap opera, was the saga of a front-line family and would lead to the Dales, the Archers, Crossroads, Coronation Street and Eastenders.

Sincerely Yours – Vera Lynn – the Forces' Sweetheart, came on after the 9 o'clock news and was a sentimental half-hour linking the men in the Forces and their womenfolk back home.

The Brains Trust with its regular panel of the cool intellectual Julian Huxley, volatile Cyril Joad with his high-pitched voice, and Commander A P Campbell with his exotic anecdotes which reflected all too accurately the plain man's superstitions provided '*education by stealth*' under the warm-toned chairmanship of Donald McCullough. "*Hardly anyone ever confesses that he didn't hear it, or if they do, takes care to give adequate reason for so doing.*" The public sent in 15 questions after the first broadcast but that soon increased to sack-loads. The three regulars would be joined by two others and could be asked anything:

> *How does a fly land on the ceiling?*
> *Why can you tickle other people but you can't tickle yourself?*

By 1943, the programme had a regular audience of 10 – 12 million each week.

The BBC Home Service also broadcast uplifting messages from evacuated children to their parents; Princess Elizabeth encouraged the children of the Empire, whilst Queen Elizabeth broadcast to the Women of America in 1941.

The Cinema

Every week in Britain some twenty-five or thirty million seats were sold.

Here in Wadhurst, slides and cartoons were shown in the Salvation Army hut [*now a pair of cottages near the Primary School opposite Costcutters*]. A film show and a prayer cost 1d. Des Mansfield remembers a man who travelled round all the villages showing films. The film, *Meet Me in St Louis,* was shown at the Commemoration Hall and Joan Griffin cried her eyes out at the sad bits. For most people in Wadhurst, however, Tunbridge Wells would be the nearest place for seeing the latest films and some of these were definitely propaganda films.

> *The Great Dictator* starring Charlie Chaplin mocked the enemy.
> *Sixty Glorious Years*, starring Anna Neagle and Anton Walbrook charted the reign of Queen Victoria and made many wonder how, with all the royal ties between Germany and Britain, things were now so politically disastrous between the two countries.
> *Target for Tonight* where all the actors were active members of Bomber Command. It was described by one person as "*a memorable film, presented in undertones, but which keeps recurring to the mind days later*".
> *One of our Aircraft is Missing* was another film promoting Bomber Command but its actors look now like a roll-call of all the people who would later become major stars.
> *Let's Finish the Job,* a documentary, was designed to persuade workers that finishing the job accurately and carefully was vital.

Next of Kin, a fictional documentary, directed by Thorold Dickinson: aimed to discourage careless talk.

The Way Ahead (Carol Reed) was made to celebrate the common soldier.

In Which We Serve (Noel Coward) was based on flashbacks to life in Britain seen through the eyes of the survivors of HMS Torrin and proved an excellent vehicle of propaganda for opening the eyes of America to the fortitude and stresses of life on the other side of the Atlantic.

London Can Take It also helped the Americans to a wider understanding of Britain's experiences of war.

Mrs Miniver, with Greer Garson starring in this saga of middle-class courage, provoked mixed reactions on this side of the Atlantic.

British film studios also produced escapist melodrama, romances, comedies and costume dramas including :

Kipps described by one Londoner as *"an entirely natural and believable love story. By the time it finished, that uncomplicated world seemed far more real than the world of shattered building and bits of charred paper from the last raid into which we emerged".*

The Man in Grey starred the exciting newcomers James Mason and Margaret Lockwood.

Henry V (Laurence Olivier) had to be filmed in Eire and was in COLOUR!

American Studios dominated cinemas generally, however, and the most famous film of the period was probably

Gone with the Wind (David Selznick), which starred the British Vivien Leigh and Lesley Howard. The latter was greatly mourned when his plane was shot down in 1943. The film was not an escapist entertainment but, lasting three hours and forty minutes, it seemed to please its audiences with its colour, costume and glamour.

Let the People Sing

The wireless helped to popularise many of the songs of the period as well as the Big Band Sound of player-conductors such as Glenn Miller. The songs of the Second World War in particular gave people a few minutes' oblivion, a laugh, the heart to carry on whether they were heard in dance halls, on the wireless or at work. The heightened emotions of War also meant that they really listened to the words and in many cases needed to believe them.

> *"We'll Meet Again, don't know where, don't know when*
> *But I know we'll meet again some sunny day".*

Wadhurst has always responded to music, and the songs of the Second World War certainly answered the need of the population for light relief.

Probably the most popular song, and certainly one of the most frequently requested on the BBC, was the sentimental, patriotic and above all optimistic *The White Cliffs of Dover* (Walter Kent 1941) immortalised by Vera Lynn.

> *There'll be love and laughter and peace ever after,*
> *Tomorrow, when the world is free.*

Many songs were looking toward a better future: *Shine on Victory Moon, When the Lights Go On Again, When They Sound the Last All Clear* (1941) but one, perhaps surprisingly popular and certainly very sentimental song, was the German *Lilli Marlene* (Norbert Schultze 1941) which delighted Rommel's Afrika Korps and also our Eighth Army. In 1942, it was provided with 'acceptable' English lyrics by Tommy Connor and recorded by Anne Shelton.

Anne Shelton

The songs of the Second World War were about optimism and they needed to be because this War was harder on the non-fighting people of Britain than any previous War. The power of music in general and popular songs in particular to distract and encourage a people quite unused to living under siege conditions was doubly valuable – for national morale and for the timeless 'play-it-again' feeling.

Songs of the First World War had never really gone away and *Now Is The Hour* (originally 1913) was one poignant return as were *Roses of Picardy* and *Keep the Home Fires Burning*.

Inevitably, sentimental songs abounded: *I'll be Seeing You* (Sammy Fain 1938), *We'll Meet Again* (1939), *All or Nothing At All* (Jack Lawrence 1940), *You Are My Sunshine* (1940) which sang about the shortages of cigarettes people were having to endure, *The Nearness of You* (Hoagy Carmichael 1940), *The Last Time I Saw Paris* (Jerome Kern 1940), *Bewitched* (Richard Rodgers 1941), *I Don't Want to Set the World on Fire* (1941), *My Heart and I* (Richard Tauber 1942), *Moonlight Becomes You* (1942), *A Lovely Way To Spend An Evening* (McHugh 1943), *You'll Never Know* (Harry Warren 1943), *Coming Home* (Billy Reed 1945).

Many of the songs were memorable as well as singable: *Let the People Sing* (Noël Gay 1939), *We're Gonna Hang out the Washing on the Siegfried Line* (Michael Carr), *Run, Rabbit, Run; Hey Little Hen; Bless 'Em All* (Frank Lake 1940), *Mairzy Doats and Dozy Doats* (1943).

Many tunes were ideal for dancing, not least *I Came, I Saw I Congaed* (1941), *Boogie Woogie Bugle Boy* (1940), *The Cokey Cokey* (Jimmy Kennedy 1942), the *Homecoming Waltz* (1943).

Songs connected with London were popular: *A Nightingale Sang in Berkeley Square* (Sherwin 1940)' *Mister Brown of London Town, The King is Still in London, I'm Gonna Get Lit-Up When the Lights Go Up in London* (1943).

Fighting Songs included *Comin' In on a Wing and a Prayer* for the RAF, *Praise the Lord and Pass the Ammunition* (the Navy), *The Lords of the Air* (again for the RAF), *Cleanin' my Rifle and Dreamin' of You* (the Army). Others, loosely connected to the Forces, were also humorous: *Nursie! Nursie!* (1939), *In The Quartermaster's Stores* (1940), and *Kiss Me Goodnight, Sergeant-Major* (Don Pelosi).

And some were simply patriotic and nostalgic: *There'll Always Be an England* (1939), recalled the quintessential "*country lane*" and "*the cottage small beside a field of grain*" before becoming more jingoistic with

> Surely you're proud, Britons awake,
> The Empire too, we can depend on you,
> Freedom remains these are the chains nothing can break ....
> If England means as much to you as England means to me.

That song is still regularly sung with great gusto in the Commemoration Hall these days.

The Pub

Traditional English socialising did not end with the outbreak of War and there was no shortage of pubs round Wadhurst, even though spirits like whisky were not readily available. There were <u>eleven</u> pubs all told: *The Old Vine* (Cousley Wood), *the Balaclava* [now Dobbins], *Red Lion* (Sparrows Green), *Castle Inn*, owned by Mr and Mrs O'Malley [later the Four Keys] where the piano was the centre of the entertainment, *Rock Robin* [these last two both on Station Hill], *the Best Beech, the Queen's Head, the White Hart* and the *Greyhound* (St James's Square), the *Fountain Inn* (Tidebrook) and the *Miner's Arms* (Snape).

"You could get half a pint of mild, a pack of five Woodbine or Players Weights, a box of matches and get change from a tanner"
[6d or 2½p] remembers Peter Wicker.

Not surprisingly, the pubs were usually full and plenty of beer was drunk. Beer and tobacco were never rationed but beer was heavily diluted. It had soared in price too because, in 1939, the excise duty on a barrel was 24/- whereas in the second half of the War it was around £7.

That did not stop the happy drinkers and Noel Carley remembers seeing some of the Canadian troops arriving at the Greyhound on their Harley Davidson motor-bikes and going home later with about eight of their comrades on one bike.

Boys and Girls Go Out to Play

Much of the entertainment of children was created by others but, from the childhood memories of local residents, it is clear that life for children could be great fun and did not necessarily need advanced technologies, nor any adult input either.

Peggy Bartholomew remembers:

> *We used to have lots of fun as children and plenty of freedom. I used to go off to play with my friend, Pat Scrubshaw, with just a bottle of water, buns and sandwiches and be gone all day. We loved playing around in the dirt!*

And Jenn Hemsley mentions particularly that "*children were allowed to roam freely, often quite a long way from home, exploring the woods and playing in the streams*".

The social life of the Sinden children revolved a great deal around the Salvation Army "*.... we enjoyed many organised activities such as paper-tracking trails and magic lantern shows – simple but enjoyable .... children played in the street the whole time and we had enormous skipping ropes and there were few cars*".

Ruth Skilton recalls a group of children called the Bulldogs, organised by the vicar's wife. They used to have tea and cakes with her.

Once lessons were over, Joyce Anscombe and her sister enjoyed skipping, whip-and-top, hop-scotch, conkers and marbles. If the weather was too bad for them, they played Cats Cradle – looping string around their fingers in a variety of different ways to create patterns, or did French knitting with an old wooden cotton reel with four nails hammered into the top, around which wool was hooked. One evening a week, a group of girls went to Nurse Dutton's house *[next to the present Chinese/fish and chip shop at Gloucester Place]* where they sang songs and played games. After church on Sundays, the Harmers would go to the home of the Misses Courthope where Panny Tyrell, the late Mrs Courthope's companion, organised choir practices. Joyce is convinced that many of these activities were organised to keep them all out of mischief.

Panny, incidentally, was one of the founder members of the Wadhurst Dramatic Club which was established in 1946, following a lively conversation in Malpass the butchers. But that's another story.

Looking back on her schooldays, Jenn Hemsley says:

> *The education was very basic and we didn't have all the equipment that children have today, but it stood us in good stead for the rest of our lives. My Mother was probably the biggest influence in our lives instilling in us the importance of a good education. Thanks to her encouragement, we all went on to have good careers and comfortable lives.*

Other games which were played indoors and provided amusement were board-games, like Ludo and Snakes and Ladders, or dominoes - but most of the time children created their own amusement.

Obviously other things made life more 'normal' and brighter for residents in Wadhurst. There were six hairdressers, for a start. It certainly must have helped too that, in December 1936, the Hemsleys had opened their flower shop in the High Street. They cultivated four acres of land and glass, growing 10,000 chrysanthemums and 25,000 bulbs for sale. They also made all designs of holly wreaths to order.

Life was not easy but any opportunities to relax were valuable:

> *A little work, a little play*
> *To keep us going – and so good-day!*
> *A little fun, to match the sorrow*
> *Of each day's growing – and so good-morrow!*

George Du Maurier

SOURCES

The People's War: Calder, Angus [1969], Jonathan Cape
Despatches from the Home Front: McCooey, C [ed] [1994], JAK Books
Voices from the Home Front: Goodall, Felicity [2004], David & Charles
Great Songs of World War II: Leitch, M [ed]
Wadhurst Parish magazine

The personal memories of local residents including
Joyce Anscombe, Jo Bailey, Peggy Bartholomew, Frank Bishop, Noel Carley, Eileen Codd, Joan Griffin, Jean Hayward, Don Hemsley, Jenn Hemsley, Ken Jones, Des Mansfield, Ken Midmer, Rosemary Pope, Ruth Skilton and Peter Wicker.

Vera Lynn - the Forces' Sweetheart

CHAPTER 15: POST WAR CELEBRATIONS
RACHEL RING

With London going wild with celebratory events for both VE and VJ Days, all of which are vividly portrayed in national newspapers along with fulsome journalistic reports, did such fervour occur in Wadhurst in response to the ending of hostilities? Photographs show thousands of people thronging the London streets and being 'carried along' up The Mall to Buckingham Palace which seemed to be where everyone was aiming: men and women dancing in the street, bunting on buildings and flag-waving, in fact all the trappings that we have come to expect when nationally we have something to celebrate. Bands played and street parties were held, or so the newspapers told us. Locally

we heard of people who went up to London to join the masses in high moods of celebration. Was this being replicated in small communities?

VE Day celebrations in Wadhurst

Exhaustive requests for people to come forward to tell us about how wildly Wadhurst celebrated the ending of six years of War and the longed-for peace, met with a disappointing response. Most, even those known to have excellent memories, said "*nothing really*" happened! Yes, we were told that, in various areas of the community, huge bonfires were lit and some fireworks let off, but memories of either spontaneous or planned gatherings or parties in the street, even indeed inside, were not forthcoming. It seemed that to be able to burn any wood one found, on a fire in the open at night, was a celebration in itself.

However, a long term Wadhurst resident, Nora Tweedley, reminisced about VE night outside the Castle Inn [*later the Four Keys*]:

> *We gathered around a piano, which was brought out of the pub on to the pavement. A huge fire was lit in the middle of the road which melted the tar and burned down telegraph poles, and a stack of wood for pit props down by the railway crossing was burnt on this fire. Troops, who had been into Tunbridge Wells in lorries, stopped and joined in the jollifications; I think they were billeted at Highfields House* [the recently-closed FTA building].

As an afterthought she added "*the landlord of the Castle Inn was Jock O'Malley who was an officer in charge of the Home Guard*".

It was as if a return to a life of 'normality', like before War commenced, and being able to do away with black-out curtaining, having lights on, and to be able to shop for goods not seen in years, were more important than jubilation on the streets. There was also sadness about those lost during the War and indeed those who had still not returned home. "*How could you really celebrate?*" they said.

Walter Hodder recalled there had been fireworks and a bonfire at Tidebrook and that Sid Farmer played the accordion, so he assumed there probably was a bit of dancing and people got some food together. He had no recollection of any celebrations for VJ Day on 15th August other than the bells were rung. This statement tied in with most people's hazy recollections.

Some who were children during the War said that, if they turned up at the Commemoration Hall, they were then given a commemorative beaker. Another, who said she was ill at the time and in bed and so unable to attend, did not receive one. A few said they were too shy to go to the Hall so missed out too. Interestingly though, all of them have vivid recollections of King George V dying, the abdication of King Edward VIII and the coronations of both King George VI and, later, Queen Elizabeth II.

One elderly lady, who lived at Woods Green, said there was a party of sorts on the green there but did not know what happened in the village or at Sparrows Green. She said the women made tea in their homes and the children had games and she laughingly recalled that they got the men to run to a board to collect a piece of string which they then tried to thread through a needle. Naturally, they could not do it, she said.

The Wadhurst School Log Book records that on 8th and 9th May 1945

> the school was closed for two days. On the second day the children had a tea party and a programme of sports was arranged for them. Expenses were paid for by the Parish Council.

Celebrations in 1947

Most people gave mention of the 'big' one scheduled for January 1947, a long time after the end of hostilities, which is detailed in the Bocking Collection. The Parish Council sent 'Welcome Home' invitations to men and women returning from the War to join in a celebratory entertainment. It appears from the lists of those to be included that 561 invitations were sent out and 312 acceptances were received back. Some did not reply.

The Parish magazine of February 1947 had a report of the event, which had been widely publicised because the Committee had invited Tommy Handley and the BBC ITMA cast, to give a performance in the Commemoration Hall for returning servicemen and some local people. However, owing to Tommy Handley's being ill, the ITMA entertainment had to be postponed at the last minute; consequently the report records what happened in lieu of the expected show.

> The long-deferred Welcome Home Gathering has at last taken place and its success fully justified the Committee in their decision to carry it through in spite of all difficulties. It was arranged that the programme should be composed of an hour and a half of 'turns', followed by refreshments and speeches, and then the distribution of individual letters of thanks and a small gift. But Tom Handley was voiceless that night, so ITMA postponed its visit and an entertainment had to be improvised at a moment's notice. Mr Francis* stepped into the breach and provided turns that kept the audience happy and amused.

The object of the gathering was, of course, to greet all who had served in the Forces; it was the community's expression of rejoicing at their return, and gratitude for their services. The Chairman of the Parish Council voiced what he felt to be the emotions of members of the parish on seeing friends and relations leave their homes, or watching the progress of the war in every aspect of which Wadhurst was represented, and then on hearing of their victorious return; he stated that those who remained at home were fully aware of the unspeakable horrors from which they had been saved and that it was the men and women in the audience, and their comrades who had saved them, and added his hope that the happy days which they so richly deserved would, in the not too distant future, come to them again.

General Sir A. Hartley and Captain C. Piper thanked the Parish Council and the Committee for the successful evening which they had organized, and for the welcome extended to them. The Chairman of the Parish Council referred in his speech to those who would never return; he said they were comparatively few in numbers, but all too many. Captain Piper in his speech suggested a moment's silence in their memory.

The distribution of letters of thanks and of the gifts then took place, the latter being in the form of an engraved cigarette lighter. They were handed by the Chairman of the Parish Council to each ex-member of the Forces as his or her name was read out, each alphabetical group being greeted with applause.

Special thanks are due to the Secretary, Mr F H Bond, to Mr Usherwood, and to Mrs Manktelow for organising the gathering and refreshments, and to Mr Francis for improvising such an amusing entertainment.

[* *Mr Francis was known locally as Doley Francis because he was the manager of the unemployment office. He could play the piano and tell a "yarn".*]

However, despite local recollections, that was not the 'special event'. Tommy Handley did actually come to Wadhurst a little later as the 14th March 1947 edition of the Sussex Express and County Herald reported. The special report by 'Rambler' waxes lyrical about the hour-long show and it seems to have been well-received by those who attended, despite the wait. The front page of the Sussex Express and County Herald showed a photograph of Mr Handley and the ITMA company playing darts in the Queen's Head prior to the evening performance in the Commemoration Hall.

Whodunit ?

The ITMA cast at the Queen's Head
[l to r] Diana Morrison [Miss Hodgkiss] - Jean Harben [Mona Lott and the talkative lady] - Lind Joyce [Bigga-Banga's daughter, Polly Palaver, and the vocalist] - Tommy Handley - Molly Weir [Tattie Macintosh] - Hugh Morton ['Sninch of Puff'] - Fred Yule [Bigga-Banga] - Jack Train [Colonel Chinstrap].

'Rambler' reported that

> *never had the Commemoration Hall stage held so many famous personalities at once. The Company sat in a circle round the microphone and presented ITMA just as they did every Thursday at the Paris Cinema in London. All were armed with scripts and as the dialogue approached their cues they stepped up to the mike, delivered their lines and returned to their seats.*

He goes on to say that the BBC Variety Orchestra was missing but that Miss Roma Clark played in the background throughout the hour long show without any relief.

In a prominent position on the front page was the heading 'Script Scraps' and the following references were made by the performers specific to the locale of their 'booking' that evening.

> *"So this is Wadhurst,"* said Tommy Handley, opening the show, which was called 'Tomtopia's Welcome Home'.

> *"Tried to score one over me did you?"* said Tommy to Hugh Morton. *"I'll have you transferred to Wadhurst football team and you'll never score at all."*

> *"He sold two pineapples and was able to buy a couple of Jonas Lane council houses,"* said Tommy Handley.

> *"Charming girl, Lind Joyce,"* said Tommy. *"She can come down Sheepwash Lane with me any night."*

> To Dan: *"You're as funny as a wet week in Hastings."*

> *"You're very sunburnt, Bigga! Were you stationed in Ticehurst?"*

> *"I can't hear what you are saying, Sir Percy. Sounds as if you are speaking from Sevenoaks Tunnel."*

> Miss Hodgkiss: *"Mr Handley, what is this disgraceful scene?"*
> Tommy: *"It's all right, Harriett. It's only Wadhurst Parish Council holding a meeting."*

All simple fun of the period, not forgetting there was no television for entertainment!

The 'Thanks' given to local servicemen and women

The evening concluded with the Parish Council Chairman, Mr H C de J du Vallon, thanking Mr Handley and ITMA for risking the journey (inclement weather of ice and snow); on behalf of the 'Welcome Home Committee' he presented Mr Handley with a cheque for £60 to go to the National Association of Boys' Clubs. Mr Handley responded by saying how much he had enjoyed his first visit to Wadhurst and that if the occasion presented itself he would do so again. Finally, Mr du Vallon presented scrolls and cigarette lighters to those who had not received them at the previous welcome home social.

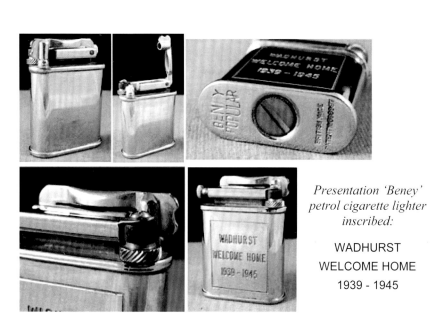

Presentation 'Beney' petrol cigarette lighter inscribed:

WADHURST
WELCOME HOME
1939 - 1945

However, apparently, there was a festering issue in the community, because not everyone agreed with the 'frittering' of the Welcome Home Fund money in such a manner and wrote vehemently on the subject. Some refused to attend; some were still overseas or at the time too far from Wadhurst to be there, so any form of celebration was premature in their opinion. No one we spoke to was overly enthusiastic about what occurred that night but then slowly reflected that "*wasn't Wadhurst fortunate that the show visited our village*". Time has wonderful healing properties on the mind.

Then Jenn Hemsley, a teenager at the time, searched her memory for recollections of celebrations at the conclusion of the War. She said that a fair few children were allowed into the very back of the Commemoration Hall for the ITMA show. Then added with a smile that, as she lived at the top of Sheepwash [*Washwell*] Lane, her garden backed on to that of the Queen's Head, and if she went to the bottom she could look through the hedge to the Hotel's garden. She knew the cast of the show were staying there so went around and got their autographs the next morning.

The words of one interviewee make a fitting conclusion to this chapter on Celebrations in Wadhurst :

> *It was such a wonderful feeling, the day peace was declared. Such a weight of anxiety and fear lifted for those in Europe, but such sadness for those who would not return and for those to whom they belonged.*

SOURCES

Our Longest Days - A People's History of the Second World War:
    Koa Wing, S [2008], Profile Books

The Bocking Collection

Wadhurst Parish magazines

The personal memories of local residents including:
    Jenn Hemsley, Walter Hodder and Nora Tweedley

THE ROLL OF HONOUR

In all three Services, during the Second World War, over 300 men and women from Wadhurst and Tidebrook, were serving all over the world. Others worked in the part-time 'Services' at home – the National Fire Service, the Home Guard, the Women's Voluntary Service and the Police Force.

No complete list exists of all their names, although the invitation lists for the 'Welcome Home' celebrations give an indication. The Parish magazine suggests the scale of the village's commitment through its returns on Christmas parcels sent to members of the Services. In 1941 parcels were sent to 121 people - 88 in the Army, 21 in the RAF and 12 in the Royal Navy; by 1943 the total had risen to 264 and in 1944 the list of addresses had increased to 300 *"but was still not complete"*.

Given these uncertainties, no list is included here, as we do not want to run the risk of leaving out names - names which should be included but of which there is no current evidence.

On the other hand, there is no such uncertainty about the names of those, from our community, who lost their lives in the service of King and country. Far too often the Parish magazine had to publish condolences and express the community's sympathy to bereaved families and friends.

In Wadhurst, their names are recorded on the War Memorial and on the stained glass memorial window in the parish church; in the church of St John the Baptist, Tidebrook, their names are cut into the entrance gateway to the church and, inside, on a memorial tablet in the nave.

WE WILL REMEMBER THEM

FROM WADHURST

Derek Francis Banfield: born July 1922, died September 1944 as a result of a flying accident when piloting a Blenheim BA 147 in Grantham. Sgt. Pilot Banfield is buried in Wadhurst Churchyard (Row C, Grave 72).

Harold James Beeney: born September 1919, died August 1944 as the battalion of the Royal Hampshire Regiment was advancing along the Canteloup – St Pierre du Fresne road. Private Beeney has no known grave and is commemorated on the Bayeux Memorial in France (Panel 15, Column 1).

Victor Marcel Bidlake: born 1918/1919, died March 1941 as a result of a flying accident when piloting a Hampden which crashed at Wroxton near Banbury in Oxfordshire. Sgt. Pilot Bidlake is commemorated at Charing (Kent County) Crematorium.

Arthur Gordon Blake: born 1922, died June 1940 on the aircraft carrier, HMS Glorious, which was sunk by gunfire from the two German battleships, Scharnhorst and Gneisenau, during the evacuation of troops from Narvik in Norway. Ordinary Seaman Blake, who had been a Boy Scout in Wadhurst and a Chorister, has no known grave and is commemorated at his home port of Chatham on the Naval Memorial (Panel 36, Column 2).

James Henry Boorman: born 1915, died 1941 during Italian and German heavy bombing on Malta. Private Boorman of the Buffs (the East Kent Regiment), a gardener at Coundon, Mayfield Lane before joining the army, was laid to rest at Imtarfa Military Cemetery, Malta (Plot 4, Row 1B).

Henry Frederick Bridger: born 1918, died May or June 1940 during the confusion of the gradual withdrawal of the British Expeditionary Force from Belgium and France via Dunkirk. Private Bridger of the Royal Sussex Regiment was buried in Esquelmes War Cemetery in Belgium (Plot 5, Row B, Grave 43).

Alexander Graeme Moncrieff Cheale: born September 1919, died in May 1940 of wounds during the defence of Oudenarde in Belgium. Recommended for a 'Mention in Despatches', 2nd Lieutenant Cheale of the Queen's Own Royal West Regiment was laid to rest at Esquelmes War Cemetery in Belgium (Plot 6, Row B, Grave 17).

Robert Bertram Roy Cook: born April 1926, died April 1945, had been a keen member of the Wadhurst ATC Flight which helped him qualify as an air-gunner. He died as a result of a flying accident, flying in a Lancaster over Owston Ferry near Scunthorpe. Sgt. Air Gunner Cook is buried in Wadhurst Churchyard (Row D, Grave 71).

Charles Henry Dodge: born March 1909, died May 1940 when the Royal Sussex Regiment was over-run near Amiens by an advancing German Panzer Division commanded by General Rommel. Lance Corporal Dodge has no known grave and is commemorated on the Dunkirk Memorial in Nord, France (Column 63).

Gilbert Roy Fazan: born September 1915, died June 1944 during action to blow up a bridge across the River Orne as part of the D-Day landings in Normandy. Lieutenant Fazan of the Royal Sussex Regiment and No. 6 Commando lies at rest close to where he died in Ranville War Cemetery, Calvados, France (Plot 3A, Row O, Grave 3).

John French: born June 1921, died April 1943 as part of the final push of Operation Torch eastwards towards Tunis to clear North Africa of the Axis Forces. Private French is commemorated at the Medjez-El-Bab Memorial, Tunisia (Face 17).

Gordon William Hemsley: born April 1921, died June 1944, as an Air Bomber in a highly secret operational squadron requiring very experienced and skilled crews, when his Halifax Mark V disappeared over Belgium. Flying Officer Hemsley has no known grave and is commemorated on the RAF Memorial at Runnymede (Panel 206).

Jack Frederick Hermitage: born August 1908, died August 1943 of malnutrition as a Japanese prisoner of war on the Burma Railway in Thailand. Gunner Hermitage of the 5th Searchlight Regiment of the Royal Artillery is buried in Kanchanaburi War Cemetery in Thailand (Plot 4, Row A, Grave 59).

Edmund Harold Keens: born March 1917, died May 1940 when the Royal Sussex Regiment was over-run near Amiens by an advancing German Panzer Division commanded by General Rommel. Private Keens, who had been a greengrocer and fruiterer in Wadhurst, lies in Abbeville Communal Cemetery Extension, Somme, France (Plot 9, Grave 14).

Leonard John Manktelow: born December 1923, died August 1944 serving with the No. 75 Anti-Tank Regiment in the area of Sourdaville during the Normandy landings. Gunner Manktelow, who had been employed as a gardener in the gardens of Mr and Mrs Keyser, Coundon, Mayfield Lane, is buried in Tilly-sur-Seulles War Cemetery, Calvados, France (Plot 9, Row H, Grave 8).

Peter Taverner Miller: born May 1908, died May 1940 when the Royal Sussex Regiment was over-run near Amiens by an advancing German Panzer Division commanded by General Rommel. He was killed while firing into the slits of a tank which had stopped and the 7th Battalion of the Royal Sussex Regiment War Diary records: *The bravery of Major Miller of "B" Company was an example to all as he led his men forward several times*". Major Miller, who had been a JP on Mark Cross Bench and had served on many organisations and committees, has no known grave and is commemorated on the Dunkirk Memorial in Nord, France (Column 63).

Donald William Muir: born February 1921, died May 1941 on board the cruiser, HMS Gloucester, which was engaged with other warships in evacuating the defenders of Crete after the German invasion. A member of the Royal Marines Band, Musician Muir has no known grave and is commemorated on the Royal Navy Memorial at his home port, Portsmouth (Panel 59, Column 3).

William George Picknell: born June 1921, died March 1944 as a submariner on board HM Submarine Syrtis probably as a result of their hitting a German mine. A former Wadhurst postman, Leading Seaman Picknell has no known grave and is commemorated on the Royal Navy Memorial at his home port of Chatham (Panel 75, Column 1).

Arthur Frank Piper: born June 1909, died August 1943 in the Combined General Hospital, Basra, of tropical illness when serving with the Royal Indian Artillery as part of PAIFORCE. Lieutenant Piper, son of the Sparrows Green building and decorating family, is buried in Basra War Cemetery, Iraq (Plot 7, Row P, Grave 6).

Edward Estill Pudsey: born February 1920, died November 1943 on a Ranger patrol in a Mosquito, flying from his base at Ford in Sussex on an operation over France. Flight Lieutenant (RAFVR) Pudsey is buried in the Clichy Northern Cemetery, Hauts-de-Seine, France (Plot 16, Row 13, Grave 17).

Frank Russell: born August 1922, died September 1943 during heavy fighting on White Cross Hill in the foothills above Salerno. Private Russell, the son of probably the last traditional charcoal burner in the area, lies at rest with his other Royal Hampshire Regiment colleagues in the Bone War Cemetery, Algeria (Plot 7, Row B, Grave 9).

Frederick William Russell: born September 1923, died August 1944 as the Wireless Operator of a Halifax on an operation to Brunswick in Germany. Fl. Sgt. Russell has no known grave and is commemorated on the RAF Memorial at Runnymede (Panel 222).

George Alastair Sales: born October 1922, died September 1943 when his Halifax crashed at Bad Munder-am-Deister, 25 kilometres south-west of Hanover. Sgt. Navigator (RAFVR) Sales and his six colleagues are buried at the Hanover War Cemetery in Germany (Plot 4, Row E, Grave 17).

Albert Edward Shaw: born December 1917, died September 1943 of malnutrition as a Japanese prisoner of war on the Burma Railway in Thailand, having previously been in Changi Camp. Trooper Shaw of the Royal Armoured Corps and 18th Reconnaissance Corps died in Songkrai Prison Camp but, while his grave was marked at the time, some markings have disappeared. Trooper Shaw's grave is probably one of the five graves of unknown soldiers in the Burma War Cemetery at Thanbyuzayat in the Songkrai section. He is commemorated on the Singapore Memorial at Kranji (Column 98), in the Book of Remembrance in All Hallows Church by the Tower of London, and in the Book of Remembrance to the Loyal Regiment in Preston Parish Church, Lancashire.

Harry William Thorpe Sinden: born June 1910, died January 1943 as a result of a premature explosion while engaging enemy aircraft in the area of Humberside. The commander of 510 (M) HAA Battery of 151 Royal Artillery Regiment at the time of his death, Major Sinden lies at rest in Battle Cemetery (Section H, Division A, Grave 19) and is commemorated on the Battle War Memorial.

Stanley Henry Thomas: born June 1922, died June 1942 when his aircraft, a Manchester, was shot down at Beekbergen, five kilometres south of Apeldoorn in Holland during an operational flight to Bremen. Sgt. Air Gunner Thomas, who had been employed at Gardners Stores in St James's Square and was a member of the Wadhurst Home Guard and a crack shot, is buried in Apeldoorn General Cemetery in Holland (Plot 4, Grave 132).

Joseph Walter Usherwood: born October 1922, died July 1942 as the result of a canoeing accident in the Bay of Quinte, Ontario, Canada during his training for the RAF. Leading Aircraftman Usherwood lies at rest in Trenton (St George's) Cemetery, Ontario, Canada (Lot 1, Plot 202, Grave 3).

Donald Eric Ogilvy Watson D.S.C.: born April 1915, died November 1942 when HM Submarine Unbeaten was sunk when returning to Malta from operations in the Mediterranean. Lieutenant Ogilvy Watson had been awarded a 'Mention in Despatches' in August 1941 and the Distinguished Service Cross in October 1941 when he was the First Lieutenant of HM Submarine Truant. Lieutenant Ogilvy Watson has no known grave and is commemorated on the Royal Navy Memorial at his home port, Portsmouth (Panel 62, Column 1).

George Sidney Watts: born January 1908, died September 1944 having been engaged in heavy fighting for some weeks at Montefiore, Gemmano, Sensoli and Ceriano ridges in north-east Italy. Private Watts of the Oxfordshire and Buckinghamshire Light Infantry lies at rest in Cesena War Cemetery in the province of Forli, Italy (Plot VII, Grave 9).

Philip Mervyn Wigg: born June 1916, died April 1944 when flying his Lancaster on a bombing raid to the La Chapelle Marshalling Yards in Paris. Squadron Leader Wigg died on the day of his son's birth and lies in a collective grave in Clichy Northern Cemetery, Hauts-de-Seine, France (Plot 16, Row 8, Collective Grave 13).

James Henry Willett: born May 1923, died July 1944 in the Secqueville en Bessin area of Normandy at a time of fluctuating battles on the Caen front before the breakout eastwards. Gunner Willett of the 71 Anti-Tank Regiment Royal Artillery is buried in St Manvieu Cemetery, Calvados, France (Plot VII, Row B, Grave 1).

Ronald Frederick Willett: born 1917/1918, died November 1941 in an attack of the Omar defences in North Africa with the Royal Sussex Regiment leading the 14/16 Punjabis against Libyan Omar. Private Willett lies at Halfaya Sollum War Cemetery (Plot 6, Row G, Grave 3).

All those connected to Wadhurst who fell are commemorated in the stained glass window in Wadhurst Parish Church.

FROM TIDEBROOK

Albert Jesse Baldock: born October 1918, died May 1940 as part of the British Expeditionary Force during the defence of Caestre covering the withdrawal of troops towards Dunkirk. Private Baldock is buried in Caestre Communal Cemetery, Nord, France (Plot 5, Row A, Grave 5).

Denys Osmond Gilbert Coote: born November 1921, died September 1944 when the Wellington bomber was brought down during bombing operations over Hegyeshalom Marshalling Yards between Vienna and Gyor, near Vep in Hungary. Sgt. Bomb Aimer Coote lies at rest in the Budapest War Cemetery, Hungary (Plot 1, Row E, Collective Grave 10).

Harry John Joffre Day: born August 1915, died October 1942 as the result of a flying accident during his pilot training in South Africa. Leading Aircraftman Day is buried in Kroonstad New Cemetery, Free State, South Africa (Plot A, Row 7, Grave 94).

John Gordon Bewley Fletcher: born November 1919, died August 1940 during a night patrol in a Blenheim from their base at Pembrey, South Wales when they crashed at Bradford Barton, Witheredge, Devon. Sgt. Air Gunner Fletcher, who had married six weeks before his death, lies at rest in Forest Row Cemetery, East Sussex (Grave 1289).

George Alexander Forsyth: born February 1913, died February 1941 when returning in his Whitley V aircraft to his station at RAF Dishforth after No. 78 Bomber Squadron had attacked Cologne. The aircraft crashed into hills in Ross-shire. Sgt. Pilot Forsyth, who was flying as second pilot to the squadron commander, lies at rest in Tidebrook Churchyard.

George Thomas Aden Lane: born June 1915, died February 1944 when his Company was left as protection for a carrier train conveying rations to another battalion and encountered extremely heavy enemy fire. Private Lane of the Queen's Royal Regiment (West Surrey) lies at rest in the Beach Head War Cemetery, Anzio, Italy (Plot 22, Row E, Grave 2).

Edward Patrick Slowe: born November 1914, died May 1940 when the 5th (Cinque Ports) Battalion took up defensive positions on the River Escaut at Wortegem, Belgium during the evacuation to Dunkirk. Lt. Slowe is buried at Adegem Canadian War Cemetery, Belgium (Plot 1, Row AB, Grave 11).

All those connected to Tidebrook who fell are commemorated
in Tidebrook Church.

They shall grow not old as we that are left grow old:
Age shall not weary them, nor the years condemn.
At the going down of the sun and in the morning
We will remember them.

Abbeville

Adegem

Anzio Beach Head

Apeldoorn

Basra

Bayeux

Bone

Budapest

Caestre

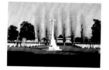

Cesena

Chatham Naval

Clichy

Dunkirk

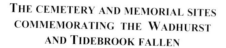

THE CEMETERY AND MEMORIAL SITES
COMMEMORATING THE WADHURST
AND TIDEBROOK FALLEN

ANOTHER SIX MEN
ARE COMMEMORATED IN
BATTLE
CHARING
FOREST ROW
TIDEBROOK
WADHURST

Esquelmes

Halfaya Sollum

Hanover

Kanchanaburi

Kranji

Kroonstad

Medjez-El-Bab

Portsmouth Naval

Ranville

Runnymede

St Manvieu

Thanbyuzayat

Tilly-sur-Seulles

Trenton

Photographs
by permission of the
Commonwealth War
Graves Commission

INDEX